Soundings

Issue 7

States of Africa

EDITORS
Stuart Hall
Doreen Massey
Michael Rustin

GUEST EDITORS
Victoria Brittain and
Rakiya Omaar

POETRY EDITOR
Carole Satyamurti

REVIEWS EDITORS
Becky Hall and
Susanna Rustin

ART EDITOR
Tim Davison

EDITORIAL OFFICE
Lawrence & Wishart
99a Wallis Road
London E9 5LN

MARKETING CONSULTANT
Mark Perryman

ADVERTISEMENTS
Write for information to Soundings,
c/o Lawrence & Wishart

SUBSCRIPTIONS
1998 subscription rates are (for three issues):
UK: Institutions £70, Individuals £35
Rest of the world: Institutions £80, Individuals £45

Collection as a whole © Soundings 1997
Individual articles the © authors 1997

No article may be reproduced or transmitted by any means, electronic or mechanical, including photocopying, recording or any information storage and retrieval system, without the permission in writing of the publisher, editor or author

ISSN 1362 6620
ISBN 0 85315 849 5

Text setting Art Services, Norwich
Cover photograph: Jenny Matthews

Printed in Great Britain by
Cambridge University Press, Cambridge

Soundings is published three times a year, in autumn, spring and summer by:
Soundings Ltd
c/o Lawrence & Wishart
99a Wallis Road
London E9 5LN

This is issue 7. *The Next Ten Years* was a special free supplement

CONTENTS

Notes on Contributors	v
Editorial: Problems with Globalisation Doreen Massey	7
The Break-up of the Conservative Nation Bill Schwarz	13
The Uncanny Family Wendy Wheeler	29
Reimagining the Inhuman City: **The 'Pure Genius' Land Occupation** Dave Featherstone	45
Economic Globalisation and the Nation State: **The Transformation of Political Power?** David Goldblatt, David Held, Anthony McGrew, Jonathan Perraton	61
Poems Okello Oculi, Daniel Wyke, Linda Chase, Jane Evans	78
Reviews Ludovic Hunter-Tilney, Christine Clegg, Timothy Bewes, Katherine Frank	82

Part II States of Africa

Introduction Victoria Brittain and Rakiya Omaar	98
States Under Pressure Basil Davidson	104
A Genocide Foretold Rakiya Omaar	109
Testimony of a survivor Augustin Ndahimana Buranga	118

Continued on next page

Continued from previous page

Moi's Achilles Heel? 121
Kathurima M'Inoti and Lucy Hannan

Photofeature: Portraits of Africa 132
Jenny Matthews

Angola under Attack: 143
Watching the Revolution Being Taken Away
Victoria Brittain

They Were Better 153
Extract from a play by Ngugi Wa Mirii

Cost-recovery, Adjustment and Equity in Health: 166
Some Lessons from Zimbabwe
Kevin Watkins

Mozambique - Under New Management 184
Joseph Hanlon

Corruption and the State I 195
Laurence Cockcroft

Corruption and the State II 198
Extract from Joseph Warioba's Report

The Role of the NUM in South Africa: I Introduction 209
Vic Allen

The Role of the NUM in South Africa: II 211
Presidential Address to the Ninth National Congress, 1997
by James Motlasi

NOTES ON CONTRIBUTORS

Bill Schwarz teaches in the Department of Media and Communications at Goldsmiths College.

Wendy Wheeler is Senior Lecturer in English Literature and Critical Theory at the University of North London. She is currently writing a book on politics, cultural mourning, and a new modernity, to be published in 1998.

Dave Featherstone is a loosely itinerant musician and intellectual who has studied and been involved with direct action politics.

David Goldblatt, David Held and **Anthony McGrew** teach politics at the Faculty of Social Sciences, the Open University. **Jonathan Perraton** teaches economics at the University of Sheffield.

Okello Oculi is from Uganda and currently lives in Nigeria. He has published three volumes of poetry and a novel.

Daniel Wyke is studying for an MA at the University of Sussex but would prefer to be writing poetry. This is his first published poem.

Linda Chase lives in Manchester where she runs a Tai Chi school. Her latest volume of poetry is *These Goodbyes*.

Jane Evans was born in 1933 and wrote poems from an early age. She is a teacher of children with hearing difficulties.

Ludovic Hunter-Tilney is a freelance researcher and writer in London.

Christine Clegg is a tutor at the University of Sussex, where she has recently completed a doctoral thesis on the subject of incest in postwar literature.

Timothy Bewes currently writes and lectures in London and is author of *Cynicism and Modernity* (Verso 1997).

Katherine Frank is a biographer currently working on a biography of Indira Gandhi.

Victoria Brittain is Deputy Foreign Editor of *The Guardian*.

Rakiya Omaar is Co-director of Africa Rights, a London-based human rights organisation.

Basil Davidson is a historian.

Soundings

Augustin Ndahimana Buranga is a survivor of the genocide in Rwanda.

Kathurima M'Inoti is a Kenyan lawyer.

Lucy Hannan is a Nairobi-based journalist.

Jenny Matthews is a photographer.

Ngugi wa Mirii is a Kenyan writer and theatre director based in Harare.

Kevin Watkins is a policy advisor for Oxfam.

Joseph Hanlon has written several books on Southern Africa.

Laurence Cockcroft is a consultant travelling widely in anglophone Africa and a founder and Board member of Transparencey International.

Joseph Warioba is a former Prime Minister of Tanzania.

Vic Allen is the author of *The History of the Miners' Union in South Africa*.

James Motlasi is President of the Miners' Union of South Africa.

EDITORIAL

Problems with globalisation

Naming the thing
There are some things which are so accepted a part of political discourse that they are taken for granted. We stop questioning them. They slide into place as background assumptions shared even between those who disagree on every other point of the debate in hand. They lie there silently, preventing other bigger issues being raised. One such taken-for-granted term in much political discourse at the moment is 'globalisation'. It is a weasel word; too frequently used perhaps, and certainly too rarely analysed politically.

In the autumn of this year, a number of reports were published on the world economy and its future, and two of them were sharply at odds. In one corner, the World Bank was optimistic in its assessment of the prospects for global economic growth and the reduction of poverty in 'developing countries' (another weasel term if ever there was one).[1] In the other corner, UNCTAD (The United Nations Conference on Trade and Development) expressed concern both that growth looked likely to be too slow significantly to alleviate poverty and that the road to growth currently being adopted (and imposed) might anyway not be successful.[2] The road to growth under dispute between these two organisations is free trade. The World Bank expresses itself as supremely confident that freeing markets and trade will lead - in the long term - to the eradication of world

---

1. *Global Economic Prospects 1997*, World Bank.
2. *Trade and Development Report 1997*, UNCTAD.

poverty. The United Nations is sceptical; it is at least hesitant in assuming any automatic link between opening up global competition on the one hand and faster growth and diminishing inequality on the other.

A host of questions and further arguments immediately arises. How is growth being measured, for instance? and should there anyway be any assumption of an automatic association between this 'growth' and decreasing poverty and/or inequality? But what is interesting too is that - behind all these questions and the crucial issue on which the reports are in dispute - there is agreement on one thing: free trade means globalisation and globalisation means free trade. In both the reports and even more so in the commentaries upon them the two terms are taken to be synonymous. This is the unspoken, shared assumption.

In our more everyday social and political discourse we use the term globalisation in a much more general way. To speak of 'globalisation' is to give the impression that in some sense the world is becoming more interconnected. That there has been a stretching-out and a re-working of the geography of social relations. And this is undoubtedly the case. However, the very generality of this use of the word obscures the fact that what we are experiencing at the moment - certainly in economic terms - is globalisation of a particular type. There can never be 'globalisation in general' - if the world is becoming more interconnected then it is doing so, and must do so, in the context of particular power relations, and governed by particular political trajectories. What we have now is neo-liberal, free-market, globalisation. It is most definitely, if we can still use these terms, a globalisation of 'the right'.

The problem is that the generalised discourse of globalisation hides the fact of this politico-economic specificity. And it also, in consequence, hides the fact that there might be other terms on which the world's economies (and thus peoples) might be integrated.

The UNCTAD Report makes depressing reading. It points to the increases in inequality both within and between countries which have taken place over the last 25 years. The numbers are numbing: the richest 20 per cent of the world's population owns nearly 80 per cent of the wealth; the gap in income per head between the top 20 per cent and the bottom 20 per cent doubled between 1965 and 1990. If we could really grasp the enormity and the daily lived meaning of these figures we could hardly go on living in the world without doing something about it. 'Globalisation' has produced both structural divides within it and massive exclusions from it. But this is due, not to 'globalisation in general', but to its present, specifically free-market, form.

That, then, is the first point: we shouldn't talk just about 'globalisation'. If we're referring to the economics of what's happening today we should give it its proper name: neo-liberal globalisation.

Globalisation as a project

This specifying of the current form of globalisation is important for another reason too. For referring to globalisation in general gives it an air of inevitability. (Of *course*, with 'history', with improvements in the technologies of transport and communications, societies and economies become more interconnected.) Globalisation in this version is a *deus ex machina*, and we had just better get used to it.

Now, while it is doubtless the case that the potential for connectivity between different parts of the world is ineluctably increasing, the nature and the terms of those interconnections are by no means inevitable. The elision between 'globalisation in general' and 'neo-liberal globalisation' rewards the latter with the apparent inevitability of the former.

And this in turn has further effects. For this discourse of inevitability serves to hide two things. First, it hides the possibility that there might be alternatives. And second it hides the agencies, and thus the interests, involved in the production of globalisation in this form. There are real acrobatics involved here. On the one hand we are treated to a discourse of how the process will happen whatever we do, and on the other hand there are massive forces at work - from the World Trade Organisation, to the IMF, to national governments in the North and national elites in the South - striving to ensure its production. World economic leaders gather (in Washington, Paris or Davos) to congratulate themselves upon, and to flaunt and reinforce, their powerfulness and yet it is a powerfulness which consists in insisting that they (we) are power*less* - in the face of globalising market forces there is absolutely nothing that can be done. Except, of course, to push the process further. It is a heroic impotence - which serves to disguise the fact that this is really a *project*.

The aim of this kind of discourse of inevitability is to render unthinkable the possibility of any alternatives. And so in the South this understanding of both the inevitability and the necessity of this form of globalisation legitimises the imposition of structural adjustment policies,[3] and the associated enforcement of export-orientation over production for local consumption.[4] And in the North, similarly, the discourse of inevitability becomes the basis for decisions not only to acquiesce to globalisation in this form ('Of course we have to have "flexible" labour markets, globalisation demands it'), but also precisely to *implement* it (the signing-up to the Uruguay Round of GATT, for instance; there was stunningly little discussion about this in the UK). This rhetoric of globalisation, in other words, is not a simple description of how the world *is*; it is an image in which the world is actively being made.

Global double-talk

Now, the image which is evoked in this talk of the inevitability/necessity of globalisation is one of a world of mobility and movement, of networks and free flows. It is a world of unbounded spaces, and it is hailed by many with breathless exhilaration as a vision of the future.

Yet quite contrary images exist at the same time. The very people who most strongly proclaim the rightness of 'free-trade', for instance, will often - in a different political context - call up an image of defensible places, of the importance of the maintenance of borders, of a world divided by nationalisms. In one breath it is assumed that 'free trade' is self-evidently a good thing and in the very next the necessity of firm boundaries is assumed in order to control immigration. Two apparently self-evident truths, two completely different geographical imaginations of the world, are called upon in turn as the political discussion requires. And so in this era of 'globalisation' boats go down in the Mediterranean as people try to act on the proclamations of a borderless world and sail to a more prosperous future. That double imaginary - in the very fact of its doubleness - of the freedom of space (for capital) on the one hand and of tightly patrolled borders on the other, works in favour of the already-powerful. At worst, it holds out a vision of the future in which the poor and already-disadvantaged are held in place and yet invaded while capital and the already-privileged have the freedom both to roam the world and to defend our fortress

---

3   See many of the articles in our theme *States of Africa*, in this issue.
4   See Duncan Green 'Latin America and free trade', *Soundings* number 5, pp73-87, Spring 1997.

Editorial

homes. The clash between worsening uneven development at a global level and the tensions around international migration must be a crucial one for the world's future.

I have written about these issues before.[5] And when I did so I used to refer to those on 'the far right'. It was easy to analyse the contradictory discourses of the likes of Michael Howard, or Portillo, or Mrs Thatcher. That was before May the first. It is dismaying now to pick up the same contradictions from Tony Blair. Not so long after the election he went to a European summit in Amsterdam, and returned in triumph bearing two things. First, he had enthusiastically sided with Helmut Kohl (and against Lionel Jospin) - he had recognised (and apparently welcomed) what he called globalisation (and which *we* must recognise as only one particular form of globalisation) and had joyfully succumbed to the constraints and necessities (eg the 'flexible' labour market) which it apparently imposes upon the functioning of our economy. But, second, he had also won for us 'the UK's right to control its own borders'. Global freedom of movement for some, but definitely not for others.

An internationalist globalisation?

There must be other ways to work our increasing global interconnectedness. I am not arguing either that we should retreat totally into protectionism, or that borders should be opened up to unlimited international migration. The point is rather to end the double-think that legitimises the coexistence of the reverse of both of these things.

What we need is a policy approach which asks what *kind* of globalisation we should be aiming for and which acknowledges the possibility of mixes of trade and migration policies appropriate to different situations. In every age there is a making and re-making of the spaces and places through which we live our lives: what need to be addressed are the power relations through which that restructuring takes place. At the moment, the apparent inevitability of globalisation in some form, and the skillful elision of this with the particular form which is dominant today, is blocking the possibility of having that debate.

---

5. For instance in *Soundings*, number 1, 1995, 'Making spaces: or, geography is political too', pp193-208.

We need an internationalist perspective on globalisation - asking not just what is good for 'Britain' (itself already a tricky-enough concept) but also what might, just possibly, lead to a slightly less unequal world. This is not an impossible task. For example, both Clare Short and Robin Cook have spoken in these terms: Clare Short has alluded to the pointlessness of giving aid to the poorest, on condition that they put more resources into health and education, when IMF structural adjustment programmes are imposing cuts in those very same services. (The contradictions between alleviating poverty and certain strategies for growth could not be clearer.) There are proposals for a better regulation of the conditions under which multinationals invest, and disinvest, around the world, and, in particular, for a rethink of the conditions which countries are allowed to impose upon them. Oxfam has written about the possibility of ethical standards agreements for transnational corporations, argued against the dumping of unwanted food which undermines Third World planning, and presented a case for social clauses in trade agreements to level the playing field. Indeed making 'free and fair' trade actually free and fair would itself be an improvement (though it would be by no means enough) - the UNCTAD Report underlines that the rules of 'global free trade' have been drawn up in favour of the richest countries. Trade in goods in which countries of the South have an advantage (clothing, agricultural produce) is heavily protected, while barriers are low for the high-tech goods and services which the richer countries mainly produce. Finally, a more internationalist approach to globalisation would demand a much more radical re-thinking of 'the nation' than could ever be engendered by the current mix of openness to capital and closedness to people.

Soundings has already carried a major article on the (disputed) extent of globalisation, and in this issue that debate is taken further.[6] We have also begun to address the issue of what kind of globalisation we have and should have. In this volume that debate is taken further in a number of the articles in the theme section on *States of Africa*. 'Globalisation' is one of the most important issues on the current political agenda. *Soundings* aims to ensure that it will not remain, as a term, a de-politicised, unexamined, assumption.

DM

---

6. See Paul Hirst and Grahame Thompson, 'Globalisation: ten frequently asked questions and some surprising answers', *Soundings* Number 4, Autumn 1996; and, in this issue, the article by Goldblatt, Held et al.

The break-up of the conservative nation

Bill Schwarz

Bill Schwarz charts the downfall of the Tories, and the collapse of the conservartive nation which lies behind it.

Three a.m. on Friday 2 May: there's no forgetting those minutes of primal joy when Michael Portillo was sunk. Wild cheers emanated from street after street. This was, finally, *the* moment when eighteen years of anger and frustration were released. In the haphazard recountings of the days which followed, it became apparent that in this moment an effective counter-community had come into being. In the relief of the aftermath the most unlikely figures came out as defectors from the Tory cause. A protracted build-up of steady loathing had cohered, the extent of which wasn't clear until the election itself. Maybe feelings like these, driven by vengeance and a raw sense of Punch-and-Judy justice, are too primitive to be associated with a sophisticated political strategy. But even for the sceptics it felt good. It felt like a liberation. The Tories, ever-more complicit in the myths of their own monstrosity and willing themselves to trump one outrage with another, had been slain.

The night itself was rich with hyperbole. Cecil Parkinson, looking for all the world like one of those benign creatures from *Men in Black* and without a clue what was going on, broke the restraint of even Neil Kinnock and David Steel, inducing in them spluttering hysterics. Tony King, abandoning the norms of punditry, declared even before a single vote had been counted that this was no landslide: it was more 'an asteroid hitting the planet and destroying all known life'. The 18 per cent swing in Crosby carried Peter Snow to the intoxicating limits of his electronic swingometer, opening the vista of hitherto unknown psephological terrains. The BBC graphics team, in homage to Luke Skywalker, zapped the blue redoubts one by one - Edgbaston, Hove, Thurrock, all zapped. History, at last, was on the move again.

The common refrain was that nothing had been witnessed on this scale since 1830, equating John Major with the unlikely figure of the Duke of Wellington. But historical comparisons like this make no sense, for to think in this manner is to ignore what politics *is* in each historical moment. In the run-up to the election the founding director of the Institute of Contemporary British History, Anthony Seldon, published a collection entitled *How Tory Governments Fall. The Tory Party in power since 1783*. Distinguished contributors were asked to consider nine factors - negative image of the party leader; strength of feeling for 'time for a change'; confusion over policy direction; and so on. This is an empiricism of cyclopian qualities. If nothing else, mass democracy, the successive reorganisation of the relations of citizenship and the interpenetration of mass politics with the mass media have transformed the very nature of politics itself. Maybe Georgette Heyer would have the imaginative capacities to transpose Peter Snow to the eighteenth century as a rakish Wilkesite enthusiast, but there the comparisons have to stop.

In the 1830s the Tories were a declining faction within the multi-national landed elite which dominated the state of Britain and Ireland. During the decades which followed the party reconstituted itself to represent the Union and empire, and against all expectations, to become a mass democratic party. The Tories fashioned, as their intellectuals liked to boast, the conservative nation. These are the historical realities - and it is this history which has been overturned in 1997.

In the 1990s it is *this* - the conservative nation - which has been broken, and which dispatches the Conservatives into uncharted waters. It has precious little to do with numbers - in this instance truth does not reside in some political *Wisden*, in which the defeat of 1997 is comparable to some far-off catastrophe. In a sense the issue is more dramatic. The strategic vision of contemporary Conservatism has become unhinged. The capacity of the party to embrace a politics of citizenship is in genuine crisis. Its carefully fashioned democratic project, which underpinned the *longuee duree* of the Conservative Party as a competitor in the field of modern mass politics, has come to an end.

The politics of the conservative nation have been replaced by the politics of Middle England. These terms, banal enough to be sure, may sound like the same thing. Or it may seem as if the difference between them is merely rhetorical, dictated by the soundbite. This I think is wrong. These terms, for all their spin, signal a shift in historical realities.

The conservative nation

The conservative nation was a complex political formation, created from an authentic conception of civilization. At its core lay the principal imperial nation: England itself. Organised around this core was the Union of the British and Irish nations. And beyond that, sharing this ideological firmament, was the white empire. The language of the conservative nation was held in place by what was perceived as a shared ethnic inheritance. For the conservative nation wasn't a nation at all. It was a multi-national and imperial confederation, made up of distinct national units, but which (with one or two notable exceptions) spoke the language of English ethnicity.

'To be a citizen of the conservative nation was to be *an ethnic*'

The idea of the conservative nation represented a political project with ethnicity at its very heart. Indeed, Conservatism embodied a politics organised to incite its citizens to *become English* - in its ethnic, if not always its national, register. How else can we understand the fact that every philosophical defence of British Conservatism for the past century turns on the potency of the nation? In the official pronouncements this can still be heard today, untransformed and unadorned. Thus David Willetts - 'Two-brains Willetts' to his friends, owing, it seems, to the repute of his colossal IQ - closes his 1997 appeal to the British electorate, *Why Vote Conservative?*, with these words: '... Conservative patriotism is not quite the same as the blood and soil nationalism of the Continental variety. We love our country because we love our institutions and the way of life they sustain.' The concept is Disraeli's, the idiom Baldwin's. Either way, the antiquarianism is evident, taking as axiomatic the putatively un-axiomatic instincts of the English.

From the late nineteenth century, when the state was slowly democratised and the Conservative Party as a mass party effectively came into being, citizenship came to be deeply imbued with ethnic obligations. To be a citizen of the conservative nation was to be *an ethnic*. It was to subscribe to the ancestral rituals encoded in the language of the crown, in the inherited verities of a nation which was genetically constitutional, and in which a concocted conception of kith and kin bound together the anglophone white races of the empire.

This was the citizen whom Beatrix Campbell (with acceptable chronological leeway) has termed 'the Home Service citizen', listening-in to the wireless with his family around him, the interior, domestic life of the nation given ideological shape by Reith's BBC. Or this is the citizen whom Virginia Woolf describes

> The good citizen when he opens his door in the evening must be banker, golfer, husband, father; not a nomad wandering in the desert, a mystic staring at the sky, a debauchee in the slums of San Francisco, a soldier heading a revolution, a pariah howling with scepticism and solitude. When he opens his door, he must run his fingers through his hair and put his umbrella in the stand like the rest.

Patently, the ethnic and patriarchal logics which held these ideals in place excluded as they included. The democratic impulse of the conservative nation, drawing the unenfranchised into the public realm of the nation, was shadowed at every turn by those who were deficient in their ethnic dispositions. At every moment the respectable citizen was confronted by an entire gallery of grotesque others who failed to function as true citizens: aliens of all stripes; hooligans and agitators; common prostitutes and good-time girls; male homosexuals; the feckless, the inebriated, the wilfully unemployed; even, in more contemporary argot, the single mother.

Yet at the same time the idea of the conservative nation could provide a genuine radicalism, creating citizens for a democratic polity which functioned by universal principles. Nowhere was this more evident in the history of Conservatism than in the person of the erstwhile Birmingham Radical, Joseph Chamberlain. He created a language which spoke to workers as workers; which denounced with bravura the customs of the ruling caste; but which turned on allegiance to empire and enmity to all manner of alien. Chamberlain's turn to Conservatism in 1886 marked the apotheosis of his Radicalism, and transformed forever the prospects of Toryism, forcing it to confront the imperatives of mass democracy. The cities of Belfast and Glasgow, Birmingham and Liverpool, are testament to the historic force of what the conservative nation, in its popular incarnation, once meant.

The rhetoric of the conservative nation - drawing on the belief of the providential nature of English history, on the mystical powers of crown and constitution, on the *liberality* of the English - may have seemed unconvincing to those hostile to Conservatism. But they conveyed a truth about the historical realities which underwrote the success of Conservatism as a mass political formation.

The decline of the conservative nation

These historical realities vanished long ago. The rhetoric alone remains. Indeed, in the current disintegration of Conservatism all that remains active in its imaginative dynamic is the ghost of this ethnic memory.

The conservative nation was founded on the twin pillars of industry and empire. From the 1950s these structures weakened, and with them the coherence of the conservative nation. The end of empire, combined with the precipitate decline in manufacturing, dislocated the conservative nation at its core. With it we witness, as Tom Nairn predicted presciently, if prematurely, the break-up of Britain. The great imperial cities and bastions of Unionism had their economic life-lines cut. This historic Unionism had given credence to identities which could be, simultaneously, Scots, Welsh or Northern Irish, *and* British-imperial. With neither industry nor empire union with England became increasingly anachronistic.

Put simply, the tribunes of the conservative nation in England reacted to this loss with a recharged radical politics in which invocations of ethnicity redoubled. We see this from the 1960s, in the protracted bid first by Enoch Powell, and then by Mrs Thatcher, to reinvent the conservative nation for new times. The corporate system which had once given life to Labour - the imperial economy based on the staple industries of the first industrial revolution, with a state formation to match - were to be uprooted. This was, one might say, a postcolonial politics which worked from a conception of ethnic life whose colonial foundations had shifted not at all.

When first Powellism and then Thatcherism cohered it did indeed seem as if they were in the business of creating a new hegemonic project. Their vision of Conservatism was based not merely on the tinkerings of electoral calculus. They were going, as Stuart Hall argued, for a radical recasting of the conservative nation. Time and again they declared that theirs was a politics which was universal in its aspiration, devised in order to break Labour and to allow all citizens to sign up to the prescriptions of a newly resurgent conservative nation. And in the election of 1970, and then again in those of the early Thatcherite period, this bid to win over the traditional Labour voter did pay dividends.

But this universalism was flawed in its very foundations. It created an idea of the nation confronted by a frenzy of enemies within and without, a radicalism driven by the imperative of exclusion. With Powell, of course, this was most evident in terms of race. But it was he, on the eve of the 1970 election, who also codified the roster of invisible enemies within - embracing not only students and kindred spirits, but also the patrician guardians of the old order. These were enemies of the conservative nation not on account of pigmentation but because they defied the deepest codes of English ethnicity, either by subversion on the cultural front, as in the case of students and the hoi-polloi of 1968, or by being insufficiently vigilant in matters of authority, on the part of the old guard. And it was Powell, in one of the great dramatic turn-arounds in British political history, who voted for the Labour Party in February 1974, in order to extinguish the spectre of Europe. This was a radicalism which reached out to an evermore indignant minority, a universalism which time and time turned in on itself.

Here, in its essentials, the language of Middle England began to take shape. Powell and Thatcher, both devout Unionists, found themselves invoking the Union, but in effect unwittingly calling upon the ancestral truths of the English. In this respect, Powell's excursus to County Down was more troubling than he had anticipated, the shared ethnic language of Ulstermen and the English doing nothing to mitigate the adventures of an autonomous, anti-Westminster Ulster nationalism. This new generation of Tory radicals in the 1960s and 1970s, owing more to Chamberlain than they ever conceived, were living out the historic contraction of England: seeing first the empire go, then the subaltern nations of what was once Great Britain, and even too some of the recalcitrant regions of England itself - those at any rate some distance from the Home Counties. If there had once been some territorial and political substance to the idea of the conservative nation, the invention of what has now come to be known as Middle England was, from the start, of a different order: 90 per cent in the mind and 10 per cent the friction of discernible geographies. It is, at most, the old conservative nation hollowed out, reverting to the image of the party of the 1830s, when all it commanded were the rural heartlands.

If the twin collapse of industry and empire destroyed the conservative nation structurally, the *coup de grace* came in the 1980s from the Thatcherite Jacobins themselves. Unhinged too was the Tory Party which - also - had been given life by the old regime. The Thatcherites unleashed a bid for hegemony which repeatedly stalled, incapable of generating a level of popular mobilisation sufficient to break the impasse bequeathed by the corporatist state. As we can now see this was a radicalism which heralded not the recreation of Conservatism for the new century, but its burn-out.

The defeat of the Heathites

There were alternatives, as there always are. A quite different strain of Conservatism can be charted, with its roots in the 'middle-way' nostrums of the 1930s. This was a tradition of Conservatism which, in the postwar world, came to be increasingly sympathetic to Europe. Churchill was an intellectual presence here - even if ambivalently, as in all his manoeuvres to underwrite a philosophical justification for Conservative Party politics. With more gusto, Harold Macmillan was critical in making this tradition happen, as was his chosen lieutenant, Edward Heath.

Too often now the divergence between the old Heathites and the prominent Tories of today is accounted for in terms of Heath's personal bile. The folklore of contemporary Conservatism thrives on new disclosures of his bad grace, and - it seems - Heath is content enough to adopt the role of folk-devil. But this is a serious simplification. The distinctiveness of Macmillan, Heath and their successors is their determination to recast the strategies of the conservative nation, and to privilege state over nation. The matter of sovereignty for them is of secondary importance. Their opponents, from Powell onwards, have championed nation against state, in a scenario in which the oppressed English - often appearing in the guise of a nation defeated - are at odds with a state in the process of incremental Europeanization. Even when leader of the party, it was uncommon to hear Heath embellish the rhetoric of the conservative nation: it was there, touching the syntax of his politics; but he showed no evidence of being transported by the rhetoric itself. Enoch Powell, on the contrary, loved nothing more than to present himself as mystic soothsayer of the English nation, uttering truths no mere politician could even *see*. Heath is happy to have on record that his deepest innermost desire was to have been a hotel-manager. Heath and Powell are different beings, with different politics: the difference is of more than biographical significance.

One of the pressing questions about the history of contemporary Conservatism is how in the past twenty or twenty-five years this Heathite project - to use a short-hand - has come to be so thoroughly vanquished. So far as Heath himself is representative of this Tory tradition, he's been written out of, and written himself out of, contemporary Tory politics. As father of the House of Commons and a former prime minister he has some prestige; as a Tory ideologue he has none.

Four reasons for the defeat of this tradition can be outlined. First, the pro-Europeans remained closely tied to the old corporatist order of the postwar settlement, understanding Britain's move to Europe as merely an extension of the existing arrangement - to be brokered from above by the sympathetic civil servants and bankers. Second, while committed to the principles of the postwar settlement, Heath and many around him found themselves, to their consternation, in practice undoing the very system to which they gave allegiance. Despite these commitments, Heath - like Wilson and Callaghan - found himself pulled into the vortex of a proto-Thatcherism, confronting the unions, allowing unemployment to rise, restraining welfare expenditure. With such policies, the Heathites' resistance to the more full-blooded Thatcherites in their midst was compromised from the outset. Third, although the Europeans inside the Conservative Party were happy to take a pragmatic line on sovereignty, the deepest rhetorical resources of Conservatism, for them as well as for their opponents in the party, still resided with the party's identification with the nation. Yet the moment they began to mobilise this language, which lay at the very heart of Conservatism, they were trumped on every occasion by those who could speak it with greater authority, summoning up the spectre of an oligarchic

'Thatcherism heralded not the recreation of Conservatism, but its burn-out'

Europe ready to gobble up little England. Fourth, neither Heath nor later generations of pro-European Tories were able to turn Europe into a popular issue, generated by a distinct conception of moral and intellectual aspiration: it is an issue which has resolutely remained in the hands of the managers.

This is a continuing story inside Conservatism. In more recent times it has been exemplified by Chris Patten. On leaving university Patten (so the story goes) wrote to both the Conservative and the Labour parties offering his services: the Tories responded more speedily, and he signed up. He started out, reputedly, as the brightest of Thatcher's critics, in direct continuation of the Macmillan-Heath lineage. But by the 1983 election his dissidence had diminished and he accepted the Thatcherite mantra that there 'had been no alternative' to the crazed deflationary onslaught of 1981-2. When Major became prime minister in 1990 Patten saw the opportunity to turn the party to a less sectional, and a more pro-Europe, outlook. In cahoots with Sarah Hogg, he devised a plan which would have transformed the Tories from the outmoded champion of the conservative nation to a more modest, more modern and more centrist party, emulating the success of the Christian Democrats within Europe itself. This was both too tentative and too late. And also, perhaps, his previous compliance with the prevailing successes of Thatcherism in the mid-1980s may have complicated his standing as a force for a new Conservatism. Patten himself lost his seat in 1992 - to the delight of Lady Thatcher and her entourage who, we are told, cheered as the result came through. But by 1992 the anti-European right inside the party was already more formidable than their critics realised.

After Thatcher

In retrospect it is clear that the decisive moment occurred in the summer of 1990, when the patience of Sir Geoffrey Howe finally snapped, and he determined on his break with Thatcher. This marked the fracturing of Thatcherism at its very centre, culminating in Howe's resignation and in his public denunciation of his erstwhile leader, which shortly after led to the rebellion which turned Thatcher herself out.

Two things followed. On the one hand, pent-up personal enmities were unleashed within the Tory hierarchy. As the collapse continued, these became ever-more influential, a substitute for politics itself. Everything came to turn on personalities and on personal scores. The hustling in the perennial leadership crises was all but entirely negative. Candidates found favour not on merit but on their capacity to destroy someone down the line more loathsome than themselves. Especially for the humiliated Thatcherite loyalists the overriding aim was to shaft first Heseltine, and then Clarke.

On the other hand, in a larger sense, Thatcherism defeated - as an ideological legacy - transmuted into a barely restrained xenophobia, given force by the battle inside the party on Europe, but signifying little else. In terms of language and rhetoric, there were obvious continuities with the earlier traditions of the conservative nation. But the substance had shifted markedly, for as we have seen the electoral strength of the party had contracted to the rural heartlands of England and to a few select suburbs. This was a politics which was defensive and sectional, driven not by the attempt to universalise its programme but by an obsession with manifold enemies and subversives. Historically, Tory democrats had never been shy about demarcating citizens of rectitude from those of more deficient disposition. The line dividing the two turned on race and ethnicity, enemies of the conservative nation being perceived as failing to conform to an ethnic ideal of citizenship. In the Conservatism which now confronts us the pale of citizenship has been drawn tight. The inherited ethnic absolutism of historic Conservatism has come home, the sole rationale for a party which speaks to a declining constituency.

Middle England

The idea of Middle England started appearing in the press in the early 1990s, and has come to signify the archetypal conservative readership of Paul Dacre's *Daily Mail*. Dacre, a one-time socialist, has been courted by the right, as one might expect, but also - with greater assiduity - by the front-liners in Blair's new Labour team. For all the significant differences between Labour and Tory on Europe and on constitutional matters, no-one in the Labour leadership has been coy in making these overtures public. The *Mail* clearly functioned as the most contested terrain of the election. The Middle England of Paul Dacre's imagination, of Labour's electoral strategy and of the anti-Europe Tory right is barely an entity which can be verified socially. It is the invention of journalists, PR wizards and politicians, with plenty of spin on it. But politics operates by such inventions, the myths and the issues inseparably one. My own sense is that whatever inroads Labour have made or hope to make on the terrain of

The break-up of the conservative nation

Middle England, at the very least it functions as one of those myths which legitimates the politics of the beleaguered Tories, alerting us to the historical transformations underway. Whatever else the notion of Middle England suggests, it signifies an ethnic politics incapable of imagining a future for itself and, insofar as this is the case, it conforms precisely to the politics of the principal ideologues of the current Conservative rump.

We can see hints of these developments in some of the formal features of the national culture. In a recent issue of *Soundings* Phil Cohen suggested that soaps contained within them a utopian impulse which genuinely speaks to a wish for community and an ethos of lived collectivity. This insight can be given a historical gloss. Citizenship in twentieth-century Britain has operated on many different sites, the cultural as much as the narrowly political. One dimension of the cultural relations of citizenship has depended upon new members of the political nation possessing the opportunity to see an image of themselves projected in the nation's media, and thus come to be recognised - by themselves and others - not merely as voters but as actors and participants in the larger theatre of the nation's imaginings. Historically, developments in the mass media have mimicked the protracted development of mass universal politics: first the Archers and Dales in the rural counties, then the petty bourgeois and respectable working Mancunians who inhabit the appropriately named Coronation Street, and belatedly the more hapless, transient and ethnically diverse population of Albert Square in the East End.

Judging by the pronouncements of the current Tory ideologues, Albert Square represents a cultural world which simply doesn't enter the Conservative field of vision. Ethnicity is a critical signifier here, at odds with the immovable whiteness which underpins the imaginings of Middle England. Even those awarded recognition in the nation's soaps, it would seem, are destined to be written out of the Tory future.

The intensification of such sectionalist sentiment within Conservatism has been extraordinary to watch. It isn't simply the preserve of a handful of individuals on the right of the party: it cuts more deeply than that, finding a ready voice in all sections of the Tory press and touching those in the putative centre of the party as well. In April 1992 the *Sun*, famously, was taking credit for John Major's election victory, announcing the following month that he was 'monarch of all he surveys'. (The paper's niftiest, if under-reported,

Soundings

stratagem during the election had been to disclose the findings of a spiritualist who had consulted the deceased on their voting intentions. Churchill, Field-Marshall Montgomery, Queen Victoria, Elvis and Sid James declared themselves for the Conservatives, while Labour had to contend with Mao, Marx, Stalin, Trotsky, Brezhnev, Andropov, John Lennon and Robert Maxwell.) Within a matter of mere weeks the *Sun* had turned against Major - first on the incompetence of his chancellor, Norman Lamont, and secondly on his prevarications over Europe. The rest of the Tory press joined the fray, reflecting and amplifying the dissension which had moved to heart of the party itself. With 'Black Wednesday', in September 1992, Major's career as a credible Conservative leader of the future came to an end - and not even his subsequent resignation as party leader and trouncing of John Redwood could put him back together again. For five years, from the summer of 1992 to the spring of 1997, Major tried to hold the party together, reconciling two antagonist traditions of Conservatism. Like Balfour before him, at the beginning of the century over tariff reform, Major's attempts to reconcile the irreconcilable finished him.

> 'Below the surface was a nationalism intent on making ever fewer pretences to represent the nation'

This is not the place to detail the growing confidence of the anti-Europe evangelicals in these five years. The party could be run neither with them nor without them, allowing all manner of pretender to emerge. Major's 'bastards' - Bill Cash, George Gardiner, Teresa Gorman and the rest - were one thing. Quite another were those who carried with them the glint of ambition for the leadership - Michael Portillo, Michael Howard, Peter Lilley, John Redwood - that is, those professing to be politicians with a genuinely national programme and national appeal.

On the specifics of Europe they could offer the party strategists nothing which wouldn't have ripped the party apart. But on other matters - on what might be termed the politics of Little Middle England - it was precisely 'the bastards' and their allies who made the running.

The bastards dominant

Look first at the BSE crisis. On the morning of Tuesday 21 May 1996 John Major took the panic decision to 'declare war on Europe' (as the *Mail* delicately opined) in order to bring an end to the European Union's continued restrictions on the sale of British beef. This marked a moment when Major himself steadfastly marched into the camp of his erstwhile enemies, the militantly sceptical opponents of the EU. For long he had been an undeclared prisoner of the Tory right, each settlement of the internal party struggle gradually pulling him further away from the centre. On 21 May he crossed the threshold.

In this he was not alone. Malcolm Rifkind, one of the new pretenders, had been bending to the right, and sanctioned his leader's shift. So too, if with a touch more circumspection, had Stephen Dorrell, a man of hitherto unblemished progressive Tory sympathies - a move, subsequently, which spelt the end of his chances for the leadership, on the slightly curious grounds that this was an opportunism too far. Even Kenneth Clarke felt compelled to support Major's tactic of non-cooperation with the EU while still attempting to trumpet the virtues of the single currency. The shift was not Major's alone: it represented a larger political realignment in which the instincts of the right prevailed.

Lying just below the surface of this realignment was a nationalism intent on making ever fewer pretences to represent the nation. The symbolic ordering of this nationalism, in the midst of the crisis over British beef, was not as arbitrary, nor as crazed, as might first have appeared. The roast-beef-eating Englishman has a long history, the no-nonsense carnivore an active figure in the myths of the English. David Willetts, in his civilised English voice, may have regretted the excesses of 'other' nationalisms, evoking an elemental belonging fixed by blood and soil. The spring and summer of 1996, however, was a time when the imagined frontiers of the English nation were marked out in the traffic of gelatin, tallow and bull semen. The blood of roast beef and the blood of the Englishman have intermingled in many symbolic repertoires of the nation. Beef. Blood. Semen. This is very far from invoking a genteel history of Englishness. It summons a more rebarbative history, in which the purity of true English stock is what makes the nation.

Secondly, one might look at the increasing prominence of Michael Howard during these years. In May 1993, after the sacking of Lamont, Howard replaced Clarke as Home Secretary. Major was trying to hold the line on Europe and allowed his new Home Secretary a free hand. Howard's appointment coincided with the heart-breaking killing of the young James Bulger. Outrage and confusion touched everyone, and Howard moved in. While the government as a whole stood paralysed, he was one of the few senior ministers seen to be *doing* something. Many of the things he chose to do, according to the country's senior judges, were about as legal as the Great Train Robbery. And previous home secretaries, the Conservatives Lords Carr and Whitelaw, ganged up in the upper chamber in an attempt to restrain him. While keeping his head down on Europe Howard, by virtue of his dedication to old style law and order, was still able to present himself as tribune of Middle England, voicing an authoritarianism which none in the cabinet felt compelled to question.

This vision of Howard as the sole activist in the Conservative hierarchy was most apparent at the party conference of 1996. The 'schizophrenia' over Europe, which Kenneth Clarke denounced and which dominated press coverage, remained suitably medicated, inducing occasional hallucinogenic outbursts on the fringes but leaving the centre drugged and listless. The main architect of this listlessness was Clarke himself, content for nothing to be seen to happen which might open public strife on Europe. The cost of this quiescence, however, was to give Howard yet more free rein.

In Howard there rested the authentic residue of Thatcherism, shorn of its radicalism, but driven by an inventive vindictiveness toward those who refused to conform to the fantasised protocols of Middle England. Whereas John Major looked back with relish to the respectable cultures of suburban England of the early 1950s, Howard emerged as the hit-man prepared to bend back the urban cultures of our own day in order to transform the world into his master's vision. In him one can see a politics abjuring universalism in favour of breaking those who fail to live up to a phantom conception of civilisation.

Thirdly, one can see similar transactions at work in Major's declarations on Unionism. In his own mind the 1992 election was won due to one principal fact: defence of the Union. As he told an audience in Glasgow two years after the event: 'It was here in Scotland that we drew the line in the sand. We declared we could not, we would not, whatever the cost, whatever the risk, compromise our deepest core beliefs and put our nation at risk'. Yet this is a Unionism which is as phantom as the imagined protocols of Middle England. After the Framework Document of February 1995 the Conservatives in Westminster couldn't even count on the Ulster Unionists - let alone the Welsh or the Scots. Notwithstanding these realities Major tried to play the same hand in 1997. On the Monday before the election, in what seemed a desperate attempt to prove

The break-up of the conservative nation

to himself the realities of the Union, he touched down with his soapbox in Northern Ireland, Scotland and Wales. Back in his more familiar *heimat* of College Green, right by Westminster itself, he issued the warning: 'You have 72 hours to save the Union'.

Aftermath

The election confirmed what his critics already knew. The old Tory vision of the Union had, by the 1990s, come to mean little more than the politics of a contracting England. The asteroid came. Wipe out occurred in Scotland and Wales. It didn't seem much to matter which faction of the party MPs supported: they were cut down in equal measure. Electorally, the conservative nation resembled nothing so much as the geographic cluster of subscribers to *Country Life*. Party membership had fallen to some 300,000 - down from the one and a half million of 1979. The average age of party members has crept up relentlessly, and currently stands at 62. Financially, as well as politically, the Conservatives are bankrupt.

The result brought the party to the cusp of vertiginous collapse. Day after day the letters pages of the *Telegraph* throbbed with the melodrama of indignation. Treachery was on many lips, including those of Norma Major. John Major himself made his exit as speedy as humanly possible, leaving the squabbling rump to sort themselves out.

In the internecine battles which followed vengeance predominated, with all the bloodletting of an unabashed renaissance drama. No

'In Howard there rested the authentic residue of Thatcherism'

sooner was an alliance made than one of its brokers reneged. The representatives of Middle England seemed past caring. Destruction of rivals meant more than political alliance on matters of policy or principle. Ann Widecombe was happy to go on public record in her determination to destroy Howard, telling the press of her intention to 'hurt him politically and to wreck his chances of the leadership', and hinting of a personality subsumed in darkness, which most of the rest of us had spotted some while back. Early on, Howard himself and William Hague stitched up a deal, which fell apart when the effects of the champagne wore off: in all the collapse of civilised norms there was comedy too.

But in all this the centre of gravity of the party was pulling to the right.

Kenneth Clarke, the upholder of the European tradition in the final days of the last Tory administrations, sensed this all too keenly when, at the last moment, he befriended John Redwood to create the dream-ticket. In the event Clarke's prognostication of two years earlier on Redwood proved telling: 'I don't think the Conservative Party could win an election in a 1,000 years on his ultra rightwing programme'. Coquetting with this 'ultra rightwing programme' did Clarke no good. Having endeavoured to hold a principled line for all his time in government, in the final moments he saw the forces stacked against him and made his compact with the right. Sufficient numbers of both Clarke's supporters and those of Redwood couldn't find the stomach to continue with their respective loyalties: defeat for Clarke quickly followed.

In the end Hague slipped through because no-one hated him enough to want to destroy him. That was his principal virtue, an act of wanton desperation, self-destruction and spinelessness on the part of those who voted for him. One can't help but agree with the pithy verdict of Edward Heath: 'no ideas, no experience, no hope'. On the other hand, Lady Thatcher came out of the wood to give Hague her imprimatur - Mrs Favisham giving Pip her blessing - in order to ensure that Kenneth Clarke would be dispatched. So far as politics touched these events Hague did all that was required to ensure that his credentials with the right held steady. On 16 June he made it known that membership of his future shadow cabinet would be restricted to those who signed up to a ten-year veto on British participation in the single currency. There was no discussion, nor any outrage. Such was the state of the party it seemed entirely uncontentious and obvious. The ploy was his own invention, codifying the post-Thatcherite instincts of Middle England into party policy. If any future Conservative government were to happen, the 'war' with Europe and all it stands for would be quickened.

Factionalism on an increasingly rightist and xenophobic platform is what the Tories face. They haven't yet hit meltdown. There is no reason to suppose that they will split to a significant degree. But the traditional slogans of the conservative nation have now proved anachronistic beyond all measure. The only alternatives in sight - Hague; Portillo, a continuing presence; Howard, Redwood and the rest still with some power and with scores to settle - look distinctly menacing. Maybe even yet the Conservatives could revive in some as yet unknown form. The idea of those cheers of 2 May coming back to haunt us doesn't bear thinking about.

The uncanny family

Wendy Wheeler

The mind/body split of the old Enlightenment is being widely rejected. The family - in its widest sense - is one place where it may be possible to rethink the importance of affect for true reason.

Family values

Not many months ago, in a *Guardian* article expressing his increasing disillusionment with Tony Blair, journalist and ex-*Marxism Today* editor Martin Jacques offered, as evidence of Blair's social conservatism, the latter's support for the family and for 'family values'. More recently, reviewing Mary Kenny's book *Goodbye to Catholic Ireland*, marxist literary critic Terry Eagleton wrote, 'For Mary Kenny all this talk of patriarchal oppression is just feminist infantilism. At the end of a reasonably well-balanced account, she reveals the true colour of her case, which is turquoise. Kenny is a greeny-blue - an Irish conservative for whom liberalism leads inexorably to anarchism and talk of human rights to drugs and decadence ... In short, Mary Kenny turns out to be Melanie Phillips with a harp'.[1] Kenny is 'a fully recovered Sixties radical who once ran contraceptives into Dublin and now promotes family values'.[2] Melanie Phillips shares with Kernny a worry about the untrammelled pursuit of liberal individualism, and the ways in which the introduction of market-type contractual relations into social relations destroys the latter. Such social relations - educational and familial, for example - were once held to be more or less exempt

---

1. T. Eagleton, 'Unfashionably turquoise', *Observer Review*, 16 March 1997, p15.
2. Ibid.

from the naked imperatives of the market, because based in large part upon strictly non-calculable things such as affection, trust and respect.

I want to argue that we can understand the concerns of Kenny and Phillips, without accepting their whole analysis or the solutions they propose (and this applies to Tony Blair too). Their concerns cannot be swiftly dismissed, since they are one expression of a widespread contemporary anxiety - which in part is a recognition of the dehumanising nature of modern capitalism. Phillips argues that the psychical structure of the selves with which we are familiar is based upon the internalisation of discipline, described by Max Weber in terms of the protestant work ethic, by Norbert Elias in terms of humanist pedagogy and the inculcation of manners from the early sixteenth century onwards, and by Freud in terms of the development of the superego. Phillips' reasoning is thus that, if we are to stop the social rot of neo-liberal individualism and the (unsocialised) infantile narcissisms which demand instant gratification, and if we are to return to deferred pleasures and to social and individual responsibility, we must reinvoke the families, education and self-discipline in which, historically, the bourgeois self has been forged.

It seems likely, however, that things have gone too far for any such returns; the postmodern is precisely the condition of fragmentation of those older selves and ways of understanding and being in the world. But are we to continue into the dystopian future of the ceaselessly fragmenting postmodernity which is characteristic, according to Fredric Jameson, of Ernest Mandel's third, globally triumphant, stage of late capitalism?[3] Or is there another way emerging in which we might be able to think about our affective lives and intimate relations? We live in a world in which at least part of the very motor of capitalism is ever to increase the fantasmatic life in which our God-empty dreams can be fulfilled by 'retail therapy' and the commodity. There is, after all, an anti-capitalist logic to the paths which Kenny and Phillips have taken, in which strong families inculcating the importance of committed affective relations are seen as sites of ethical resistance to the irresponsibilities of 'my right to gratification', whatever the cost to 'you'.

The moral soil which Jeremy Bentham took for granted, and upon which he

---

3. Fredric Jameson, 'The Cultural Logic of Late Capitalism', in Jameson, *Postmodernism or, the Cultural Logic of Late Capitalism*, Verso, London 1991.

formulated the utilitarian calculus of happiness, has, over the intervening two hundred years, become much less substantial; the pursuit of unconstrained self-interest has become widely acceptable. Greed is good. As far as the family is concerned, is the choice, then, one between serial relationships, broken families, and, too often, hurt adults and children on the one hand; and, on the other the oppression, inequality and, for modern women at least, the unacceptable pressures of the traditional gendered division of labour within the bourgeois family?

Why is the family so often such taken-for-granted 'bad news' on the left? Why does the phrase 'family values' appear to command such easy and widespread scorn on the left, especially when people on the left are just as likely actually to be living in families as anyone else is? What is the point, or political usefulness, of condemning 'family values' when the family remains a hugely psychically and emotionally potent social form? Yes, the family certainly has been the site of oppressions various, and affections private to the point of pathology; yet, and in spite of the increasing numbers of people living alone (although not necessarily by choice), the majority of people still seek out the particular goods of intimate affection and sexuality offered by the shared household. Certainly this remains true of British women, as the recently published *Values and Visions: The What Women Want Social Survey* indicates:

> The subject of relationships came up again and again in the survey: it was a matter both of concern and joy, and clearly central to women's lives. In fact, more women in the UK are marrying or cohabiting than earlier in the century, according to Central Statistical Office figures for 1995. They show that 17 per cent of women born in the 1920s were still single by the time they were 30, compared to only 8 per cent of women born in the 1960s.
>
> Relationships are taking different forms and are more often not permanent. During 1993-94, 56 per cent of women in the UK were married and five percent cohabiting; 18 per cent were widowed, 6 per cent divorced and 2 per cent separated.[4]

In this 1996 survey of 46,000 women in the UK, women's main preoccupations

---

4. P. Smith, 'Section 6: Relationships', *Values and Visions: The What Women Want Social Survey*, eds. B. Vallely & I. Cowe, Women's Communication Centre, London 1996, p117.

were better and more equal relationships with men. Perhaps most importantly of all, most people still want to have children, and the family is where these children will be brought up. And, of course, *all* intense affections - whether sexual or not - are prey to great difficulties in contemporary societies; this is very often because we have lost the languages we once had for encoding and understanding various kinds of more or less intimate relationships; indeed, nearly all our relationships are increasingly less formalised and uncertain.

The research and statistics quoted above indicate that most women do still want to live in successful close affective relationships with men. These, along with committed same-sex relations which may or may not include children, and households headed by a lone parent, are all *families*, and the left needs to find a way of talking about them which is not simply damning: given what most people want and do, and especially where raising children is concerned, *what would the alternative really be?*

Nonetheless, and as many commentators have noticed, we have not yet found a new way of articulating the relationships we want (and perhaps now also fear) under postmodern conditions. Where children are concerned, workable solutions to these weakenings and loosenings of affective relations are very hard to find. Driven by the libertarian spin of 1980s neo-liberal languages of self-interest and self happiness, regardless of the well-being of others, the older ethos of responsibility to the other - whether pragmatic or Lévinasian - is clearly not surviving very well.[5] Solutions that might work for adults (half and half care; proximate living) may well be disturbing for children, particularly young ones, and the amount of general distress caused by the social acceptability of seeking personal satisfaction at more or less whatever cost seems to be widespread. People are *worried* by the breakdown of the family because they see it as a major source of acculturation. The history of pedagogical conduct literature in Western societies since the early sixteenth century suggests that the development of humanist Enlightenment was closely tied to an ethos which involved the disciplining of children, under the over-arching guidance of fathers, from much younger than had been standard practice in the Middle Ages.[6]

---

5. See Zygmunt Bauman's discussion of the Lévinasian 'face to face' in Bauman, *Postmodern Ethics*, Blackwell, Oxford 1993.
6. H. Cunningham, *Children and Childhood in Western Society Since 1500*, Longman, London 1995.

Contemporary anxieties about the state of the family are almost certainly a direct response to a centuries old tradition in which acculturation - the inculcation of good manners and control of the passions - and the developing ascendancy of civil, as opposed to violent martial, societies have been experienced as more or less directly linked. The gradual development of bourgeois civil society from the sixteenth century onwards, and, from that, the rise of liberalism and capitalist democracy, are interdependent phenomena. It would be surprising if, in however befuddled a way, this history of connected social and political forms was not experienced as important. What *other* explanation could there be for widespread anxiety about the breakdown of the family if not that it will lead to much wider social breakdown? Indeed there is an argument - too long to enter into here - which has sought to tie the fate of democratic societies quite closely to familial structures.[7] What is clear, however, is that one aspect of that centuries-long tradition of acculturation is waning fast, and that is the predominance given to the power of fathers over mothers. Since the immediate post-World War Two period, and perhaps for very obvious reasons, almost all childcare advice has centred on the importance of mothers, and of gentle love rather than authoritarian discipline, in early child care. This affectionate parenting should not, of course, be confused - as it too often has been perhaps - with the failure to set necessary boundaries.

Social anxiety and cultural symptoms

If one had to identify the major social anxieties and preoccupations of Britain in the mid to late 1990s, I think these would be very likely to be, in order of priority: law and order - especially the apparent breakdown of these on council estates housing large numbers of the unemployed and never-employed young men; education - with a focus upon primary and secondary schooling; and child-rearing - particularly where that is being done by single mothers. At first glance, these may not seem to be particularly directly linked; but if you turn the sequence

---

7. Briefly, the Frankfurt School took the view that the 'brief intermezzo' of true liberalism in the nineteenth century was dependent upon a strong and enlightened father. After World War Two, the psychoanalyst D.W. Winnicott argued that only by valuing and protecting the 'transitional' work of mothers could democratic societies hope to preserve the psychical conditions necessary to their survival.

around, it becomes clear that what these social anxieties describe quite precisely is an anxiety about the trajectory - from infancy, through schooling, to productive and informed citizenship - of those people who are recognisably *not* being caught by the work ethic and associated self-disciplines of civility. But this anxiety is not simply about the disadvantaged themselves; it has such an intense purchase because it seems to paint a picture of the dystopian future we can all expect when all the things which forge the bourgeois soul no longer work. In other words, the fact of disadvantage is troubling in itself, but the *punch* of these related issues, which so exercise public debate these days, comes from the ways in which they tell us something about the failing future of the *bourgeois* self. Feckless men on sink estates and single 'welfare mothers' seem to provide a very obvious challenge to the ethos of 'proper' work and the ordered family, but it is hardly amongst these groups alone that these problems arise. The majority of families headed by a lone parent (overwhelmingly women) are the result of much wider social changes in which familial commitment is weaker, and divorce is acceptable. Disadvantaged people have become the *visible* site of a 'problem' - about the family - which is *actually* rampant, but much more hidden, amongst the middle classes themselves.

Both Norbert Elias and Raymond Williams have written about the structures of feeling informing the development of bourgeois life. In *The Civilizing Process*, Elias offers a detailed survey of conduct literature from the sixteenth to the eighteenth century - especially the much reprinted 1530 treatise *De civilitate morum puerilium* (On civility in boys) by Erasmus - in order to argue that the long transition from the emotional and physical violence and volatility of medieval life to the civility, order and 'sympathy' of modern life, and to the structures of feeling which we associate with the rationality of Enlightenment (ordered forms, whether in logic or aesthetics; proper conduct; empathy with others, as in the cult of sensibility), is effected by the increasing pedagogical emphasis on self control, the containment of aggression, and good manners - especially in boys, towards whom the bulk of this conduct literature is directed. In order to be civilised, one must, in particular, control one's affections and one's body, especially where the physical boundaries of the latter are traversed - as in eating, shitting, belching, farting, spitting and so on. What Elias describes is what Mikhail Bakhtin, in his Introduction to *Rabelais and His World*, writes of as the move from the 'open' medieval body to the 'closed' classical body of the seventeenth century and beyond.

When we consider what it is that is closed, fixed, and oppressive about the bourgeois family, it is worth asking what it is that is 'oppressed' or 'suppressed' within it. Girl children were largely left out of the pedagogical impulses of humanism and Enlightenment. It is, thus, arguable that what is suppressed is, as it were, something 'medieval' which came to be more closely associated with girls and women - i.e. 'irrationality' and a predominance of the passions. What has historically been privatised in the modern family form is the life of the affects. Yet it has been women, and their attentions to the world of feeling and social connectedness, who have kept an *economic* arrangement *psychically* and *emotionally* viable. The family is a site of both oppression, free labour, and reproduction for capital, *and* of resistance to capital's calculating-machine model of life. The paradox is that capital has depended intimately upon the, largely female, sustenance of affective 'medieval' life in order to make and to preserve the affective bonds of the (bourgeois) family as an *economic* unit necessary to capital's continuation. Here capitalism promotes the non-calculable affections which, everywhere else, it has been determined to banish in pursuit and rationalisation of efficiency. Treating people like human beings has not, generally, been deemed profitable. Now, however, things are changing.

No turning back

We are living in extraordinary times. I can understand perfectly well the logic which leads Melanie Phillips to argue for a return to 'proper' families and the inculcation therein of the work ethic and the associated self-controls through which the Protestant work ethic and early capitalism flourished; but the fact is that one cannot turn the clock back. We are moving towards different, more self-reflexive, understandings of our postmodern condition. In fact, what I want to argue here is that we are on the brink of discovering - largely through recent developments in neuroscience, and in related, new, understandings of mind, human reason and intelligent action - a whole new way of thinking about ourselves and our relationships to the rest of the living and inanimate world. In these new understandings, ethical behaviour will not simply be (as it has increasingly been in humanist self-understandings since the sixteenth century) the result of an internalised aggression manifested as self-control and good manners, in which the individual suppresses his desires in conformity with the mores of the group; rather, ethical behaviour will spring from a gradual, increasingly widespread, but absolutely fundamental reconceptualisation of human mind and human well-being. In the coming conceptualisations of what it means to have a mind - especially, a self-conscious and self-reflective intelligence (although I think that we may not want to restrict our understanding of mind to *self*-consciousness) - the cartesian individual who is isolated in the *cogito*, and who thus conceives of himself, imagines himself, as separated from all others, including that most intimate other - his own body - will be re-understood as something absolutely embodied in the world and intimately and sensually connected to it.

> 'The *post*modern is exposed as the disavowed condition of being *modern*'

At the very point at which many of us worry about the new Labour embrace of market economies and top-down managerialism, it seems more than likely that the future will belong to a species of socialism; for it is in the socialist and proto-socialist tradition that connectedness, and an ecology of collective life and continuity with the natural world, has historically been thought. Just when it seems that neo-liberalism and the market has triumphed, we actually find ourselves at the threshold of ways of thinking about human mind and reason - as ineluctably embodied in the world - which will eventually quite dramatically modify the ways in which we go about our daily lives (including in families) and will decisively limit the terrible powers of capital which have been ravening onward again in the last twenty years. We may well have entered a new third phase of capital after World War Two, but recent scientific developments - in neurobiology; in the mathematics of propositional logic and Artificial Intelligence; in related theories of new economics which advance more holistic ways of calculating happiness and well-being; and in health research which indicates that the healthiness of a population depends upon a minimising of relative inequalities within the population - suggest that our understanding of ourselves, as people and as economic actors, is in the process of quite radical change.

Left thinking has, of course, produced theories of connectivity based on class, but it has often been indifferent or hostile to thinking about these connectivities on smaller or more local scales; the impetus to do so has come almost exclusively from two sources: feminism and ecology. Both of these have, of course, been critical of the hierarchical modes of domination associated with the patriarchal family and with the nature-mastering modes of modern technology and science, but neither have forgotten or been contemptuous of the very small and local connections that are the living stuff of the larger picture.

The unconditioned heart

It is generally thought that the postmodern refers to a time and a condition of fragmentation, uncertainty, and scepticism in relation to the possibility of Truth. Some of this has been over-stated; there are a great many things - trivial in the wide scheme of things but significant enough for most of us - that we *know*, in all useful senses of the word, to be true. The postmodern, as condition, exposes the uncertainty of a Godless and morally ungroundable world. As such, the *post*modern is what modernity - via its great narratives of spiritual and scientific progress towards the good - tries to cover over. In other words, the *post*modern - finally exposed as the disavowed condition of being *modern* - is something to be faced and to be worked through. The paradox, if it is one, is that in order to be thoroughly and courageously *modern*, we must first be able to encounter our condition of being *post*modern without trying to run away from its difficulties, and from the fact of the loss of all the things which the processes of modernity have taken away - especially the comforting things, such as the certainties of tradition, a non-alienated symbolic life, and a sense of being at home in the world (however fraught).

In recent years, a term has come into use which I think captures something of the positive possibilities of this postmodern transitional period, rather than the fracturing, unbindingness and cynicism usually associated with postmodernity. This term is 'reflexive modernity'; it means an expanding of the inner space delineated by the term 'modernity'. It means the detailed reflecting upon what it means to be a self, upon what it means to have some relatedness to others, upon what it means to occupy a space in the world amongst other human and non-human creatures and forms of life; but this reflection centrally includes a reflection upon reflexivity; that is to say, a more subtle reflection upon the *side-effects* of any action. What this means is a self-reflexive engagement with the *incalculable*. Whereas modernity sought to rationalise the world, postmodernity - or reflexive modernity - engages with the non-calculability of the world. As Ulrich Beck puts it: 'Modernisation no longer conceived of only in instrumentally rational and linear terms, but as refracted, as the rule of side-effects, is becoming the motor of social history'.[8] Reflexive modernity means a reflection upon experience which is not measured simply in terms of the coolly rational and 'mathematically' calculable. This latter form, or idea, of rationality - one which ignores the very obvious *affective* purchases of symbolic life, for example - is what Gerald Edelman has referred to as 'the first Enlightenment'.[9] What the term 'reflexive modernity' captures is the encounter with modernity as a form of loss (of tradition, of belief, of certainty), but one which moves beyond the very real nostalgias and melancholias of fracturing and splitting postmodernity, and goes towards the proper mournings of a *new* modernity. In this, we become able, in myriad forms, to reflect upon the ways in which we can *save* our human-ness. Saving our human-ness means reflecting upon what makes the quality of our lives truly human: that is to say, it means reflecting upon the *non-calculability* of our lives. In as much as this is an expansion of the project of Enlightenment, it is modern; but, in so far as it is a rejection of calculability, it is postmodern, reflexive, and constitutes a *new* modernity.

It is hard to find a serious commentator these days who has not noticed the 'postmodern' turn to non-rationalism. Derridean deconstruction and Foucauldian genealogy, for example, have offered influential critiques of the rationalism associated pre-eminently with cartesian scepticism and, later, with Bentham's 'calculable man'. The motor of this critique of reason lies, I believe, in something absolutely integral to modernity, which is the split between head and heart. As Ernst Cassirer pointed out,[10] the dominant spirit of eighteenth-century Enlightenment was logical and essentially mathematical - scientific, we might say - and, by the end of the eighteenth century, a revulsion against the calculating spirit of utilitarian materialism manifested itself in the Romantic urge towards what Wordsworth called 'relationship and love'.

This opposition - utilitarian rationalism and reforming enlightenment on

---

8. U. Beck, *The Reinvention of Politics*, Polity Press, London 1997, p3.
9. G. Edelman, *Bright Air, Brilliant Fire: on the Matter of the Mind*, Penguin, Harmondsworth 1992, p171. 'We may well hope that if sufficiently general ideas synthesizing the discoveries that emerge from neuroscience are put forth, they may contribute to a second Enlightenment. If such a second coming occurs, its major scientific underpinning will be neuroscience, not physics.'
10. E. Cassirer, *The Philosophy of the Enlightenment*, tr. Koelln & Pettegrove, Princeton U.P., Princeton N.J. 1951.

the one hand, and the romanticism of the organic utopian society (a sort of future-orientated conservatism) on the other - gave form to the great debates of the nineteenth century and beyond: Wordsworth and Coleridge; Thomas Carlyle; Matthew Arnold; J.S. Mill; Ruskin; William Morris and so on. Recently, we have seen its political outline clearly again in the new Labour creed of the inclusive bindings-up of a stakeholding society which were offered as an antidote to the unbinding deregulations of Thatcherite neo-liberalism. The seeds of Blairism can be seen in the first New Left of the 1950s, particularly in the cultural analyses made by Raymond Williams.

> 'The inclusive bindings up of a stakeholdong society are an antidote to the unbinding deregulations of neo-liberalism'

This impulse to rethink the culture as a whole was also the spirit which gave birth to Woodstock and the Summer of Love in the 1960s, and which returned, in the 1990s, in the more commodified hippyism and mysticism which remains around us today. In the 1990s, New Age mysticism and the Age of Aquarius went mainstream. People who were EST (Erhardt Seminar Training) and Exegesis cultists in the 1970s now make a packet out of management consultancies. The rejection of cold-hearted utilitarian rationalism is widespread; and, for those of us who have watched neo-liberalist managerialism and laissez-faire market economics tear apart the social fabric, the return to the heart - and to a sense of the connectedness of mind and body, body and world - may seem like an appealing thing.

The old terms of the cartesian split between body and mind are not only attacked by contemporary romantics and mystical management consultants; hard-headed calculating science is turning its attention to holism too. As I indicated above, recent research - from neuro-biologist Antonio Damasio, and mathematician Keith Devlin, for example - also seeks to illuminate the error of cartesian dualism and scientific method.[11] Damasio shows that rational behaviour is always dependent upon affective, bodily, information; Devlin - whose mathematical specialism is the propositional logic used in

---

11. A. Damasio, *Descartes Error: Emotion, Reason and the Human Brain*, Picador, London 1995. K. Devlin, *Goodbye, Descartes: The End of Logic and the Search for a New Cosmology of the Mind*, John Wiley, Chichester 1997.

computer programming - argues that human intelligence is always embodied, in part intuitive, and derived from the affects: the dream of computer intelligence (as opposed to lightning-speed calculation) is just that - a dream; and this is precisely because of the very *embodied* nature of human knowledge. Both Damasio and Devlin argue that our ability to make rational decisions is dependent upon the myriad experiences of being embodied creatures; no computer can have that experience. Computers are programmed according to logical propositions mathematically encoded - of the sort 'if A then B' - and no set of mathematically logical propositions is capable of encoding the potential context-dependent complexity of even the simplest of human interactions; these latter call upon enormously complex, not necessarily conscious, responses of memories, visceral responses in the past and the present, and visceral responses to minute changes of expression, posture and so on in others. Only creatures with bodies and memories of bodies can do this; and only creatures with self-consciousness can reflect on their own responses in order to make complex judgements. Reason, and intelligent mind, are always intimately dependent upon body and affect - that is to say, upon *feeling* in *all* senses of the word.

So far so good. Very many of us have felt that the cartesian distinction - in which what was certainly true was self-conscious mind, whilst body, object and world, were something else and less certain - was wrong. Descartes had to introduce his two proofs of God to guarantee the truth of our perceptions of the object world (including our own bodies), and Kant said that we can never know the truth of reality in-itself, but only the world as it appears for us. Clearly, what is important about the turn (or return) to an understanding of mind as embodied is that it offers to restore to us a sense of being as *being in the world*. This is the sense at which both ecological and mystical or pantheistic understandings of being grasp.

Recent moves from within the hard sciences - neurobiology with Damasio, mathematics with Devlin, and, a little earlier, the physics of Fritzjof Capra, and eco-science generally - offer to restore relationships between spheres (basically those of science, morality, and art) which have become separated in modernity. These developments in modern science echo earlier anti-Cartesian claims, made at the end of the eighteenth century, concerning - from Jacobi, for example - the impossibility of grounding knowledge in anything other than intuition or 'the leap of faith'.

Thought through, this renewed sense of rational being as always embodied *being-in-the-world* enables a new reflection upon every aspect of human life and relations. To understand that, when you are a part of the lives of friends, colleagues, lovers, children, you are *really* a part of their mind and being - that is: mind as an ecology of body-mind, and mind-body as an ecology of body-world - is to see one's place, the place of the individual, in the workplace, in the home, in the community, in social and political actions of all sorts, very, very, differently. For one thing, such a view *deprivatizes* affective life. To understand that mind is embodied - and that what I *sense* (see, hear, touch, taste, smell) *is a part of my mind* - is to have a very different view of the world from the atomised Cartesian view.

At the worst, in a litigous culture, one can imagine the possibility of family members, or employees, suing on the grounds of 'affective disruption' (the old hippy expression 'mind-messing' was an early conveyor of the 'ecology of mind' view). Where scientific evidence could be brought in support, one can entertain the not wholly gratifying picture of a distressed employee suing a soul-less corporation for 'messing with my mind' - and winning. Might this not increase a trend, which Paul Heelas has noted, towards the increasingly widespread use - amongst absolutely mainstream companies and institutions - of New Age techniques in management? It is worth quoting Heelas at a little length in order to give the full flavour of the *already* changed perceptions of mind, self-consciousness, and interaction which are being taken absolutely seriously by both capitalist institutions and academic researchers:

> As long ago as 1984, the European Association for Humanistic Psychology, together with the Human Potential Research Project of the Department of Educational Studies of the University of Surrey, ran a large conference on 'Transforming Crisis'. Luminaries such as Peter Russell, 'one of the first people to take human potential workshops into corporations' according to conference material, were involved. The Croydon Business School, to provide a more recent illustration, has run a two week event, in association with the New Age Skyros Institute, on the subject of 'Innovative Management'. (IBM's Tom Jennings was one of the distinguished staff.) And Ronnie Lessem (1989), of City University Business School (London) has written a volume

extolling the principles of 'metaphysical management'. Thinking of my own university, it will be recalled that the Centre for the Study of Management Learning, together with a New Age consultancy (Transform), has run a conference entitled 'Joining Forces: Working with Spirituality in Organizations'. And in the States, influential author Michael Ray is Professor of Creativity and Marketing at Stanford University. Furthermore an increasing number of articles on New Age management and business are appearing in academic journals. The *Journal of Managerial Psychology*, for example, recently ran a special issue on 'Spirituality in Work Organizations'.[12]

At best, one might imagine that selfish behaviour - as an insult to, and assault upon, the very *minds* of others - might become much more profoundly socially unacceptable. Whatever the view of the post-Cartesian self, the effects will certainly be more profound than has widely been recognised. The claim to have been subjected to passive smoking will pale into insignificance alongside such possibilities as the claim to have been subjected to passive violent objectification in the mind of another!

Of course, this is a sort of knowledge which is already partly known - criticism can never articulate anything that isn't already, in some sense, a part of knowledge and the times - and it is quite well understood by some people in some sorts of relationships. For example, we - some of us - can grasp quite easily, and act upon, the idea that emotional violence is experienced *affectively* in precisely the same way as physical violence; or even that it may be worse where their is no *physical* sign of trauma; fewer people are happy with the idea of an ecology of the workplace, or with the idea of structural managerial violence, or the violence of offices, or the violence of housing, or the violence of social and legal systems - least of all, perhaps, those responsible for running them. To extend reflexivity (an economy of *side-effects*) into the spheres of work and politics might improve both the *real* quality of life *and* efficiency, but it would do so by measuring both these things differently - i.e. holistically. (A challenge here to what might constitute *really* reasonable criteria for monetary

---

12. Paul Heelas, *The New Age Movement*, Blackwell, Oxford 1996, p66. The epigraph to Heelas' book is 'Only connect' (from E.M. Forster's *Howard's End*, i.e. 'only connect the prose and the passion').

convergence in Europe?)

Thinking holistically in a reflexive and more subtle way seems to be a generally good thing; the problem, it seems to me, lies in how the holism is *imagined*. The trouble with the thinking of wholes lies in the move from 'total' to 'totalitarian'. I think it likely, for instance, that early romantic accounts of mind or spirit as embodied being, combined with the Hegelian narrative of being as dialectical becoming, were influential in the formation of scientific discourses of inheritance and progress as expressed in the nineteenth-century science of heritable characteristics, from which eugenics emerged. Here, romantic philosophy combined with modern science to produce the 'irrational rationalism' which manifested itself in the *Übermensch* doctrines of National Socialism.

Thus, the postmodern turn to romantic critiques of a limited, disembodied and abstract form of reason as the only source of rational knowledge about the world, and the postmodern rejection of a solely objectifying science which refuses to see the absolute interconnectedness of things, still leaves us with the problem of imagining what Theodor Adorno called a 'togetherness of the manifold' which is not a form of, potentially totalitarian, violence. The only form which I can imagine - and I am certainly not alone in this - would be an ecology in the fullest and widest sense. To recognise that we are not, in fact, atomised individuals, but that we are part of, that we *effect* and *affect*, all the forms of social and natural life in which we think and act, would be radically to reconceptualise our social and political relations.

I think that there is already plenty of evidence - across the world - of the development of these kinds of ways of thinking that I have been talking about. The danger - as deep greenism, amongst other things, has shown - is of various forms of totalitarianism. To acknowledge reflexively a more subtlely holistic world in which human reason is always also body, affect, and intuition - and mind *is* in the world, not locked inside the skull - is not necessarily to open the doors to chaos or to great surges of unmediated emotion. But it will be as well for us to recognise what the dangers are, and where they lie. In fact, I think that, as far as our own politics go, some people probably do recognise the dangers of the new romanticism, and it is this - not necessarily well-theorised - recognition which accounts for what I call 'the Blair-Smirnoff Effect', in which one experiences moments of dizzying uncertainty as to whether what one is watching is a pussy-cat or a tiger. 'From Bambi to Kim Il Sung in six months' probably said it all quite early on. Let's hope that Buddha Blair's Third Way steers a path somewhere in between.

Finally, taking care of affective relations, and understanding that proper - as opposed to dessiccated - rationality *includes* affect, is what families - and especially, perhaps, the women in them - try to do. That this is always fraught is inevitable. Home and family can be mobilised for reactionary ends, but they are also, for us, and as Marianna Torgovnick has argued, very often the site of our utopian ideals of a place where our very difficult human-ness is acceptable and negotiable.[13] As Angelika Bammer also points out, the idea of 'home' is one of the 'recuperative gestures of our affective needs'.[14] However much the family has been a site of patriarchal oppression, it has also, in modernity, been the *only* institutionalised place where such affective life-work has been done. I can see no reason to be scornful about the historical importance of this sphere - however imperfect it has been.

Largely, the imperfections of the modern family - its oppressions, and its quiet violences - have derived from its uncanniness: what is homely, comfortable, safe and familiar (*heimlich*), can too easily turn into what is hidden within, secret and, thus, potentially, frightening (*unheimlich*).

The future, however, is eco-shaped and resistant to the closed off, to the secret and to the private. Not only should progressive people on the left be able to develop a positive understanding and language in relation to the affective work done in families (most often by women, of course), but they need to understand that this affective work, this understanding of mind as embodied, and of body as enworlded, *is being deprivatised*; it is spreading out of the family into the much wider world. Hopefully, it will alter the face of capitalism forever.

---

13. See Angelika Bammer, Editor's Introduction to special issue *New Formations*, 17, (Summer, 1992): The Question of 'Home', pxi.
14. *Ibid.*

Reimagining the inhuman city
The 'Pure Genius' Land Occupation
Dave Featherstone

The Pure Genius occupation represented an innovative form of politics. Dave Featherstone analyses its strengths and weaknesses.

Mike Davis commented in his discussion of the dark side of contemporary Los Angeles that as the 'walls have come down in Eastern Europe they are being erected all over our cities':[1] there are scars in every city now. Our cities increasingly flaunt their 'inhuman character'; poverty and wealth existing in vicious proximity, the formation of urban landscapes razed by the incessant demands of the car and the increasing disappearance, enclosure and surveillance of public spaces.[2] The task of creating truly human forms of urbanisation has never clamoured as violently as it does today in the cities of Britain. In the context of such hostile directions of urbanisation, the occupation of a piece of derelict land, owned by Guinness and marked for development, by activists associated with the land rights campaign The Land is Ours in Wandsworth between May and October 1996 was innovative, welcome and necessary. It was an important event for many reasons, but it was riven by tensions and problems which demand being engaged with.

---

1. Mike Davis, *City of Quartz*, Vintage, London 1990.
2. Walter Benjamin, *Charles Baudelaire: A Lyric Poet in the Era of High Capitalism*, Verso, London 1973, refers to Parisians living under Haussmann as becoming 'conscious of the inhuman character of the great city.'

Soundings

On 5 May, 1996, about 200 activists moved on to 14 acres of ex-industrial land at Gargoyle Wharf beside the Thames adjacent to Wandsworth Bridge. The aim of the occupation was to form a demonstration site illustrating possible uses of derelict and wasteland in Britain's cities which are more sustainable and socially equitable than existing ones. Activists moved prefrabicated structures on to the land - including structures to house communal debate, make-shift dwellings, and prefabricated compost toilets. Large quantities of compost were moved on to the site so gardens could be constructed and planted, enabling vegetables to be grown healthily and successfully on land which was concreted over and potentially still contaminated. Some activists stayed beyond the first weekend/ week, but a loose community of about 50 people formed on the site in an ad hoc way out of a mixture of local homeless folk, travellers and activists. This community came to be known as 'Pure Genius'. People on the site were encouraged and helped to build low cost and low impact housing with materials mainly from the detritus of urban society, often found in skips near the site: some of these structures had strikingly innovative character and designs.

The land, which had been derelict and enclosed for seven years, was the site of an old brewery which Guinness had acquired as part of its asset stripping of Distillers during its murky takeover of that company. Guinness had sought planning permission to build a supermarket on the land, an application which was later turned down. The site's location illustrated London's brutally socially polarised character: a social polarisation in this case entrenched by the policies of Wandsworth's - radical right dominated - Conservative Borough Council. Adjacent to the site, along the Thames, was a luxury waterfront housing development. The site's backdrop was a badly maintained social housing project separated from the site by a busy main road: its inhabitants largely welcomed and were supportive of the occupation. Over the period of dereliction a rich pioneer ecology had developed on the site: a survey by London Wildlife Trust found more than 300 plant species, including many rare in London. Merely opening up such a piece of land was an important effect of the occupation, making it a resource which a deprived local community could use rather than being alienated and excluded from.

There are three elements of the occupation which I believe are significant. First there is the innovative way in which the campaign moves the direct action movement on to a terrain where it can begin to expand its own agenda rather

Reimagining the inhuman city

than being fixed within the structure of constant opposition. Second are ways in which it provides an active interrogation of what it is to live in this land in the late twentieth century, celebrating events in English/British history which have often been ignored or dismissed, in a way which can wrest some of the terrain/experience of Englishness away from the right. Thirdly, there are the ways it suggests for the broad green movement to engage with urban politics in the environment and social justice.

Directions for direct action

The direct action movement, a fractured and fluid network, burst into the 1990s provoked by the Government's road programme, and found itself incensed into unity by the Criminal Justice Act. While at times it has been strikingly innovative, its influence and imagination have been constrained by a tactic of response to agendas and ideas formed by the government and private capital. Although alternative voices around the direct action movement have forged spaces in which they can speak and crystallise (like *Squall:* the magazine for (as)sorted itinerants), opposition and fragmentation have hindered its ability to articulate a will to shape society. Such problems are partially intensifying as parts of the movement's politics become hardened and fixed - a direction symbolised by the rise of the tunnel as a main part of the resistance - illustrative of a tendency towards being rebels against *any* future rather than being part of imagining and constituting a new one.

The argument of Gramsci, that advanced capitalist societies depend for their legitimacy on the 'spontaneous consent given by the great masses of the population to the general direction imposed on social life by the dominant fundamental group' can inform our ways of thinking about how social/political movements can challenge and reshape this direction.[3] Dominant groups elicit this 'spontaneous consent' by constructing hegemonic power relations which, through a complex interlocking of political, social and cultural forces, diffuse their own lived system of meanings and values throughout the whole of social life. This process works through institutions, such as media and education rooted in civil society, which shape the ordinary thoughts of the mass of the population:

---

3. Antonio Gramsci, *Selections from Cultural Writings*, Lawrence & Wishart, London 1985, p12.

the legitimacy of the state is also bolstered by the law and the use of force in times of crisis/conflict.[4] Thus power is not brittle and rigid - as it often seems to be conceptualised in the anti-roads movement - but is fluid and amorphous; it urges, incites and solicits as much as it punishes. To challenge the direction of such societies one must contest at the level of the terrain on which hegemony is secured: i.e one must consider not only the economic, but also the moral/intellectual arguments which can prove decisive in transforming and shaping the ordinary thoughts and actions of people and social groups.

The 'Land is Ours' occupation represents a significant development towards developing a will and praxis to shape society; rather than squatting land in the route of a proposed road, it has taken the initiative to define for itself which land and which issues are important. Through this it forms the germ of an alternative hegemonic formation which connects disparate forms of struggle and begins to find spaces around which it can take a 'leading' role in society. This is not in the narrow sense of providing ordinary political leadership but in the much deeper and wider sense of actively illustrating/forging directions which society could take, through engaging with and attempting to shape the common sense of the moment.

In the present situation the ideological project of Thatcherism has succeeded in making free market monetary values seem almost 'natural' - the only and 'spontaneous' way in which the world is conceptualised - attaching this to a regressive vision of a society based around a fixed notion of the family. New Labour, though placing different accents on certain areas, has not broken with this central emphasis on the market and the family. Defined as it is against radical democratic ways of modernising the labour movement, in government it is allying this emphasis on the market and the family with paternalistic and hierarchical attitudes towards people, rooted in a Fabianism that has long structured the Labour Party where people are passive subjects to the wills of bureaucrats and experts. Policy programmes like 'Welfare to Work' are illustrative of this. In their refusal to forge spaces which allow the ideas of the young unemployed to be integrated into their conceptualisation and construction, they are not being structured in a genuinely open way. Thus there continues to be a

---

4. This description of hegemony is taken from Raymond William's chapter on hegemony in *Marxism and Literature*, Oxford Universuty Press, Oxford 1997.

49

Soundings

vacuum for the articulation of ideas which can challenge and reimagine dominant and accepted values in innovative and inspiring ways.

This space is being partially filled by a small subset of new social/political movements like The Land Is Ours, which have stressed linking direct action with the battle of ideas. A fine example of the way the occupation engages with this struggle is the way the campaign recaptures certain languages and gives them a different accent to the one with which they are usually encoded. In reclaiming the 'stolen language of self help' from the way Thatcherism articulated it to a selfish and monetised individualism, it opens the possibility of restoring the idea of 'self-help' as one of the core ethics and values of a flourishing and socially aware alternative.[5] In doing so it illustrates how problems like homelessness can be engaged with in direct ways where dwellers have control over their own housing and micro-environment and where people have exposure to the immediacy and empowerment associated with direct action, in a supportive atmosphere. It develops an ethic which can create forms of housing directly responsive to people's desires and needs. This offers a way beyond both the bureaucratic colonisation of lived space which is the legacy of post-war social housing policy in Britain and the individualism of Thatcherism.

'It challenges the official versions of English History as inherently uncontested and not riven by struggle'

Contesting Englishness

A contestation of dominant interpretations of 'English history' is integral to the identity of The Land Is Ours. The occupation of the site at Wandsworth was timed to celebrate the fiftieth anniversary of the post-war squatting movement, when demobbed soldiers squatted disused barracks and military land on finding themselves homeless. Celebrating this anniversary and events like the Diggers' squatting of St George's Hill in 1649, alongside invoking the troubled memories of processes such as enclosure, is important, because it challenges the official versions of English history as inherently uncontested and not riven by struggle. Major landowners still derive legitimacy from the

---

5. Colin Ward, *When We Build Again: Let's have housing that works!*, Pluto Press, London 1985.

production of the idea of England as a 'green and pleasant land' where the status and territory of land owners was uncontested, a discourse which represents the mass of the people as unchanging and not active in the creation of their own history or landscape. A similar contestation of history has been an important part of the road protests. Its creative, cheeky culture has thrown up icons like the Union Jill, symbols which offer tentative resources for the construction of oppositional imaginations informed by a 'pluralistic, post colonial sense of British culture and national identity'.[6]

This whole reappropriation of history is still beset, though, by a tendency to sediment experiences of dissent into sealed constructions of ethnicity and place. The result of this, as in other celebrations of English dissent, like E.P. Thompson's invocation of the 'freeborn Englishman', is to deflect attention away from the way dissent in England was shaped by its place in transatlantic systems of exploitation and cultural exchange, leaving the impression that it evolved organically from its own transformations. If these interrelations are taken seriously, I think it is possible to draw on the complex history of dissent in Britain to ground an oppositional imagination which is inclusionary and pluralistic. What was important in Wandsworth was that the diverse nature of people living on the site - including travellers, black British, urban homeless - showed that The Land Is Ours had not substituted land owners for an ethnically purified 'ours'. Such an interrogation of the past and of the symbols of the past allied with a pluralistic reality, can rupture the potent image of an undivided English people which was used by Thatcherism to attack as un-English 'alien insiders' - the miners as the enemy within - and outsiders - 'immigrants' - who might 'swamp' our national culture.[7] This is a construction New Labour has also largely based itself upon (eg Blair: 'Britain can and will be a great country again'. 'This is the patriotic party because it is the people's party.')

Articulating the right to the city

The ideological division between the country and the city is long standing and pervasively structures the contemporary green movement. Even as this division

---

6. Paul Gilroy, *The Black Atlantic*, Verso, London 1993.
7. The introduction to Stuart Hall's *Hard Road to Renewal*, Verso, London 1988, has a fine discussion of Thatcherism's relation to and production of populist nationalism.

becomes more and more blurred in reality, it seems its importance as an ideological/ cultural boundary becomes more pronounced. The green movement's tendency to root itself in the values of an imagined idyllic country side based in a rather rigid gaze to the past, which castigates the city as a virulent pathological excresence, has led to a poverty of green perspectives on cities and a reticence to seriously engage in urban issues. This is related to the way the green movement has rarely integrated the ideas or experiences of the poor into its theory or praxis around ecological issues. Where there have been innovative positions developed around ecological and urban issues, they tend to have emerged from alliances which have ruptured and expanded the movement's intellectual boundaries. Inspiring examples in Britain are the road protests against the M77 and the M11 Link Road, where itinerant activists have intersected with local working class communities in Glasgow and East London; and in the US Environmental Justice movement where poor black and hispanic communities have mobilised against the racism structuring location of hazardous waste sites which threatens to make their localities 'ecological sacrifice zones'. These movements have found it necessary to engage with the nature of capitalist urbanisation because it is frequently in such marginalised urban locales that the multiple oppressions arising from the inter-relationships between poverty and ecological problems are lived.

In reconstructing cities in a way which would facilitate their appropriation by their inhabitants, it is crucial to recognise that cities are the result of inter-relating processes working at many different scales. It is necessary to interrogate the unjust processes which create unequal distributions of wealth and unequal access to decision making: as, after Iris Marion Young, 'a focus on distributions is insufficient if it ignores the broader structural and institutional context within which decisions are made'. The direct action at the M11 and the M77 struggled against the result of decision-making processes which internalise the spatial inequality of cities like Glasgow and London. The Wandsworth occupation began to untangle and illuminate questions about the ownership of land and the way companies like Guinness are able to dominate the process of planning. The circulations of money which shape the city depend on intertwining relations between the worlds of planning, linked to local state administration, and of developers conceiving 'for the market with profit in mind'. The result of this alliance is a 'brutal functionalism' which would raze the entirety of the banks of the Thames into car parks, Sainsbury's and luxury flats.[8] The occupation was important in that it explored the possibility of using direct action, with its attendant strength of spontaneity and immediacy, both to illuminate, and alter, the processes through which unjust decisions are being made rather than just protesting against the unjust outcomes. It illustrated some of the processes which exclude the felt needs and lived experience of local people, especially working-class and other people lacking cultural capital, from shaping the direction of cities and their particular micro-urban environments.

The loss of the feeling by the citizens/ inhabitants of a city that they have the ability to achieve what is possible in their urban environments has had a pervasively debilitating effect on imaginations about progressive change. What the French philosopher and sociologist Henri Lefebvre called 'the right to the city' crystallises this absence. He conceived of this as a right to direct and shape the character and direction of the city through forms of participation and appropriation which are distinct from, and transcend, the right to property and the right merely to visit the city.[9] Expelled from the centrality of the city by the omnipresent walls of property and the enclosure of public spaces, and also expelled intellectually and symbolically from the representations of the city which pervade and structure official decision-making processes, marginalised groups find their ability to form this 'meandering cry and demand' crushed. A reality of the city is created which drifts above people's desire and right to appropriate and direct urban life for themselves without the mediation of profit.

> 'the M11 and M77 were the result of decision-making processes which internalise the spacial inequality of cities'

The Wandsworth occupation crystallised this desire, this demand for the city to become more than an entity divorced from its citizens'/ inhabitants' lives. It acted, albeit briefly and ambiguously, as a node for the demonstration that through direct action people can begin to assert this right, illustrating that people can recolonise and begin to shape their own lived

---

8. Henri Lefebvre, *Writings on Cities*, Blackwell, Oxford 1996.
9. Ibid.

spaces and environments, rather than have these lived spaces colonised and striated by abstract forces of planning and profit. It began to wrest away imaginations of cities from the narrow constraint of profit - opening up whole areas of people's imaginations about the possible directions of the urban environments in which they live which at present are given no space to develop. In this way the site had the potentiality to become a discursive space where people from the surrounding community could come and discuss the direction of their area without the rigidities, banalities and exclusions that pervade the formal political process. It suggested embryonic ways in which campaigns and institutions shaping cities can be structured, in an open and radically democratic way, breaking the rigid structures and languages that usually cage debate about planning.

In its everyday existence the site also illustrated directions beyond the rigid division and commoditisation of functions and different parts of life, in societies where domains like culture and leisure are being collapsed into the economic, through celebrating and mingling different parts of life and existence. The boundaries of art, work, access to 'nature' and, through the site's gardens, production of food on the site were blurred. It also illustrated how the city could be reappropriated as a forum of uncommodified leisure and play - although in doing so it illuminated how deeply these concepts are related to exisiting ethics and definitions of work. It showed how difficult it is to root notions of festival and play in a community suffused by the banality and boredom which pervade the everyday existence of many experiences of unemployment and homelessness, because of the tendency for such notions of festival to become dystopian through being pervaded by the kind of teleologies of escape associated with hard drug use.

Eviction and internal problems

On 15 October at around six o clock in the morning bailiffs entered the site to carry out an eviction on behalf of Guinness. They were supported by Metropolitan Police attired in intimidating riot gear, with shields, helmets and long handled batons, although resistance was almost entirely nonviolent. As evicted residents walked away over Wandsworth Bridge. JCBs were indiscriminately bulldozing people's homes and trashing the site's vegetation. The eviction stimulated much discussion about the site, much of which focussed on its internal problems: articles by John Vidal and George Monbiot in *The Guardian* of 16 October concentrated on 'how few pissheads it takes to wreck a site'. It is accepted that the site itself had serious problems, but there has to be an effort made to relate the internal problems of the site to the way that the occupation was constructed and conceptualised.

Many socially damaged people were knocking around the site: including people with mental health problems, people who'd been pushed out of social services care and folk with severe drug and drink problems. This is illustrative of the way that it was a social movement which, like many of the road protests and groups like the Exodus collective in Luton, is composed as much by 'forced outs' as 'drop outs'. This was exacerbated in the 'Pure Genius' case because the occupation happened in an area which was simultaneously socially polarised and socially fractured. It therefore lacked the embryonic forms of community and social and institutional bases out of which demands like 'the right to the city' could be formed and articulated. This has a dramatic impact on the way a campaign functions and is constructed. Trying to create a community with and alongside socially damaged people is a mentally and physically draining process. The very act of daily reproduction of a site like 'Pure Genius' in such difficult social conditions is something which saps the energy of a community and makes it nearly impossible for it to have any positive direction. At the same time it becomes easy for people with problems to be scapegoated as the reason for the problems of the site and for attention to be deflected away from ambiguities in the formation and conceptualisation of the campaign.

One of the key differences of contemporary societies from the kind of societies in which nonviolent direct action was pioneered by activists like Gandhi, is that they are increasingly 'Societies of the Spectacle' - societies characterised by a constant stream of disembodied images divorced from meaning.[10] Campaigns like The Land is Ours never cease to be conscious of having to orient their action to the eye of the media and let their form of action be dictated by the need to conform to the desires of this eye. They constantly risk becoming just another image in the raging stream of disembodied signs. Planned as a one week demonstration site which if possible would evolve

---

10. Guy Debord, *The Society of the Spectacle*, Black and Red, Detroit 1967.

into a community, the occupation was conceived with a short time scale because of the limited time people could commit: it was also an unexpected benefit when people were actually able to stay on the site and were not immediately evicted. This week long demonstration site, though, is vulnerable to depiction as a kind of 'eco-challenge Anneka': direct action as visual soundbite.

Many of the people who were involved in the organisation of the occupation have backgrounds in the media: including several current or ex-journalists and at least one media persona, George Monbiot. This made it natural for the occupation to be at one level a well organised media stunt. The occupation captured media attention wonderfully - obtaining favourable and supportive coverage in both the national and local press - but the short term structure which evolved to achieve this created a condition from which it was virtually impossible to create a socially sustainable community. It attempted to create the material conditions needed for an ecologically sustainable community, without at the same time providing the means for facilitating a socially sustainable community. The way the community was rapidly thrown together hindered the development of the minimum amount of sortedness and internal communication, as well as democracy, that a site has to have for negotiation of life there - and for some form of negotiated exclusion to work.

A genuine commitment did exist throughout the life of the site to it being a pluralistic community which would enable homeless folk to build their own dwellings and gain a permanency denied to them elsewhere. The campaign, however, was structured by a naive projection that people could come in, and form the bare structure of a community which they would then leave for an ill-defined section of other people like 'the homeless' to fill. This rested on a simplistic view of the conditions that homeless people face. It expected them to be able to adapt quickly to life in a very different situation without considering the stresses that drink and drugs use, homelessness, mental health problems, and lack of direction and low self-esteem, etc, would place on the everyday life of such a community. There were also only sketchy ideas about how the site could become self supporting - unlike the inspiring social alternatives like some of the Amsterdam squats, which have formed their own embryonic micro economies largely independent of state benefits.

Soundings

Gramsci argued that the ideas which gain the greatest popularity are not necessarily those which are most coherent, but often those which possess a certain 'logical elasticity'.[11] The green movement with its bewildering array of inflections of opinions appears to be one such movement: the direct action network is often no different. The attempts of the 'Pure Genius' site to tackle problems of homelessness alongside problems of inner city ecology are a symptom of a tendency to suggest that one can simply add social justice problems to an environmental concern and easily come up with an adequate solution. The objective is crucial, but in avoiding deeply interrogating social problems, and the complex interrelations between social justice and ecology, it becomes easy to drift into a situation where nebulous and problematic notions like community become 'flags of convenience' under which disparate groups of people can unite. It is not surprising that what results is not particularly coherent or successful.

What the 'Pure Genius' experience perhaps illustrates best is the way an abstracted vision of small communities has become accepted as the dominant alternative adopted by the contemporary green movement, without the short-comings of such communities being adequately discussed. It has not engaged with the capacity that small communities have for allowing the reproduction of the petty 'tyrannical bitterness' that pervades our everyday lives, and the tendency for such communities to form and cement their identity by exclusion and chauvinism.[12] One reaction to the social problems which the site experienced is to advocate the formation of socially purified communities, which some of the road protest camps - the Fairmile camp in Devon - approach. These are communities where outsiders are not welcome and not integrated into the life or decision-making processes of the site. It is presented as the necessary alternative to sites riddled by those who are seen as unsorted, folk who are usually termed 'lunchouts' or 'brewcrew'. In wishing to transform our society we have to start from 'attending violently to things as they are in the present'. We start from socially divided communities, and to create socially purified ones of our own is a disastrous and pernicious strategy.

The weakness of the kinship structure that emerged at Wandsworth, with

---

11. Gramsci, *op. cit.*, pp405-406.
12. Iris Marion Young, 'Together in Difference', in J Squires (ed), *Principled Positions*, Lawrence & Wishart, London 1993.

very little development of shared goals or structures of mutual aid, illustrates the fact that mediation by face to face relations is not necessarily liberatory, and is also very difficult to foster and develop. What needs to be thought through are ways of keeping the militant concern and commitment to particular places - which was present throughout the Wandsworth occupation - but fostering it through networks of flows of people, techniques and ideas generated by direct action and other movements, and through interaction with the areas which surround it. This would constantly challenge and regenerate the community, working against tendencies towards fixed chauvinisms and parochialisms. If emergent structures of internal democracy and kinship are encouraged to develop more organically and securely - and in more open and genuinely radical democratic ways - then action with those representing community in different forums can be more sinuously related with people's vastly differing needs and desires. This could prevent the tendency for the division between the imaginations and articulated needs of people and planners be reproduced within the campaign. One activist spoke of his annoyance that people outside the community had been negotiating to build relatively expensive 'ecohouses' on the site, when he had constructed his own dwelling for under £100, inspired by a Scandinavian design. This is symptomatic of a wider failure to integrate the views of forced out and marginalised people into the actual planning and conceptualisation of the occupation itself.

This necessitates having a notion of people as riven by all sorts of complex divisions and differences rather than perhaps the rather homogeneous image which was adopted in the Wandsworth case. Unless the complexity of this notion is interrogated and integrated into the structure of campaigns and institutions, the aim of a fluid polyphonic process shaping the city will be replaced by a different elite, colonising lived space whilst presenting itself as representing the interests of others but in reality only articulating *its* own 'right to the city'. The kind of more open structure needed to achieve this may be approximated by the current direction of the The Land Is Ours, which is evolving towards a situation where its role will be to facilitate more organic grassroots campaigns and articulate links between them and other organisations rather than parachuting in artificial communities overnight. In order to avoid sedimenting itself in to a rigid, fossilised centre it is in the process of reconceptualising itself as a federation of interrelating but autonomous local groups and groups struggling along particular axes.

We live in societies in which the boundaries between people and nature are being constantly transgressed and broken down. One of the possible responses for the green movement in the shadow of such transformations is nostalgically to invoke values of an imagined past when societies based around small communities were close to, and in harmony with, nature. But to attempt this would be a regression; these ideal communities in reality were often suffocating. As Frantz Fanon demanded, there can be 'no question of a return to nature'.[13] The task we face is the much harder one of envisioning 'a different and less hostile order of relationships among people, animals, technologies and land'.[14] This necessitates taking urban environments seriously and engaging with the complex forces which are shaping them in increasingly hostile and unjust ways.

At best, sites like Pure Genius can become nodes which illuminate the dark forces shaping our cities; which can crystallise the demand for the right to the city; and can begin to establish some collective ground from which to articulate this right in what are fractured and divided communities. Through direct action techniques like land occupation they can stimulate the starting point for an interrogation of and reconstruction of the boundaries of daily life, becoming nodes of the struggle to 'command and educate the common sense of the age' and move it in a progressive rather than reactionary direction - towards values based on social and ecological respect; a slow and a molecular process but also an urgent one.

This essay is based on limited involvement at the site. It is also based on ideas developed in a dissertation written after living at Pollock Free State in Glasgow. Thanks to Land is Ours activists and Soundings *editors for comments on earlier drafts.*

---

13. Frantz Fanon, *The Wretched of the Earth*, Penguin, Harmondsworth 1990, p253.
14. Donna Haraway, Introduction, *Primate Visions*, Verso, London 1989, p15.

Economic Globalisation and the Nation State
The transformation of political power?

David Goldblatt, David Held, Anthony McGrew, Jonathan Perraton

What is the extent of globalisation in the late 1990s? And what are its effects on politics?

For all the voluminous output of the last decade or so, the debate over globalisation shakes down, pretty much, into two schools of thought: hyper- and sceptics. Hyper-globalisers argue that we now live in a world in which social processes operate predominantly at a global scale. National economies, polities and cultures are immersed in a sea of global flows. As a consequence, significant national differences are being eroded and a homogeneous global economy and culture is emerging; the sovereignty and autonomy of nation-states have been radically reduced. Such claims have provided tempting targets for the more sceptically minded. Casual empirical inspection reveals that for all the increases in global flows of trade and investment, the majority of economic and social activity continues to occur on a more restricted spatial scale. Historical evidence suggests that contemporary forms of international economic and social interaction may not be unprecedented. It is not at all clear that it is all over for nation states and nationalism.

How has this rather academic debate about globalisation influenced politicians in the West? Neo-liberals welcome the emergence of truly open global markets, celebrate their efficiency and delight in the corresponding diminution of an essentially malign state power. Mainstream Social and Christian Democrats tend to accept the globalisation thesis and restrict themselves to trying to initiate and coordinate the technological, infrastructural and training policies which ensure that a nation remains internationally competitive and attractive to capital. In Western Europe they are among the leading advocates of European economic and monetary union - in which pooled sovereignty is expected to be rewarded with a generalised return of power to political institutions rather than markets. Many of those on the left of social democracy argue that globalisation is an ideological fig-leaf for a process in which governments have willingly passed power from the democratically legitimised sphere of politics to the unaccountable realm of the market. A similar view can be heard from conservative nationalists of various kinds: Gaullists in France, Buchanan and Perot in America, for example, have argued that an economic defence of the nation should be allied to a cultural politics of fervent nationalism. So who, if anyone, is right? Is the contemporary world economy really something new? And what are the implications of this for state power and democratic politics? What actually is globalisation anyway?

What is globalisation?

Globalisation describes growing global interconnectedness: a stretching of social relations across space to the point where they are transcontinental or inter-regional, such that day to day activities in one part of the globe are increasingly enmeshed with events happening on the other side. Globalisation is not an end point, it is a process. It does not just apply to economic activity but to the spheres of politics, culture, law and military affairs. Each form of globalisation has its own distinctive logic, dynamics and geography in different historical periods. One cannot read off a general account of globalisation from any one of them. But how can we describe these stretched social relations? We can distinguish between different historical forms of globalisation in a number of ways: the geographical extensiveness of networks and flows - how much of the globe these relations and social flows traverse; the intensity of these flows and interactions relative to more spatially limited interactions; the degree to which these flows and interactions impact upon the policies and power of national and local actors and institutions; and the degree to which global networks have acquired an entrenched infrastructure of interaction (telecommunications, transport, legal frameworks) and have been institutionalised.[1]

Obviously not all social relations have reached global proportions: to talk of a 'global age' or 'global civilisation' is sheer hyperbole. In any case, the political power that arises from state institutions has always been territorially delimited, although it is only with the advent of nation states that the external reach of legitimate authority has been tightly circumscribed by internationally agreed and internally determined and policed borders. As such, global flows run across the territorially delimited networks of power that emanate from nation states. Networks of economic and cultural interaction have never neatly corresponded to the political space of states, be they city states, nation states or imperial states. Nor have they overlapped and interacted with national patterns and networks in uniform ways. States have always been constrained by, and had to cope with, external forces and spatially extensive networks of economic, military and cultural power. Moreover, while nation states do claim the sovereign right to legislate independently for, and rule over, a given territory and people, the extent of that claim has rarely, if ever, actually corresponded to the real capacities of states to determine autonomously the character of national economic policy or to implement it successfully. So what, if anything, is new about contemporary globalisation? We explore below the historically distinctive features of contemporary forms of economic globalisation in three areas - trade, finance and multinational companies.[2]

---

1. It is also important to note the patterns of *hierarchy* and *unevenness* within these networks, for access to global networks and sensitivity to their impacts are radically unequal. We address these matters in, D.Goldblatt, D.Held, A.McGrew and J.Perraton (forthcoming) *Global Flows, Global Transformations: Concepts, Arguments and Evidence*, Polity, Cambridge.
2. Other central forms of globalisation - from the environment to law and security questions - will be left aside here. We examine these matters in *Global Flows, Global Transformations*.

Trade

Trade has always flowed across borders, civilisations and states, binding economic fortunes together as well acting as a conduit for ideas, technologies and social practices. The pre-modern civilisations of Latin Europe and Islam contained extensive trading networks that cut across political boundaries of all sorts. Islamic expansion into South East Asia and European expansion from the sixteenth century onwards created global and cross-civilisational loops of exchange. However, the geographical extensiveness of trade was not matched by a social or economic intensiveness. At the start of the nineteenth century, the best estimates of global exports as a percentage of global output suggest a figure of only 1 or 2 per cent.[3] It was the nineteenth century that saw international trade flourish. Geographically it grew between the industrialised nations as well as flowing under imperial auspices between metropolitan centres and underdeveloped peripheries. For developed economies the average export-to-GDP ratio rose to around 11 per cent in this era and for individual trading nations, especially in Europe, the ratio was much higher.[4] The First World War and the inter-war depression saw a collapse in international trade, the erection of substantial trade tariffs, imperial trading blocs and other import restrictions. Thus the post-1945 era began with a much less extensive and less intensive trading order, legally more closed and infrastructurally more depleted, than fifty years earlier.

However, since 1945 a very *extensive* trading system has emerged. Statistical comparison suggests that almost all nations are trading with a larger number of other nations and that while trade within regions has climbed this has been complementary to and supportive of more extensive global links.[5] While the majority of trade occurs between OECD states, this is changing fast. Industrialising economies in East Asia and Latin America are taking a bigger share of world trade; the collapse of Communism has brought a swathe of countries into the global trading system; liberalisation in China, India and other developing countries looks set to expand trading relations more extensively than ever before. The growing transport and communications

---

3. S.Kuznets 'Quantitative aspects of the economic growth of Nations: Level and structure of foreign trade, long term trends', *Economic Development and Cultural Change*, 1967.
4. A. Maddison, *Dynamic Forces in Capitalist Development*, OUP, Oxford 1991.
5. T.Nierop, *Systems and Regions in Global Politics*, John Wiley, Chichester 1994, ch.3.

infrastructure of contemporary trade has diminished the costs and uncertainties of exchange and reduced the investment required to enter foreign markets. The legal infrastructure of this system, set by GATT and its successor the WTO, has created a system which is more open than previous systems; and tariffs are significantly lower. Despite protectionist rumblings, the use of non-tariff barriers to restrict trade, and a multiplication of regional trading agreements, trade continues to grow faster than global output.

International trade is now worth around $5 trillion a year which adds up to about 20 per cent of global output.[6] For individual Western economies, the ratio of trade-to-GDP regained nineteenth century gold standard levels by the early 1970s and has now surpassed them, reaching at least around 30-40 per cent of output and in some cases much higher. The US ratio remains comparatively low but it has evolved from being a virtually autarchic economy to a reasonably open one in the last twenty years. In addition, it should be noted that much of the output growth of the last fifty years is accounted for by government expenditure which is rarely traded. If comparisons are made on the basis of GDP minus government expenditure, as a proxy for tradeable GDP, then the *intensity* of contemporary export output ratios for the private sector in national economies comfortably exceeds that of the last century.

International trade has extended beyond primary and capital goods to all forms of manufacture and to many services as well. While previously there was almost negligible trade in services, it now constitutes around 20 per cent of international trade and acts as a significant conduit for the diffusion of cultural products, icons and practices. As such, few economic sectors are completely shielded from competition in domestic markets; most are dependent on exports for profitability or foreign imports for key plant or components. The imported content of manufactured output rose between 1899 and 1985 from 16 per cent to 29 per cent in the UK, from 3 per cent to 24 per cent in the USA, and from 8 per cent to 46 per cent in Sweden.[7] For OECD countries, except Japan, the majority of trade is now intra-industry, entailing the exchange of similar products. This trade has transformed consumer industries so that many firms now sell to international rather to national markets. Much of the intra-industry trade is

---

6. WTO, *International Trade Statistics Yearbook*, WTO, Geneva 1995.
7. OECD, *Structural Adjustment and Economic Performance*, OECD, Paris 1987, p271.

accounted for by intra-firm trade as components and semi-finished manufactures move between production sites in different parts of the world.

Contemporary international trade is therefore more extensive, if still uneven, than during the late nineteenth century. While it exhibits regional patterns, these are complementary to growing global interaction. Its intensity relative to global and national output is greater, leading to fiercer international competition in domestic and foreign markets for national economies and firms in most sectors of economic activity. Finally, contemporary international trade is facilitated by a more institutionally entrenched and technologically sophisticated legal and communications infrastructure than in any previous epoch. However, this does not constitute a set of perfectly open global markets; intra-firm trade introduces significant deviations from the textbook model of global competitive markets.

Finance capital

The movement of finance across political borders has a long history. Early forms of international banking and insurance were central to the growth of international trade. International loans helped keep the states of early modern Europe at war for centuries. The equity markets of London and Amsterdam were closely integrated in the eighteenth century. The clearest analogue of today's system of global financial flows was that of the nineteenth century gold standard era. Established and organised under the auspices of British imperial hegemony, the value of national currencies and thus the volume of money in circulation were tied in principle to the value of gold. If a country ran a trade deficit, gold would flow out, the money supply would fall, and this reduced demand for imports while also reducing the price of domestically produced goods so that the country could become competitive again. The reverse process occurred when a country ran a surplus. However, in practice exposure to the strictures of the gold standard was mitigated by defensive and protectionist trade policies, while monetary adjustment was far from automatic. The richer nations often ran large surpluses and some emerging economies large deficits, but high levels of foreign investment allowed this to persist without straining the gold standard system. In addition, there were huge migratory flows of unemployed labour from Europe to expanding economies in the Americas. This certainly relieved some of the pressures of adjustment.

Much foreign investment involved states raising capital on the international markets by issuing bonds. In the 1920s over 50 states were issuing bonds on Wall Street, a figure that collapsed in the 1930s and remained low well into the 1980s. Viewed in this perspective, the financial dislocation of the inter-war years, which saw the collapse of international financial transactions, and the Bretton Woods system of the post-war era, which combined an international system of fixed exchange rates with strict national controls on capital movements and was only fully operational for thirteen years, are the exceptions in a longer history of open and extensive capital flows.

The Bretton Woods system was compromised at an early stage. In the 1960s national capital controls were steadily evaded through growing Euro-currency markets in which national currencies, deposits and assets were traded in offshore locations. International bank lending was revitalised by the recycling of petrodollars that followed the OPEC oil price hikes. Evasion of national capital controls, aided by new telecommunication technologies and combined with a political revaluation of the virtues of free international capital movement, led to the steady dismantling of capital controls and a loosening of the defensive regulation of national financial markets: in the late 1970s in the US and Canada, in the early 1980s in Japan, Australasia and the UK, and the rest of Western Europe in the late 1980s and early 1990s, partly in response to the provisions of the Single European Market. In the mid-1990s cautious liberalisation continues in many developing economies and in Eastern Europe.

'The clearest analogue of today's system of global financial flows was that of the nineteenth century gold standard era'

What is the contemporary scale of global financial flows? Foreign exchange comes closest to the model of a perfect open global market, with almost instantaneous and costless electronic transactions across borders. Daily turnover has climbed from around $10 billion a day in the early 1970s to around $50 billion in the 1980s and to the astronomical $1 trillion a day in the 1990s. The ratio of foreign exchange turnover to world trade has climbed from 10:1 in the early 1980s to over 60:1 today. The most recent estimates of turnover from the Bank of International Settlements suggest a climb to over $1.2 trillion a day.[8] Against this, the entire foreign reserves of the OECD

---

8. BIS, *Annual Reports*, Bank of International Settlements, Geneva various years.

are a mere $650 billion. Alongside these markets international bank loans grew at a rate of 12 per cent a year in the 1980s. Annual international lending has climbed from negligible levels in the early 1960s and a mere $20 billion a year in the 1970s to 10 times that level in the 1990s. The outstanding net stock of loans has risen to around $4.6 trillion. Translated into a percentage of world output, the net stock of international loans has risen from less than 1 per cent in the 1960s to over 16 per cent in the 1990s.[9] This rising tide of international lending is reflected in the level of foreign assets and deposits in national banking systems, the internationalisation of banks themselves and the increasing penetration of foreign owned banks in domestic money, equity and security markets.

A huge increase in Western governments' borrowing has boosted the international bond markets. Annual issues of international bonds now comprise over 70 per cent of the international capital markets and the cumulative value of the stock of bonds now exceeds $2.4 trillion. Annual issues have risen from less than $20 billion in the early 1970s to over $300 billion in the 1990s. Furthermore, the percentage of government bonds held by foreigners has risen across the West in the 1980s and early 1990s. In the cases of Britain and Germany, the rise has been substantial, from around 10 per cent to 20 per cent. In France, the rise has been dramatic, from less than 1 per cent to 45 per cent.[10]

Both the international issue of equities and the cross-border trading of equities has steadily risen through the 1980s and 1990s driven by privatisation programmes and multinational expansion. International issues in 1995 were $45.6 billion. In 1996 cross-border sales reached around $125 billion. As a consequence, there has been a marked increase in the foreign composition of pension fund and insurance company holdings and a diversification of the national markets and assets drawn upon. Over the last decade foreign holdings amongst UK companies rose from 10 per cent to 20 per cent while in the more insular Japanese and American sectors the increase was even sharper from less than 1 per cent to around 6 per cent and 10 per cent respectively.[11]

Although international bank lending was the dominant element of

---

9. UNCTAD, *World Investment Report* 1994, United Nations, New York 1994, p128.
10. BIS/IMF sources quoted in *The Economist*, 7 October, 1995.
11. See, 'World Economy and Finance', *Financial Times* 27 September 1996, p3 and p15. and *The Economist*, 1995, p11.

international capital markets in the 1960s, it now constitutes a much smaller element of international financial transactions. Bond and equity markets are also dwarfed by the emergence of derivative markets. The demand for assets that allowed hedging against risks and market volatility, combined with technical innovations and intense competition amongst financial institutions, encouraged the growth of international derivatives markets. The price of these financial assets is based on, or derivative of, movements in the value of other assets - bonds, currencies, stock market composites, and interest rates. The value of existing contracts in these complex 'products' has risen to over $25 trillion from less than a $1 trillion in the early 1980s, often trading on highly volatile markets. The jury remains out on the degree of instability that these markets might inject into the global financial system - but they are certainly capable of wiping out the most venerable financial institutions.

Compared to the gold standard era or the early Bretton Woods system, the contemporary globalisation of finance capital is more extensive and intensive than any other period. More currencies and more types of asset are traded more frequently at greater speed and in greater volumes than in earlier eras. The infrastructure of exchange is more institutionalised and more advanced technologically. The sheer weight of international capital movements relative to global and national output and trade is unique. The range of financial instruments, domestic financial markets and domestic financial institutions engaged with international transactions is greater and their enmeshment profound.

MNCs and FDI

Multinational corporations are the linchpins of the contemporary global economy. This, if nothing else, distinguishes the current epoch from the gold standard era. The late nineteenth and early twentieth centuries certainly witnessed very high levels of international investment and possessed complex, international corporations - some of considerable antiquity - coordinating finance and trade. However, contemporary MNCs, while falling short of the footloose global actors in neo-liberal accounts of globalisation, are quantitatively and qualitatively more extensive in their operations, more intensive in their importance and more significant as economic and political actors than their predecessors. Around 20,000 MNCs account for between a quarter and a third of global output, 70 per cent of international trade (a significant part of which is intra-firm trade), and they dominate foreign direct investment (FDI) - investment which acquires operational power over corporations rather than the veto power of portfolio and equity investments. MNCs also account for a very large part of international technology transfer. This occurs as a by-product of FDI and more directly through joint ventures and alliances, international patenting and exploitation, licensing and know-how agreements. MNCs are both customers and active participants in international financial markets. Their demands stimulated the development of euro-currency markets and the multinationalisation of banks. They also issue international bonds and equities. MNCs are significant purchasers of foreign exchange and derivative products designed to hedge risks. When cash flow is high they may be significant speculators in financial markets.

Although there were significant FDI flows before the First World War, FDI flows relative to economic activity are comparable, if not higher, today. Estimates suggest a ratio of all international investment flows to GDP of around 5-7 per cent for the UK before 1914.[12] Data is peculiarly untrustworthy in this area as records do not separate out FDI from other forms of investment and definitions of direct investment have varied wildly between national statistical agencies. Nonetheless, a bench-mark figure can be generated from the best available estimate on the composition of those capital flows which suggests that 35 per cent of that investment was controlled by MNCs, the rest being held by scattered portfolio investors.[13] This gives a proxy ratio for outward flows of FDI to GDP of around 1.5 - 2.5 per cent. Given that UK overseas investments accounted for around half of all global investments, no country would have a figure higher than this and most much lower. Along with the UK, Germany, France and America were the main investors while the recipients shifted from the US itself to a number of developing and colonial economies who received two-thirds of the total capital.

After the First World War, depression and international disruption terminated

---

12. A.Green and M.Urquhart, 'Factor and commodity flows in the international economy of 1870-1914: a multi-country view', *Journal of Economic History* 36 (1), 1976.
13. J.Dunning, 'Changes in the level and structure of international production: the last one hundred years', in J.Dunning (ed), *Explaining International Production*, Unwin Hyman, London 1988.

European investments, but American companies like General Electric and Ford established significant European plants. Since 1945 growth has come in a number of waves, the origins, destinations, and forms of which have varied. American expansion in the 1950s focused on European manufacturing, factories in Latin America and global oil industry investments. In the 1960s and early 1970s investments began to flow from Europe, particularly from certain sectors - like textiles, clothing and footwear - which avidly sought low cost labour. This was followed by explosive growth in FDI in the 1980s led by Japanese and European firms seeking global economies of scale, access to international technology and a foothold in the markets of the US and other European economies. In the 1990s there has been a slower growth of investment but a greater geographical diversity of investors and hosts. MNCs have emerged in industrialising economies of East Asia, while capital has flowed to Eastern Europe and the Pacific Rim. What is the scale and geography of these flows?

The total stock of outward FDI grew from $67 billion in 1960 to $1.7 trillion in 1990. It now exceeds $2 trillion. Of that 70 per cent could be accounted for by just 6 countries (US, Japan, Germany, France, Netherlands, UK).[14] During the 1980s boom in FDI, outward flows relative to GDP were in line with or surpassed UK rates before the First World War. In the peak years of the late 1980s the ratio of outward FDI to GDP in Germany and Japan was 1.6 per cent and 3.1 per cent respectively, while in Britain and Sweden peak outflows were over 4 per cent and 6 per cent of GDP.[15] In terms of destination, around three quarters of current FDI is within the OECD. However, the early 1990s have seen a new wave of major investments into the hitherto closed economies of China and Eastern Europe, whilst a number of developing countries (India, Brazil, Mexico and Chile) have become both more open to FDI and more attractive locations for MNCs. Investment has, like trade, spread beyond primary and manufacturing industries into services as well - around a third to a half of inward and outward investment flows in the OECD are in the service sector.

Despite the growth of foreign direct investment, the global character of

---

14. UNCTAD, *World Investment Report 1995*, United Nations, New York 1995.
15. GDP data based on IMF, *International Financial Statistics*, IMF, Washington. Capital flows data based on OECD, *International Direct Investment Statistics Yearbook*, OECD, Paris various years.

MNCs described by hyper-globalisers has been challenged. Sceptics have argued: that MNCs are regionally rather than globally biased in their patterns of investment, trade and production; that a majority, in many cases a large majority, of assets, employment and sales remain located in the home nation; that core decision-making personnel, management culture, institutional ownership and highest value added production remain nationally concentrated. These claims need to be carefully evaluated.

> 'The contemporary global economy is different because MNCs play a much more central role today'

Statistical indices of regional bias reveal only a slight regional preference in patterns of trade and investment, amongst MNCs from some countries. Alongside regional expansion there has been a pattern of global expansion and investment, albeit a pattern heavily concentrated on Europe, North America and East Asia. While the foreign percentage of MNC's assets and outputs can be as low as 20 per cent in some sectors, there are many areas where it is much higher. In any case 20 per cent may be enough to have a significant effect on the fortunes and behaviour of a company. Facing a saturated domestic market and/or intense domestic competition, 20 per cent of sales may be the difference between overall profit and loss, 20 per cent of assets may be the key to achieving competitive economies of scale, 20 per cent of employment overseas may be the key to lower global unit costs that ensure survival. Unlike the nineteenth century, MNCs (both home based and overseas plants) now account for a much larger proportion of domestic employment, production and capital formation in advanced capitalist countries - figures that with some variation have risen throughout the 1980s and 1990s.

However, contrary to the hyper-globalisers, MNCs are not footloose, stateless, truly global operators. First, the sunk costs of investment, particularly in hi-tech manufacturing, are significant enough that regular relocation carries large economic penalties. Second, FDI is often undertaken to ensure local market presence, avoidance of non-tariff barriers and access to locally developed innovations; none of these can be achieved by footloose exit. Third, some domestic markets are just too big for any company to be able to walk away from. Finally, while a few corporations may approximate to the truly global company, systematically scouring the planet for improved rates of return, MNCs display a very wide variety of forms of international organisation and coordination. Measuring the presence (as the hyper-globalisers do) or the absence (as the sceptics do) of a single model of MNCs cannot be considered as proof for or against the economic globalisation of investment and production networks.

In conclusion, we can argue that the contemporary global economy differs from that of earlier epochs because MNCs play a much more central role today than they have done in the past. In particular they have established international networks of coordinated production that are historically unique, and have done so across a wider range of sectors than in the past. They have come to play a greater role in the operations of advanced economies than ever before; their actions and interests shape the flow, form and location of investment, the conduct of trade and the development of technologies.

Implications

This survey of contemporary economic globalisation suggests three things. First, to conceive of globalisation purely as the existence of open global markets, globally orientated consumers and global footloose corporations misconceives globalisation as an end-point rather than as a process, as a uni-dimensional rather than as a multi-dimensional phenomenon, and fails to capture the diversity and variety of global economic interactions. Second, while it is clear that the gold standard era witnessed a significant intensification of economic globalisation and that much of the post-war era has involved a process of catching-up, today's global economic system overall is more extensive and intensive than in the gold standard era; it links national and global economies, markets and firms together more tightly; and it possesses a more entrenched infrastructure of interaction. Third, the precise geography of global economic flows and the hierarchies of relative power within them have shifted. So something has changed, but have these changes diminished the power of nation states? Answering this question requires a more sophisticated analysis of power than either hyper-globalisers or sceptics deploy. A number of points need to be made.

First, power is a relative concept. We need to focus on how globalisation shifts the balance of power between states and other actors. The balance of power and thus the relative autonomy of states varies according to the type of economic strategy they are pursuing and the actors and institutions beyond the nation state that are involved. States are engaged with the global economy as direct market actors (for example, central bank operations in currency and bond markets); as legal and administrative regulators of markets both domestically and in the context of international economic institutions like WTO or the European single market; and, as taxing and spending agencies that both provide much of the infrastructure of global economic interactions and pick up the pieces of its effects in terms of welfare and public services. In this regard, the most important shift in power has been the historic expansion of exit options for capital in financial markets relative to national capital controls, national banking regulations and national investment strategies, and the sheer volume of privately held capital relative to national reserves. Exit options for corporations making direct investments have also expanded but less so. Nonetheless, the balance has shifted in favour of capital *vis-a-vis* both national governments and national labour movements who, whilst not powerless, must attend more closely to the economic and political requirements of financial markets and MNCs.

Second, it is rarely the case that globalisation has rendered any policy impossible or eradicated autonomy. Rather, it is more effective to look at these changes in terms of the shifting balance of costs and benefits of any given policy. National governments retain the capacity to invoke protectionist restrictions of various kinds on trade. However, the benefits of doing so have been reduced by the increasing dependence of national firms and markets on imported inputs and the costs of doing so have increased as states have become more tightly enmeshed in international free trade commitments with substantial retaliatory powers available to participants. Similarly, governments may choose to pursue fixed or managed exchange rate policies and, through central banks and legal regulations, retain the tools for doing so. However, the costs in interest rate terms of maintaining an exchange rate has climbed as the exit options available to capital have increased. The cost of choosing one's own interest rate are now considerable and include loss of control over the exchange rate, openness to market volatility and, given the shortage of reserves, acceptance of the international financial market's perception of the soundness of assets denominated in the national currency. At times these changes have pushed the costs of certain policies so high that they have become virtually inoperable. For example, expansionary macro-economic strategies may incur considerable costs in the form of high interest rates that are likely to make this path unsustainable over the medium term.

Third, power can be thought of in behavioural and structural terms. In the case of the former, power is actively and continuously executed by an individual agent in response to a particular policy. In the case of the latter, power is unconsciously and collectively executed as the unintended consequences of the sum of a multiplicity of actors directed and channelled by the rules, institutions and systems in which individual agents operate. The examples of labour, social and environmental regulation illustrate this. In behavioural terms, globalisation affects such policies as multinational corporations may actively resist their implementation, seek to water down their provisions or threaten to shift their investments. However, a much more powerful constraint upon the social regulation of the market is the emergence of global networks of free trade and competition in which the threat of corporations already using cheap foreign labour indirectly raises the perceived potential costs of instituting certain reforms.

Fourth, it rarely makes sense to think about state autonomy in terms of individual policies. Governments invariably, if often haphazardly, seek to implement economic strategies which deploy a complex mixture of policies. The market assessment of the credibility and sustainability of such policies varies between states and over time. While governments face considerable uncertainty over market responses, the absence of a sustained consensus on the 'rightness of policies' creates some room for manoeuvre for politicians if they can 'win the argument' with market makers. But there are limits to this. The impact of globalisation is often to render particular strategies or policy packages more problematic or less effective rather than simply to constrain or delimit individual policies. It has been argued that the globalisation of financial markets has rendered expansionary economic strategies involving high levels of government borrowing more and more problematic. This may be the case where governments seek finance to conduct a generalised reflation or to fund what markets perceive to be uncontrollable levels of welfare expenditure (Italian state pensions, for example). However, where borrowing is tied to tight fiscal polices, or in the case of the Reagan administration to massive rearmament programmes, then international financial markets appear more willing.

Fifth, economic globalisation undermines the domestic political coalitions which have traditionally underpinned progressive social and economic policies by profoundly altering the sectoral economic and political interests and the relative economic and social power of social groups and classes. The dependence of an increasing number of firms on overseas markets and investments may diminish the pool of powerful supporters for protectionist policies. The growing importance of MNCs in funding research and development makes it impossible not to include their interests in the calculation of national technology policies. In this sense, globalisation transforms the political arena within which states have to operate; building domestic coalitions based on a shared national interest may become more difficult.

Thus, the overall impact of globalisation on the autonomy of nation states is more complex than both hyper-globalisers and sceptics would allow. State autonomy has always been limited and constrained by global forces and international actors. However, it is reasonable to assert that states today do face a more complex array of global constraints and problems than hitherto. In addition, they must also face a wider range of international actors. They are more deeply enmeshed in global networks of interaction. Crucially, they have seen their own expansion in size and absolute power diminished by the relatively greater increases in the direct power, exit options and collective structural power of international actors and global forces.

The claims of hyper-globalisers and their sceptical critics miss much of what is distinctive about contemporary economic globalisation and its political consequences. Nation states still remain immensely powerful. Indeed, in the military domain they may be more powerful than ever before. Nation states certainly have access to huge economic resources, sophisticated bureaucracies and new technologies of information gathering and control. Yet globalisation is not a mere ideological construct, it has real and discernible material features. Why now, given (as the sceptics believe) a more limited intensification of globalisation, and given more enduringly powerful nation states (than the hyper-globalisers would allow), does the autonomy, democratic accountability and legitimacy of nation states seem so uncertain? Perhaps this is because for three or four decades Western nation states had just sufficient power, relative to domestic and global forces, that governments were able to deliver enough of their electoral programmes to secure their legitimacy. But it was always a fine call. It has only required the smallest shift in relative and structural power between states and markets, due to processes of globalisation, to demonstrate that the autonomy of democratically elected governments has been, and is increasingly, constrained by sources of unelected and unaccountable power.

What does this mean for democratic politics? Neo-liberals will celebrate this power shift, for they never had any intention of bringing these forces within the scope of their deracinated conception of democracy. Conservative nationalists will not attempt to bring these forces within the rule of the nation state either. Despite claiming to represent the nation they have never been very concerned with letting the nation do any ruling. This leaves us with Social and Christian Democrats who, as the sceptics point out, are probably overcautious about their capacity for exerting greater political control over global forces. While a more robust national politics, the formation of institutions of geo-economic governance and strengthened supranational political institutions in Europe would constitute an attempt to swing the balance of power back from markets to states, it is far from clear that the proposals on the table will create arrangements which would be more accountable or democratic. And as the Greens are constantly reminding us, the voracious appetite of the global economy may consume us all before we have had a chance to do anything about it. Economic globalisation has not only shifted the balance of power between states and markets; it has also changed the stakes of the game.

Four Poems

Promises

Another sunset lands upon us.
Cold fingers of night creep over our exits;
driving us away from market-places
of human tempers.
And soon sleep
closes doors of our todays;
opening windows for tomorrow
to look at shows in the nude,
as she waits for her turn.

Before the sun went away
a little boy sat loading,
stretching
releasing
loading
stretching
releasing stones from his catapult;
drawing misses each shot;
falling short with each aspiration;
limp and puffing with each release;
ending his outing shouting:
'you coward
don't run away
tomorrow I will get you
you will see!'

He went into the arms of night
full of his promises to the sun.
And so when a bomb upon his tender
form made a hit
each piece of him in flight
hoped the others too held their promise;
chanting:
'Lak lyec pe pek i wonnere!
Tusks of the elephant are not heavy
for the owner!'

Waking, I rushed shouting at the sun:
'Will you tell your tomorrows to protect the promises
in small children or you will see the fire,
you indifferent traveller of Pharaohs!'

I was at it
when night put his hand over my mouth,
tucking yet another promise from mankind
under his armpits.

Okello Oculi

Cargoes

Visiting you I'd board a ship that's sailed
around the world for eighty years, weighed
down with obsolete machinery but laden
still with cargo from another age.

Urgent your need to own and mine to know.
I'd will you strength to force those locks, to share
with me the secrets of your lifetime's hoard
before the final shipwreck took its toll.

Visiting now I find a ship that's foundered,
all hands, all cargo lost. Now from my shoulders
strangely a burden slips. Your wreck unplundered,
my ship's discharged, my journey disencumbered.

Jane Evans

Champion

Saturday. Returning from a jumble-sale
with boxing gloves swinging from my wrist.
Redolence of sweat, sting of cracked leather

and tang of blood, ducking to avoid
my opponent's soft-hurting, air-filling
uncounterable and untiring blows.

On *World of Sport* in the kitchen, Ali
went down in the fifteenth. I fumed
and got back on my feet, again and again.

Daniel Wyke

Risk

We could, you know,
go right out into the street today -
broad daylight, not much traffic.
We could maybe even hold hands
or snuggle our chins a little
into each other at the bases of our necks.
We could peck each other lightly on the lips.
We could put our open palms on each other's hips
as we walked along with our arms draped
around each other's waists, casually.

We could just go ahead and do it.
People would probably point and gasp
and shout and the police would be likely to come.
I would be arrested and taken away in a van
or maybe held hostage by the angry crowd,
jeered at, spit on, stoned to death.

We could just give it a try.

Linda Chase

REVIEWS

Altered States
Ludovic Hunter-Tilney

Thomas Pynchon, *Mason and Dixon*, Cape, £16.99

In 1756, while making his *Observations on the Present State of Affairs*, Samuel Johnson wrote disparagingly about French and British boundary disputes in the New World:

> The forests and deserts of America are without landmarks, and therefore cannot be particularly specified in stipulations; the appellations of those wide extended regions have in every mouth a different meaning, and are understood on either side as inclination happens to contract or extend them. Who has yet pretended to define how much of America is included in Brazil, Mexico, or Peru? It is almost as easy to divide the Atlantic Ocean by a line as clearly to ascertain the limits of those uncultivated, uninhabitable, unmeasured regions.

According to Johnson, the great cartographer of the English language, America is quite simply unmappable: at best, it is rendered unintelligible by the conflicting babble of its inhabitants; at worst, it defies any form of geographical enclosure at all. It is, in a word, meaningless.

A decade later, between 1763 and 1767, Charles Mason and Jeremiah Dixon drew their eponymous line between Pennsylvania and Baltimore (another boundary dispute, this time between the owners of those states). At least one part, then, of Johnson's 'unmeasured regions' had been brought into the realm of European knowledge, a process of definition that provides Thomas Pynchon with the basis for his latest novel, the baldly-titled *Mason & Dixon*. Loosely employing an eighteenth century style and vernacular, Pynchon affectionately charts the years of partnership between his protagonists (astronomer and surveyor respectively) while registering something of Johnson's dismay at the roles they play in the gradual cultivation of the 'wide extended regions' of pre-revolutionary America.

The novel itself is narrated by a genially unreliable story-teller, the Reverend Wicks Cherrycoke. It is 1786, the year of Mason's death, and Cherrycoke is responding to his nephews' demands for an unprecedented 'tale about America'. In terms of duration, his yarn knocks Marlowe's Thames-side telling of *Heart of Darkness* for six: Pynchon's novel weighs in at a hefty 770 pages. Nonetheless, Cherrycoke's family audience remains more or less indefatigable and provides a post-independence counterpoint to the events of his narrative by frequently interrupting it.

Cherrycoke starts his tale with the first of Mason and Dixon's expeditions, to the Cape of Good Hope. Here they encounter libidinous Dutch settlers, witness the casual brutality of the slave trade and observe the transit of Venus. Then on to St. Helena, where Mason works with an unhinged colleague, Nevil Maskeleyne, the future Astronomer-Royal. The tone of Mason and Dixon's relationship is set early on, for they are that most traditional of Hollywood clichés, the mismatched couple. Mason is a dour widower, in permanent mourning for his wife Rebekah; Dixon is a pleasure-seeking Geordie Quaker. Their travels across the globe and along their boundary line are marked by both incessant squabbling and, true to Hollywood archetype again, a growing friendship. Indeed, their final meetings together are imbued with a sentimentality that, unusually for Pynchon, succeeds in becoming genuinely affecting.

Much else in *Mason & Dixon* is more reliably Pynchonesque. Vaudevillian ditties, cartoon-like capers, erudite allusions, paranoid delusions, scores of characters, puzzling erections, sentences swelling - with dashes ... and ellipses: all here, in profusion. An array of fantastical conceits populate the novel's landscape: a talking dog, a mechanical duck, a golem, lessons in flying, enormous vegetables, Jesuitical inventions and so on. Pynchon's verbal and intellectual inventiveness constantly astounds: the wheeling tangents his narrative describes provide a desperate resistance to the plodding, quotidian linearity of the novel's central trope, the Mason-Dixon boundary itself.

It is precisely this resistance that most animates *Mason & Dixon*. Pynchon is evoking a world that has been measured out of existence, that has been calibrated 'into the Network of Points already known, that slowly triangulates its Way into the Continent, changing all from subjunctive to declarative, reducing Possibilities to Simplicities that serve the ends of Governments'.

Governments may change, but their power remains tied to such secular certainties: no sooner are the Penns and Lord Baltimore bustled out of their fiefdoms than the Mason-Dixon line takes on a newly-divisive lease of life as the border between slave-owning and free states. In other words, Mason and Dixon's colonial partition finds renewed expression even after the parturition of the United States as an independent nation.

Coincidence ... or something more sinister? As any dedicated paranoiac would attest, the only successful conspiracy is the one that becomes so pervasive as to be all-encompassing, a literal second nature. In *Mason & Dixon*, Pynchon locates the mapping of places, the standardising of time, the measuring of earthly and astronomical boundaries, as forming such a conspiracy. The post of Astronomer-Royal is an apt example: it was created in the seventeenth century with commercial interests (improved navigation) specifically in mind. This, then, is a confluence of scientific investigation with economic and imperial expansion. Revelations about the state or working of the world ride roughshod over people's perceptions and experiences: popular upheaval against the loss of eleven days when converting to the Gregorian calendar takes on a less irrational hue in this novel. Nonetheless, *Mason & Dixon* does not share the grand guignol paranoia of Pynchon's earlier *Gravity's Rainbow*, with its formulation of a shadowy 'They' ordering proceedings. Intrigues, politicking and Machiavellian manoevering all stud the narrative, yet the most important piece of plotting in *Mason & Dixon* remains that of the line itself.

Pynchon's literary invention in *Mason & Dixon* is not, however, deployed in direct opposition to scientific invention. His imaginative exuberance instead resists the tyranny of straight lines, enforced closures, ways of classifying experience that seek to strip it bare of illusion: Mason and Dixon's growing disillusionment with their work stems from a realisation that they are a part of this process. Pynchon would doubtless concur with the mixture of science and mysticism that can be found in Alexander Pope's intended epitaph for Isaac Newton: 'Nature, and Nature's Laws lay in Night./God said, *Let Newton be!* and All was *Light.*' But *Mason & Dixon* also strives for a more harmonious interplay between light and darkness, the known and unknown (like, say, the constellation of the night sky). One imagined ending to the novel sees Mason and Dixon surveying a line across the Atlantic, the reductio ad absurdum that Samuel Johnson invokes in his *Observations*.

Appropriately, Johnson is among a clutch of historical figures who make fleeting appearances in the novel. His *Dictionary* is itself a collection of lines drawn through the endless Atlantic of the English language, a lexicographical endeavour that will always be at once defeated and invigorated by the boundless elasticity of its subject matter. Similarly, Pynchon's fiction in *Mason & Dixon*, by recording the eradication of an America that might have been, seeks finally and admirably to recollect it imaginatively.

Kissing Time Goodbye
Christine Clegg

Kathryn Harrison, *The Kiss*, Fourth Estate, £14.99

Towards the end of *The Kiss*, Kathryn Harrison's autobiographical account of a sexual affair with her father, there is a moment in which she tells him that she can no longer endure the desolation that her life has become: ' "My life," I tell my father, "sucks. But I mean really, really sucks." ' Her father responds by suggesting that they stop having sex: ' "If it's the sex, we don't have to do it. It's just a means of expressing our commitment to each other. If it's not good for you, we'll find another way." ' What is striking about this strategic attempt to keep things going, one way or another, is that if sex between them were to cease, then their relationship would no longer be incestuous. If it were no longer incestuous, then it might revert to the familiarity of an 'ordinary' father-daughter relationship which is what the daughter is wanting, and which is what she has never had.

'Ordinary' fathering, for this daughter, would mean the continuity of a friendly contact sustained by simply keeping in touch: telephone calls, birthday greetings, and so on. This is not what her father has in mind. Harrison's father left when she was a baby, leaving his memory as a mark of absence and grief between the little girl and her mother. When Kathryn is twenty he returns to claim her in the primacy of the sexual 'kiss' of the title; for this father, giving up 'the sex' does not mean giving up the special confines of an intimacy which has been defined by an uncompromising 'commitment'. He has a relationship with society, with the world beyond the limits of the obsession with his daughter. He has work (he is a minister of the church), and a second family (a wife and other children), which he has no intention of giving up. Meanwhile Kathryn, his first-born daughter, is designated as 'his girl' in the most proprietorial terms. What he would exact from her is the entirety of her life, and he does this with the impeccably perverse logic of a demand for unconditional 'love', in which she represents his entitlement, his reproductive gift to the world; a gift that he feels no obligation to part with: ' "... *I gave you my flesh and blood, my spirit. It is my heart that beats within you. I have as much right to you as any one, as much as you have to yourself...*"'

As the affair with her father begins to unravel, divided family loyalties are exposed. Harrison's hair - a lock of which appears on the cover of her book - becomes a symbol of this clash of loyalties. Harrison's mother, who is dying of cancer, wants her daughter's long hair to be cut, as much as she longs for the affair to finish. Conversely Harrison's father wants the hair, which he adoringly attends, to stay. The lock of hair which adorns the cover of *The Kiss* represents the breaking apart of Harrison's coupling with her father and a move of reconciliation with a mother who was always out of reach. The mother's final, deathly kiss draws a line around the mother and daughter in a bond which excludes the father, just as the daughter and father had excluded the mother.

One of the influential ways in which the incest taboo has been understood is that it underpins the structure of marriage and social alliances whereby, for the sake of culture, 'women' are given up, by the men of the family into which they are born, to other men. The benefit of this arrangement is that a bond is forged between men. Since this theory of exchange appears to lock 'women', without volition, into a decidedly heterosexual and interminable circulation, it has been the subject of extensive feminist debate. In revealing so clearly the way in which her father's demand for commitment locks her outside of society, and outside of the experience of being 'ordinarily' in the world, Harrison's narrative reinflects the critique of onerous social structures which is central to that debate. Harrison's desire for what 'other people have', for the conventions that are normatively granted in marriage through social structures of recognition - who is legitimately designated as a husband or wife - comes to represent what it would mean to be free from all that is so profoundly antisocial about being committed to her father's keeping. It is in the realisation of the limits of a paternal sexual fantasy made manifest that Harrison shows up the impossibility of the daughter's desire.

In the Freudian sponsorship of the Oedipal fantasy, the condition of *becoming* an adult in culture is that the unconscious wish for the beloved parent must be denied. In the instance of anthropology, the condition of *being* an adult in culture is the recognition of who is permitted in sex and marriage and who is forbidden. As much as these influential theories may be incompatible on the question of desire, they say something similarly fundamental. To be an adult in culture means something has to be given up. We cannot have what we want. For Kathryn Harrison, not having what she wants means giving up on the fantasy of having an adequate love from her father. As it is, his love is both too much to take - sexual - and never enough - paternal. The 'big body' that now comes between her and the social has never been in the right place. Like the fictional Lolita, enshrined by her 'senior partner' in an endless string of tacky motel rooms, Kathryn Harrison finds herself with 'nowhere else to go'. In the face of isolation from the life and work of her own generation, incest, with or without the sex, starts to look like death.

Harrison's account of incest has largely been acclaimed in aesthetic and confessional terms - it speaks of traumatic secrets, and it does so with great artistry. Because of its literary qualities, and because of the way it avoids being drafted in as an incest survivor narrative, the fact that it so clearly takes the measure of the complex provenance of the incest taboo might be overlooked. *The Kiss* is, undoubtedly, an elegant transformation of something deeply horrible, but it is no less incisive for that. In this it is not unrelated to the genre of incest survivor narratives, such as Charlotte Vale Allen's *Daddy's Girl*, and Sylvia Fraser's *My Father's House*, which testify to father-daughter incest. In all of these texts, writing represents not only the act of writing 'out' the trauma, and a breaching of the incest taboo by revealing the family secret, but also the act of becoming a professional writer as a means of living through the experience.

What differentiates Harrison's memoir from many incest survivor narratives is that she was a woman of twenty when the sexual relationship with her father began. Unlike Fraser, for example, Harrison is not writing of the anguish of recovering buried sexual memories of what happened *to* her as a child, or as an adolescent; theoretically, at least, she was a consenting adult. It is this question of consent which tilts *The Kiss* towards another framing of the representation of incest. The idea of consenting adults appears to draw the subject of incest away from the predominant influence of feminist debates about child sexual abuse, and into the more diffuse area of libertarian transgressions and sibling passions (Anais Nin's adult affair with her father, and the filial passions of Byron and his half-sister, spring to mind here). Herein lies the difficulty with Harrison's memoir. She is initiated into the affair with her father through a kiss which takes place as they part company in an airport departure lounge. The question of what transforms this familial kiss into something other both haunts the book and, enigmatically, encloses the difficult subject of the daughter's sexual desire. In a very real sense this serves to highlight the question of consent. In law, children are deemed unable to give or to refuse consent. Judiciously, we draw lines of responsibility and culpability between adults and children as a means of protection (which only too often fails miserably). What Harrison shows, and I think this is why her book is important, is that even as adults we remain in some primal sense our parent's children, and the ability to 'know', or to imagine, what we are consenting to may be no more available to us at twenty than it is at ten.

Risky Business
Timothy Bewes

Ulrich Beck, *The Reinvention of Politics*, trans. Mark Ritter, Polity £45.00 (hb), £12.95 (pb)

Ulrich Beck's elegant theories about 'risk society', his reflections on the 'chaotic' experience of love, and his reconceptualisation of postmodernity as a condition of 'reflexive modernisation', have attracted considerable attention well beyond the borders of his own discipline. A sociology professor at the University of Munich, Beck has been courted by German politicians, was appointed to Helmut Kohl's ambitiously-named Commission on the Future, and is reported to have met with Tony Blair on several occasions. A book explicitly addressing the political implications of 'reflexive modernisation' was probably necessary for Beck to consolidate this widening interest in his work, and his latest English publication is an attempt to provide exactly that. Eloquently written, and drawing on a wide range of source and theoretical material, *The Reinvention of Politics* extends the analysis offered in his 1986 book *Risk Society*, with the benefit of a retrospective view upon two symbolic and poignant events which occurred in 1989: the Chernobyl nuclear reactor disaster, and the collapse of the Berlin Wall.

Chernobyl and the Berlin Wall illustrate and, for Beck, confirm the truth of the two most important assumptions of the theory of reflexive modernisation. The first of these is oracular: nature no longer poses the principal, or indeed any significant risk to mankind. In fact, nature no longer exists as such; the process of world colonisation, which continued throughout what Beck calls the period of 'industrial modernisation', is complete; nature now exists only as 'naturalisation' - the artificial creation of 'certitude', a desire to forget the complexity of the world by recourse to a dream of innocence, a benign oblivion. Beck hereby gives a historical interpretation to one of the persistent theoretical tropes of postmodernism: the nature/culture opposition *has dissolved*; we are living, now, in a world in which all certitude is 'constructed'. Thus 'back to basics', religious fundamentalism, neo-nationalism in Europe, along with communitarian movements, represent 'counter-modern' tendencies which *refuse* what is an unprecedented condition of 'liberation' from ideological certainties, by imaginatively re-investing the world with simplicity. In a society the only significant threats to which originate entirely from within society itself, certainty, says Beck, is a mental condition fraught with danger. In the risk society, knowledge is best replaced by 'doubt' - a humbler, truer disposition, for which the ecological consideration of the future, on a global scale, is a more significant long-term goal than the myopic preoccupations of ideological antagonisms.

Second, with the disintegration of the Soviet Bloc, the premises of conventional politics fall into incoherence. 'Left' and 'right' are redundant categories: 'With the loss of the East-West orientation,' writes Beck, 'politics is becoming a silent movie, or, more accurately, a sound movie without the soundtrack. People move their lips and pound the keyboards, but nothing comes out!' (p149). Parliament as it currently operates - the arena of the political system - is obsolete, a moribund institution. Politics proper, says Beck, now takes place in a 'sub-political' realm, which may include anything and everything that is not Parliament: industry and small businesses, individual consumers and activists, science and technological research, workers in schools and hospitals - in short, all that was previously understood to be the private sphere now has a greater impact upon social change than the political institution. 'Side effects', says Beck, have replaced instrumental rationality as the 'motor' of social transformation. The implication is that social transformation is no longer feasible on a macrological, that is to say, structural scale, but only micrologically, internally, at the level of the existential, the emotional, or at best the local and specific.

Thus the political system, in the risk society, is to be remodelled as a domain of 'intersystemic mediating institutions' - committees, in short, intended to foreclose upon imprudent judgements and 'irresponsible' activities. Reflexive modernisation is a condition in which modernity has lost faith in its own industrial expansion - justifiably so, implies Beck. The concept of politics as inspiration-led, expansionist as a matter of principle, motivated by grand visions and the desire to remake the world according to the dream of a charismatic individual (for example), has been entirely discredited. Politics is devolving to the sub-political sphere, where individuals, as 'tinkerers with themselves and their world', are the new political agents. Two worlds, says Beck, belonging to two different epochs - industrial and reflexive modernity - currently exist side by side. 'On the one hand, a political vacuity of the institutions is evolving and, on the other hand, a non-institutional renaissance of politics'. 'The individual' continues Beck happily, 'is returning to society' (p98.

For some time now, commentators have bemoaned the 'depoliticisation' of modern politics. Ulrich Beck, almost uniquely, recognises the truth of this depoliticising process, *and endorses it*. 'The political constellation of industrial society is becoming unpolitical, while what was unpolitical in industrialism is becoming political.' The realm of the 'sub-political', which subsumes the old distinction between politics and non-politics, is one of 'responsible' action which is reconciled to the decline of over-arching ideologies, and the condition of 'individualisation' to which all men and women are 'condemned'. Individualisation, as Beck reiterates, denotes not alienation or social disconnectedness, but simply this *fact* of redundant industrial certainties and ideologies, the absence of metaphysical truths, and the obligation of individuals to construct new certainties - in terms of personal biography, identity, commitments and convictions, for example. Decision-making, in reflexive modernisation, is everything. Ideology, not merely in classical Marxist terms, but in post-structuralist Althusserian ones as well, has been overcome;

yet this is a condition of inescapability, not of choice, on the part of citizens in the risk society.

Similarly, history, despite Beck's objections to the contrary, is conceived as having a linearity and a direction that is completely at odds with a traditionally Marxist or Hegelian concept of 'dialectic'. A third assumption of reflexive modernisation is that science, in the form of genetic research, is on the brink of discovering the human blueprint - or at least, that such a discovery is possible and ultimately inevitable. This discovery, part dream, part nightmare, as Beck concedes, will make possible and necessary 'a new quality of politics', in which 'everyone rules himself and his progeny and can directly implement the rules that govern him (intolerance, images of others, fears) under his own direction (arm in arm with the 'genetic counsellor' assisting him).' 'Research is already underway', he continues, 'looking for genetic features that favour violent behaviour, in covariance with environmental influences, of course.' Yet that final, appended, sub-clause is devastatingly unconvincing. History, for Beck, is virtually at an end; the scenario envisaged by Dostoevsky's man underground, whereby man, having discovered the laws of nature, will no longer be responsible for his actions, is imminent - except that for Beck this discovery must be reconceptualised as a liberation from the orthodoxies of the past, an unprecedented devolution of responsibility onto the individual, who is enlightened as to the origins of his impulses and beliefs as never before.

It can be seen that Beck's theory of reflexive modernisation is, in certain ways, more apocalyptic and 'periodising' than the concept of postmodernity, which he rejects, partly on those same grounds. My suspicions about the theory of reflexive modernisation as a whole begin to collect at this point. The perceived totality, or near-totality of our objective knowledge is a notion which recurs at certain stages in history, and is a beguiling misperception for the simple, self-evident reason that we cannot know the extent of what we don't already know. This seems too obvious to be worth stating; yet Beck's theory of the end of the age of industrial modernisation is predicated upon this assumption that modernisation, having 'consumed and lost its other' - having, in other words, proceeded to the point of self-exhaustion - has turned on itself and become 'reflexive'.

This loss of faith on the part of 'modernity' seems more like a renunciation of the political obligation to hold fast to the possibilities of reason and modernity, in all their difficulty and riskiness, than a decision taken at the terminus of knowledge, or one based on the rational calculation of risk. Risk, I would say, is the *condition of possibility* of modernisation; risk is indispensable to reason and to politics - and this is a universal quality, not specific to the late-twentieth century. Life is of course less risky now than at any time in the history of civilization - this, perhaps, and not the prevalence of risk, is the root of our current political malaise.

It is irrational, likewise, to subscribe to the idea that nature is now a mastered domain. Numerous examples attest to the truth of this - from the volcano in Monserrat and disastrous flooding at Frankfurt-on-Oder this summer, to the tornadoes in Texas last May - yet the most important refutation is a theoretical one: knowledge is not a finite objective; the field of investigation is never entirely divorced from the enterprise of knowledge, but is constituted by it; it expands and mutates, as human endeavour advances and encroaches. There is no final frontier, just as there is no real attainable point of Absolute Knowledge.

The apparent 'sanitation' of modernity, and of politics, is an important note in the theory of reflexive modernisation. The 'dark side' of modernity is a recurring theme in modern literary criticism; Diderot, Kierkegaard, Dostoevsky, Nietzsche, Kafka, Adorno, Horkheimer, Foucault, are all mentioned in Beck's work, yet his treatment of them is peculiarly programmatic. In his final chapter, 'The Art of Doubt', Beck performs an analogous operation to his treatment of the nature/culture opposition earlier in the book; this time, however, the object is the distinction between certainty and uncertainty. In his expatiation upon the virtue of doubt, Kafka is the first to be cited explicitly, and Beck quotes from his self-strafing *Diaries*. In Kafka's self-loathing, says Beck, 'it is possible to hear and experience an echo of the liberation from the yoke which the maintenance of the grand facade of the self has represented for its exponents to this day' (pp162-3). Thus Beck's attempt to save modernity is matched by this extraordinary attempt to 'tame' Kafka, to expunge what is relentless and pessimistic in Kafka's despair, and transform it into a pragmatic relativism. Pages later, Beck writes of the possibility of harnessing a 'reflexive' doubt which, directed towards doubt itself, is able to 'drive away the caustic and destructive sides of doubt'.' But as a reading of Kierkegaard, or for that matter Hegel, makes clear, doubt without despair is not doubt at all; Beck's attempt to harness doubt in this way is too easy, and one is reminded of Richard Rorty's methodological institution of irony. Of Montaigne, his model for a productive, liberating and 'subversive' doubt, Beck writes: 'There is no difficulty for him in uniting being a nihilist with being a Christian ... Precisely because he cannot recognize and distinguish what is the truth, he clings to whatever permits him to lead his life.' This pragmatism ultimately scuttles the theory of reflexive modernisation, since its effect is to advocate a way of thinking that is permanently qualified, permanently mediated, and therefore instrumental and reactive.

The most urgent imperative, Beck says, approaching his conclusion, is to discover a source of criticism which argues 'completely in step with its times' - and he names this source as 'self-confident doubt'. I would in no way dispute that this book, or this conclusion, is thoroughly in step with its times; 'self-confident doubt', as a euphemism for institutionalised caution, describes very well the temper of British politics in the 1990s. These are neurotic times, and this book suffers from the association. That one should be *out* of step with one's time, however, is not only an imperative for any reinvention of politics at the present moment, but should be a criterion of all truly political engagement.

Writes of Passage: Narratives of India
Katherine Frank

Sunil Khilnani, *The Idea of India*, Hamish Hamilton, £17.99
Arundhati Roy, *The God of Small Things*, Flamingo, £15.99

The Idea of India is, as Sunil Khilnani says, an 'essay' on India since 1947, but of a completely different sort than those produced by V S Naipaul, Ved Mehta and, more recently, Gita Mehta. Khilnani isn't interested in anecdotes or verbal snapshots: what he produces in a mere two hundred pages of text is a new kind of historical/political narrative: lean, elegant, and sharply analytical. Rejecting both imperial and nationalist simplifications on the one hand and, on the other, diverging from what he calls 'the pointillism of the new historians', he explores instead the deeper currents that underlie the torrent of events in recent Indian history. And he taps into these currents by examining various perceptions, notions, manifestations and symptoms of contemporary India in four chapters that focus on democracy, planned development, Indian cities and the nature of Indian identity.

The title *The Idea of India* may seem fashionably postmodern, but note that Khilnani's 'idea' is singular, not plural: this is not a book about representations of India. Khilnani is interested in what forces contrive to make India a unified whole, and central to his argument is a Nehruvian vision of democracy. Against the odds, in a society founded on the inequality of the caste system, largely poor and illiterate, and with 'a staggeringly diverse citizenry', democracy has survived in India. This, Khilnani holds, 'is the single most remarkable fact about post-1947 India, distinguishing it from almost all the new nation states that emerged out of the disintegration of European empires.'

Khilnani is interested in ideas rather than people, but the hero of the long chapter on democracy, and indeed of the book, is Jawaharlal Nehru - the main architect of Indian democracy - while his daughter, Indira Gandhi, is presented as a serious threat. Khilnani's discussion of the ways in which Mrs Gandhi centralised power, treated provincial governments, dismantled the Congress Party and undermined the constitution, is the best analysis of her rule that I've read. As Khilnani concludes, under Indira Gandhi 'the meaning of democracy [was] . . . menacingly narrowed to signify only elections.'

And yet, even after the Emergency, elections were held and democracy survived - a powerful testimony to its resilience and underlying strength in India. Because he is not interested in personalities, Khilnani doesn't speculate on Indira Gandhi's motives and the extent to which she was aware of what she was doing. Nor does he explore the biographical influences which shaped Nehru's vision of democracy. But the vision itself is the lynchpin of the 'idea of India' and it recurs throughout the book. Khilnani explores it most fully in his discussion of Nehru's *The Discovery of India*, a book which undoubtedly influenced Khilnani's own. It was here that Nehru evolved his unique pluralistic vision of Indian identity which was based on his understanding of the Indian past as 'a tale of cultural mixing and fusion, a civilizational tendency towards unification.' It is precisely this deep rooted capacity for accommodation and inclusion that makes Partition, in Khilnani's words, 'the unspeakable sadness at the heart of the idea of India'.

Khilnani, however, is not merely an apologist for Nehruvian democracy. *The Idea of India* is a critique as well as a defence. And it is most critical in the chapters devoted to Nehru's programme of planned industrialisation and India's cities. 'India in the 1950s,' according to Khilnani, 'fell in love with the idea of cement.' Dams and modern cities like Chandigargh were to be 'temples of the future'. But India has failed to become the industrial giant Nehru envisioned while Chandigarh has degenerated into 'a museum piece in need of protection from its own violently quarrelling citizens and the ravages of the climate'. Today liberalisation, not planning, is the discourse of economic discussion, and Bombay and Bangalore the booming Indian cities.

If democracy is the protagonist of *The Idea of India*, the antagonist or counter-force is the recent rise of Hindu nationalism which proffers an anti-Nehruvian vision of Indian identity that is exclusive rather than inclusive: an 'Indianisation' based on the forging of 'one nation, one people, one culture'. Hindu nationalists and their party the Bharatiya Janata Party (BJP) have embarked on a struggle 'to capture the state and purge the nationalist imagination, leaving it homogenous, exclusive and Hindu'. Since the mid 1980s the BJP has been steadily gaining strength, culminating, of course, in the 1996 general elections when it briefly gained control of the government.

But the rise of the BJP and Hindu nationalism was most frighteningly revealed in the 1992 destruction of the Babri Masjid at Ayodhya. If Partition is 'the unspeakable sadness' at the heart of India, then Ayodhya is its running sore. Khilnani ends his chapter on Indian identity by delineating the options: 'India's history has shown two broad possibilities of dealing with diversity: a theoretically untidy, improvising, pluralist approach, or a neatly rationalist and purifying exclusivism. . . . The present generation of Indians . . . must decide what they wish to build out of the wreckage of Ayodhya's Babri Masjid.'

India, then, is at a crossroads. This is a cautiously hopeful book which appears at a time when people tend to be either wildly enthusiastic or desperately gloomy about the future of India. It is written from a dual perspective by an Indian who has been educated and continues to live and work in Britain, and this penetrating double vision makes it seem both dispassionate and heartfelt.

It is a relief to report that all the hype surrounding the publication of Arundhati Roy's first novel, *The God of Small Things*, and the exorbitant advances paid to the author on three continents, are richly deserved. This is a brilliant book, though not the flawless one some critics have been touting it as. It is overwritten, marred by stylistic tics (one-word sentences, capitalised words for emphasis, pretentious repetitions) and laboured images such as the moth who recurrently perches on the heroine Rahel's heart. These, however, are forgivable excesses which call attention to themselves in an otherwise perfectly structured and modulated book. They sink into insignificance in the face of the heartbreaking story Roy tells.

It is hard to sum up what exactly that story is: the story of a Syrian Christian family in a sleepy, lush Kerala town, the tale of twins - Estha and Rahel - 'a rare breed of Siamese twins, physically separate but with joint identities', the journey from acute, wide-eyed childhood to adult understanding and despair. *The God of Small Things* is all these, but it is also, obliquely, a book about India, about politics and caste, about the God of large as well as small things 'in a country ... [where] Worse Things kept happening'. And Roy's genius is to tease out the connection between personal turmoil and the 'insane, unfeasible, public turmoil of a nation'. She does this not in anger or scorn (*vide* Rushdie) but with a haunting compassion. Her characters are hounded, pursued, destroyed by History. The God of Small Things is 'the God of Loss' and the loss is forever.

This is what Estha and Rahel grow up to understand and the knowledge effectively destroys them too. The book takes place in two time frames: 1969, when the twins are seven, and 1993 when they are thirty-one. In between Estha, the male twin, has stopped communicating because of the betrayal forced upon him as a boy, while his sister Rahel has succumbed to emptiness. As maimed adults, they are still linked in their twinship, but it is now a 'hideous grief' that binds them: 'the terror' they witnessed and innocently participated in as children has blighted their lives.

Though this is a palpably Indian novel - one steeped in a particular historical moment, culture and landscape - Rahel and Estha's passage from innocence to knowledge is, of course, universal: Every Child's journey, Every Adult's handful of dust. And this, finally, is what makes *The God of Small Things* such a rare and profoundly moving novel. Roy transports us to Kerala, immerses us in the world of a bizarre family running a pickle factory overlooking a river, their untouchable retainers, and a militant communist movement, which in their weird juxtaposition lead to devastation. But having transported us so far, Roy brings us home in the end to the familiar god of small things - the god of loss - in our own hearts.

SOUNDINGS PART 2

States of Africa

INTRODUCTION

Victoria Brittain and Rakiya Omaar

The collapse of the old state of Zaire - the embodiment of decay and corruption in Africa - and its rebirth as Congo, was, apart from the end of apartheid, the most symbolic and heartening event on the African continent for the three decades since colonial rule cracked and began to dissolve. (Basil Davidson examines the hopes pinned on Laurent Kabila, Congo's new leader and a man identified with the independence struggles of thirty years ago, p104-8)

The transformation of Zaire into Congo was an event which had its roots in an extremely weak state, Zaire, and in the 1994 genocide in neighbouring Rwanda, which together swept away the ancien regimes in both countries. (Rakiya Omaar and Augustin Ndahimana Buranga describe the unimaginable torment of the survivors, and the struggle to prevent the rewriting of history which could still allow the culture of impunity to prevail; this would force Rwanda to relive the horror and destabilise the entire region, pp109-117). The two regimes, in Zaire under Mobutu, and in Rwanda under Juvénal Habyarimana, are sadly illustrative of the degraded post-colonial leadership which Africans have endured, and which the rest of the world has accepted with the implicitly racist premise that Africa could expect nothing better. Idi Amin of Uganda and Samuel Doe of Liberia, for instance, ignorant brutal men who should never have led their villages, never mind the countries which they brought to their knees, were actually supported by Britain and the US. Neither could have survived without continuous Western support. Both were driven out of power, and in Doe's case killed, by their own people's disgust and anger at the suffering and shame they had inflicted on the country. But by the time they left, they had wreaked such political, economic and moral havoc on their countries that recovery, even under the most auspicious circumstances, would take decades. Liberia is still reeling from the consequences of Doe's

Introduction

misrule.

Country after country buckled under a system of misgovernment in which one man sought to personify the state, bringing some countries, like Liberia and Somalia, to virtual disintegration. The private and public misuse of power, and the absence of ethical leadership, allowed the state to monopolise political space and to benefit from the absence of institutional sources of criticism. Instead, the nation's resources were harnessed to serve the seemingly insatiable greed for power of those ruling the country.

Within a month of Kabila's arrival in Kinshasa and the flight of one of the continent's richest and once most powerful men, two more West African countries were up in flames. Sierra Leone faced a coup led by a group of desperate young soldiers who could no longer bear the humiliation of their poverty and the ethnic politics of the newly elected Head of State; while Congo Brazzaville was torn apart by heavy fighting in the capital between rival ethnic militia loyal to the two principal contestants in the approaching presidential elections. The Central African Republic was still in the grip of ethnic violence from rival groups of soldiers.

The fault lines along which so many conflicts in Africa have erupted - ethnicity and regionalism - have led many Western observers to argue that tribal animosities are a permanent feature of African politics, which have their own dynamics irrespective of the broader political framework. But there is nothing inevitable about the creation of *political* ethnicity. Idi Amin, Samuel Doe and Mohamed Siad Barre of Somalia, amongst others, manufactured ethnic differences and manipulated fears and rivalries as a strategy of building a political constituency; thus laying the foundations for a future explosion and made orderly and effective government impossible for years, if not generations.

Mobutu destroyed his own country's wealth and well-being with the connivance of Western business. For over twenty years, and at the behest of successive American administrations, he hosted mercenaries and let his country be used as the staging point for a terrorist war against Angola which has destroyed its hopes. (Victoria Brittain describes the forgotten days of dignity in a country proud of its socialism, pp143-152.) To please his friends in the darker quarters of French intelligence - and as a bargaining chip against ending his days as an international pariah - he went along with the genocidal project of the Rwandese authorities to wipe out the

Tutsis of Rwanda for ever. For his own reasons he encouraged his army units in the east to assist in the destabilisation of Uganda by a dissolute band of former Idi Amin men.

For years none of this was considered worthy of protest in the West, or in the United Nations, or even in the Organisation of African Unity. Again, as with the leadership question, Africa could expect nothing better. Even apartheid South Africa's long years of destabilisation of its neighbours brought little condemnation and no action from the rest of the world.

Behind the indifference lay the shadows of the cold war. The ideological struggle between the Soviet Union and the United States was transported to Africa, which became the bloodied battlefield for proxy wars, particularly in the Horn and southern Africa.

The French, with a long tradition of continuing control of their former colonies, similarly found autocratic rulers - such as Houphouet Boigny of Ivory Coast, Omar Bongo of Gabon, Gnassingbe Eyadema of Togo, and King Hassan of Morocco - to their taste. All over the continent dictators flourished and democracy was still-born in the post-colonial phase.

With the lack of democracy went lack of development. Education, health and transport were the poor relations in budgets dominated by the military; and the small ruling elites, both civilian and military, were almost invariably corrupt. (Tanzania, one of the countries least known for corruption, produced the Warioba report which revealed a picture recognisable across the continent, pp198-208.) Mobutu's export of his country's wealth as a personal fortune was different only in scale from what happened in a huge number of African countries. It is little wonder that almost all the Least Developed Countries, as ranked by the UN or the World Bank, are in Africa.

But when Yoweri Museveni and a dozen of his colleagues went into the bush and took up arms against Milton Obote at the end of 1980, it was the start of a new era for Africa. The trigger was a scandalously rigged election which the Commonwealth had declared free and fair. Museveni was a young intellectual, the product of Dar es Salaam University in its vibrant radical years, and much influenced by time spent with Samora Machel in the Mozambican bush, as Frelimo wore down the Portuguese colonial soldiers. The romantic ideals of the 'New Man' which Frelimo lived by in those days, and the heady success of the guerrilla war, left Museveni determined to challenge the political rules of money and force which the political class in Uganda thought inevitable. No-one believed he could possibly win a guerrilla war in Uganda. Not only was there no precedent for such a war post-independence, but Uganda was landlocked and no neighbouring country would act as a rear base for the rebellion. But, emphasising the importance of self-reliance, Museveni proved that a rebellion whose aims and *modus operandi* responded to local needs, could succeed without outside support. When he took the reins of power in January 1986, few believed that he could raise Uganda from the ashes, still less act as a lighthouse for a younger generation of African politicians.

In power Museveni has been the catalyst for, and in some cases has given material help to, new regimes in Rwanda, Eritrea and Ethiopia, as well as Mr Kabila's Congo. There is a new generation of African leaders from these countries - Paul Kagame of Rwanda and Issias Afeworki of Eritrea in particular - who are as confident and clear-sighted as Museveni, and, like him, give no deference to powerful Westerners. These leaders came to power after years of struggle and privation, and with a popular base won in those struggles (except in the very particular circumstances of post-genocide Rwanda). Their success on the battlefield, against adversaries with more resources and weapons, is a crucial factor in their confidence. It was their support - political, moral, logistical, and in some cases military - together with some from the Angolan armed forces, which allowed Kabila to carry off a feat in Congo in six months that none thought possible.

Museveni has carried off politically a challenge to Western conventional wisdom which none thought possible. One of the defining characteristics of Museveni's Uganda is his resistance to the existence of traditional political parties. Insisting that the proliferation of parties in Africa has brought not elections, but rather tribal selections, his government has introduced a system whereby members of parliament seek votes in their personal capacity and represent their constituents, rather than parties. Compared with the botched multi-partyism forced on neighbouring Kenya, which has been deformed into an anti-democratic framework, as Lucy Hannan and Kathurima M'Inoti recount on pages 121-131, Museveni's no-party state holds some important lessons for the future political map of Africa.

In South Africa - often seen as the natural leader of the continent in its post-apartheid phase - Thabo Mbeki talks of the Africa Renaissance, but in

South Africa reconciliation has been less than completely successful and the compromises with the old regime leave shadows over the future James Motlatsi, leader of the miners union, puts forward a critique of the ANC's economic policies (pp211-223). Motlatsi's article touches too upon the question of whether there has not been too much of a rush to reconciliation, under Western pressure. Can a nation realistically reconcile in such a short period of time after such a long period of horror? The question is: at what price and at whose expense?

Africa's seeming inability to resolve its political problems is, in part, a reflection of its marginalisation in the world economy. Even in crises where African leaders have been politically ahead of the UN in their analyses and willingness to act, for example during the Rwandese genocide of 1994, the continent's lack of economic muscle made it impossible to translate the rhetoric into effective action. It is a similar story at the national level. (For example Kevin Watkins describes how Zimbabwe's health service, the pride of the post-independence period, has been battered by the demands of Structural Adjustment Policies.) This picture of declining state capacity in social services, repeated all over the continent, leaves Africa set in a trend which is directly contrary to that which produced the much-vaunted Asian economic miracle in countries like Malaysia.

The lack of economic opportunities has not only led to unprecedented emigration and the exodus of qualified and experienced people. By allowing the deterioration of public services, many governments and nations have become vulnerable to foreign pressure and foreign agendas. But it is not only governments which have become dependent on external economic assistance. The civic institutions that are needed to permit alternative voices to emerge and play a role in shaping a country's political future also rely, to a large extent, on foreign funding. Resources from Europe and North America keep many church organisations, academic institutions and non-governmental organisations afloat. This trend, which has come to be known as 'donorism' comes at a heavy price (as Joe Hanlon's article makes clear, pp184-194). The very forces necessary for the growth of democracy are obliged to respond to the needs, if not the demands, of a foreign rather than a national constituency. The increasingly pointed questions that are asked in Africa about the impact of foreign relief organisations reflect frustrations about the extent to which the priorities and perceptions of Africa are determined by outsiders.

Introduction

As more Africans struggle to achieve the future they have been denied, but believe they deserve, there will, without doubt, be new waves of turmoil. The level of violent explosions may well be highest in countries - such as Kenya - where the West has propped up autocratic rulers as guarantors of 'stability'. Out of the violence, and the peaceful efforts of many on the continent, must come the institutions that alone can safeguard the lives and well-being of future generations. The self-confidence of people like Yoweri Museveni and Issias Afeworki, and their vision of an Africa reliant on itself and capable of deciding its own destiny, is important for a continent that has felt diminished by a succession of leaders who have betrayed its hopes. But good leaders are not enough; they must leave, as their most important legacy, institutions shaped by the needs of ordinary men and women in Africa. That will be the most important break with the past, and the only basis for an enduring future.

States under pressure

Basil Davidson

Basil Davidson argues that the Kabila regime in the Congo is very good news for the African continent.

If I insist that recent events in the former Belgian Congo confirm the approaching end of an epoch in the history of the African continent - an end to the epoch of territorial imperialism - I shall expect to be accused of sentimental optimism. And besides, who thinks that territorial imperialism matters a damn? Nowadays we know all too well that economic imperialism is what rules; and no-one in their right mind supposes that economic imperialism is near its end. All the same I still think that this ending of territorial imperialism is a fact - if, needless to say, it really is a fact - of great and pregnant meaning. Let me, briefly, argue the case.

To begin with, then: yes, it is a fact. These one-time student innovators came out of the forests of the Kivu region, a few months ago, and proceeded to chase the incumbent neo-colonialists, the one-time Belgian imperialist spy Mobutu and all his gang, to defeat and disappearance; and there is no present sign that the defeat will be reversed. But this man Kabila: won't he just degrade like all the others? Or, if he doesn't degrade, won't he be eliminated (like Pio Pinto, for instance; like Amilcar Cabral; like so many others who stuck to their innovating plans until the assassins came for them)? Well, we shall see. No ground for sentimental optimism here. But the fact, so far, is that nobody has tried, or rather, those who have briefly tried (such as Savimbi's men of the so-called UNITA 'movement' from neighbouring Angola) have failed. By all the signs, Kabila and his friends are in for a good run. The further fact, very large in its implications, is that Kabila and his friends are responding to a political scenario that now becomes notably different from before, and by no means in the Congo alone. Consider only that this vast sprawl of a country has not been a political state, a state-unit in any recognisable sense, for very many years. On the contrary, apart from a few islands of mineral and export-crop production, the Congo has long since 'gone back to bush': meaning, in the old colonial phrase, has reverted to the everyday self-rule of and for local populations. Little is known about this decades-long 'interregnum', for the local populations have evidently felt no need to write about themselves. But when we discover more we shall surely see that these local populations have nonetheless been able to provide for themselves. And this will be seen to have happened because these populations have recalled the customs and disciplines of their pre-colonial and therefore pre-Mobutist history of self-government. The Congo demonstrates that these Africans have not forgotten how to govern themselves; and this will be the sense in which 'the end of territorial imperialism' has a real meaning.

※※

It is, of course, by no means sure that this 'real meaning', if perceived, will be found acceptable in our old imperialist countries. For accepting it has then to mean accepting another but much more far-reaching proposition: that there was indeed a time when these Africans, before the European dispossessions, did know how to govern themselves, and, if our anthropological and other serious texts and analyses are anything to go by, knew this with an impressive stability and success. But at this point in the argument, no doubt, we have to plunge a little into the specifics of our own culture such as we have received it from our imperialist ancestors. Nothing is more certain than that this notion of pre-colonial political success in Africa, in 'tribal Africa', will be generally rejected in old imperialist countries with gravely head-nodding scorn, for everyone knows that pre-colonial Africans were no better than they should be: why otherwise should our forebears have embarked on the great colonial civilising mission? Now you may at once object that nobody any longer really thinks like that save on the wilder shores of political extremism. But from my experience the truth is rather that nobody any longer *admits* to thinking like that. The depths of inherent British paternalism in this connection are very deep, and those of most European cultures are probably deeper still. No such paternalism - *read*, no racism in the common usage of the term - in Sweden, Norway, or Denmark - or other such non-imperialist countries? Well, I wonder. For 'us', in any case, the outright imperialist decades weigh far more heavily than can be comfortable. Whenever any English person presents her/himself with enlightened views about the prospects for Africa I find myself bound to remember my old and kind instructor Dr Leopold Mottoulle in the Belgian Congo of half a century ago. As chief medical officer of the then great mining conglomerate, the Union Miniere, Mottoulle had performed a civilising marvel: he had banished the migrant labour system in those mines invented and imposed by their European entrepreneurs (Belgian, French, and other), and, at some expense to their profits, had ceased to allow the mines to borrow the British system of annual or bi-annual 'recruitment' of rural labourers. This was a savage system which laid waste to rural welfare and stability; and Mottoulle, who valued both those qualities, would have nothing to do with it.

Yes, but Mottoulle was still a convinced imperialist in our own familiar sense. He wrote what no-one nowadays is ready to admit even though the inner thought remains intact. As regards the whole great colonial enterprise (he wrote in 1946, and repeated to me in conversations of 1954),

> the coloniser must never lose sight of the fact that the Negroes have the minds of children ... The European must in all circumstances show himself a calm an thoughtful chief, good without weakness, benevolent without familiarity, and above all just in the repression of faults as in the reward of goodwill.

Excruciating, no doubt: but surely recognisable in our own world of today, if in far more 'tactful' language? Perhaps I exaggerate. Yet most current personal attitudes, in Britain, do seem to reveal a very general disbelief in any African capacity to make progress in the management of African affairs. Africans may *try*, it is agreed, but they will not succeed. Or, if they do succeed, this will be only by following a European or North American precedent or lesson. Left to themselves, there is bound to be failure and confusion. (Or, of course, worse.) So far as the press is concerned, even our more thoughtful broadsheets can be seen to share this automatic attitude. Those who were broadly in touch with the realities of Congolese affairs (and with due reservations I include myself, who at least was one of those long awaiting Laurent Kabila's reappearance from the Kivu forests) were also those who saw that Kabila and his friends almost surely held the key to post-Mobutist reconstruction. If they could survive many years of virtual banishment from any public presence, and still retain the essence of the ideas and convictions which had carried them through the anti-Lumumbist persecutions and corruptions of the 1960s and after, then they would have something new and different to show to their country and to the world.

We shall see. Of course: perhaps! But while our journalists are (quite reasonably) digging up the evidence for Kabila-ist shortcomings during those long and lonely years of banishment and virtual isolation, the fact remains, today, that Kabila and his friends are well on the way to installing a peaceful scene in their troubled land, and may, on the internal evidence, quite possibly succeed: at any rate during the foreseeable future, and that will be no small thing. Yet our ingrained paternalism still prevails. Even as history-minded a newspaper as *The Guardian* feels it well and wise to take Kabila in hand. To come to any good, we read in a first leader of 19 May, 'Mr Kabila needs to show mature political judgement'. Reading this, one is induced to wonder how this man (and his friends in Congo) could possibly have got through the empty years if they had lacked that quality of judgement? To put in no higher, Kabila is after all the only 'Lumumbist' who managed to survive assassination or its equivalent in the decades of CIA-directed dictatorship. We read further that 'Kabila has much to learn and a track record which is shaky at some points and blank in others'. Perfectly probable: but, if so, shouldn't we be rather careful not to give advice out of our own ignorance? Admitting that leader-writers have to write leaders even when they have nothing useful to say (and I too have been a leader-writer, though for *The Times* and not, alas, *The Guardian*), this kind of automatic scepticism does seem to lead back to our customary paternalism; and the root of the matter, as it seems to me, rests in the stubborn power of cultural stereotypes. These have to be confronted; but they are deep embedded, and excavation is hard. Other peoples, of course, have the same difficulty: not least, Africans. In one of his memorable papers about the beliefs of the Kalabari, a people who live in the Niger Delta, Robin Horton tells an altogether convincing story about Kalabari reactions to their first sight of Europeans. Demonstrating a rooted condition of cultural paternalism, this story is all the more impressive because the Kalabari have otherwise shown themselves to be an ingenious and stubbornly experimental people. 'The first white man', we learn, 'was seen by a Kalabari fisherman who had gone down to the mouth of the (Niger) estuary in his canoe. Panic-stricken, he raced home and told his people what he had seen: whereupon he and the rest of the town set out to purify themselves - that is, to rid themselves of the influence of the strange and monstrous thing that had intruded on their world.' Nowadays, the Kalabari no longer see Europeans as strange and monstrous: or, rather, they no longer admit to this. We are all Europeans now. And now, in our own time, we may at any rate claim to be reaching and perhaps entering a post-imperialist epoch; but, if this is so, we have yet to reach and enter a post-imperialist culture.

※

That we are not there yet may be seen, for example, from reactions to this institutional crisis in the Congo. All the same, there is a novelty at work. It is that no powerful authority appears to expect 'the West', meaning in practice the USA and the European Union, to repeat their Bosnian (and other such experiments in 'knowing better') adventure, and send in troops and political administrators bearing solutions to crisis. We are evidently, at last, going to leave Africans to settle their own troubles and clear up their own confusions. After the spectacle of European interventions in Africa over the past century and more I am not at all sure, dear reader, that I can quite bring myself to believe this good news. But I am going to try, and, if I may say so, I strongly recommend you to do the same.

A genocide foretold

Rakiya Omaar

Rakiya Omaar argues that repeated failure to punish Hutu mass murderers feeds a culture of genocide in Rwanda. And a survivor of the genocide gives his testimony

Théoneste Karangwa lost his father, Marc Mirambo, at the age of three. He was killed in 1964 in the commune of Cyimbogo in Cyangugu. Marc and his brother, Munyakazi, were arrested by policemen after a local militia known as 'The Young Ones' (*Abajenesi*) had identified them as Tutsis. The *Abajenesi* had been created by the ruling Parmehutu party. One of the leaders of the militia was Jean Nsengumuremyi. Many Tutsi men were arrested during the same swoop. Hutus who had been arrested as common criminals were let out during the day to dig graves for them, just below the commune office of Cyimbogo. While they waited to die, they were beaten regularly by their grave-diggers.

On the 'day of judgement', the men were led out to face a huge crowd. The mayor had chosen a cross-section of the Hutu population from Cyimbogo to decide the men's fate. All Tutsis who worked in the local administration were condemned to death and thrown in the graves that awaited them. The victims included Marc Mirambo and his brother. In recognition of his part in the killing of Tutsis in 1963-64, Jean Nsengumuremyi was appointed as head of Cyimbogo's communal police force. Over the years, he became known as a formidable hunter of Tutsis, earning him the nickname of *Kinigantama*, 'the slaughterer of lamb'.

Théoneste became a wealthy businessman in Cyangugu's commercial capital, Kamembe. Thirty years later, Théoneste was burnt alive in Kamembe, on 7 April 1994, the first day of the genocide. Jean Nsengumuremyi travelled to

Kamembe to ensure that Théoneste died, only to discover that the deed had already been carried out. It was important to Nsengumuremyi to let neighbours know that he had not allowed Marc Mirambo's son to escape. He contacted the militia responsible for Théoneste's death, and managed to retrieve his watch, parading it as proof of his murder.

Nsengumuremyi went on to kill many other people during the genocide. He acted as a godfather to the local killing squad, teaching them the lethal skills he had accumulated over a thirty-year period. When the slaughter began in his sector on 9 April, he assembled young Hutu males to give them a lesson in how to deal with Tutsis. A young man was his first victim; Nsengumuremyi twisted the left arm sharply to highlight the position of the heart and then pierced him with a sword. As in the past, he expected to be rewarded. Instead, the government that sponsored the genocide lost the simultaneous war against the Rwandese Patriotic Front (RPF). For the first time, he felt fear of justice. He fled in July 1994 and became a 'refugee' in Zaire.

In April-June 1994, more than a million Tutsis were killed in Rwanda, the harvest of a long history of crimes without punishment. In the words of a priest who has had several narrow escapes since 1963, 'In Rwanda, genocide of Tutsis was taught and assimilated, to the point of becoming instinctive'. The ideology and the know-how had been maturing since the first anti-Tutsi killings of November 1959. The hundred day genocide of 1994 was unusual only in its efficiency, speed and the breadth and depth of popular participation.

The lessons began in 1959, developing into an art - and a sport - that has been passed from one generation to another. Some prisons today harbour three generations of a family accused of mass murder in 1994. The men and women who designed, encouraged and implemented the genocide of 1994 drew moral justifications, political conclusions and practical guidance from the manner in which earlier anti-Tutsi pogroms had been planned, carried out and excused. They knew that no-one would be punished. The seeds sown in 1959 were reaped in 1994 when genocide became a family affair and a communal project. Husbands and wives collaborated, brothers worked as teams and parents took their children along on killing sprees, as if on a family outing. Doctors, nurses, teachers, local government officials, and even priests and nuns, worked in groups to ensure the extermination of Tutsis, fraternities bound together by the blood of genocide.

A genocide foretold

Two of the men indicted by the United Nations International Tribunal are father and son. The father, Elsaphan Ntakuritimana, was the president of the Seventh Day Adventists in the region of Kibuye, and a pastor at the Parish of Ngoma. His son, Dr Gérard Ntakuritimana, was a doctor at the Hospital of Ngoma, next to the parish. Thousands of Tutsis had sought refuge in the parish; the women and children were placed inside the church while the men, including more than sixty Adventist pastors, remained in the courtyard. Elsaphan had encouraged local Tutsis, in particular his fellow Adventist pastors and their families, to seek protection at the parish. On 16 April, Dr Gérard, armed with a rifle, shot at the entrance door of the church and led the militia as they macheted the women and children, using his rifle as a backup. Elsaphan, to whom the pastors had written an appeal for help, came and told them 'to die like men, not children'. People rushed into the hospital, and were immediately disoriented by tear-gas. The coughing and sneezing enabled Dr Gérard and his militiamen to identify the survivors and to kill them off. In the following weeks, father and son collaborated in a series of military assaults which wiped out more than 50,000 Tutsis on the hills of Bisesero in Kibuye. Several other men indicted by the Tribunal worked closely with their fathers during the genocide.

'Parents took their children on killing sprees, as if on a family outing'

The first organised massacres of Tutsis took place in Rwanda in November 1959, encouraged as a political duty by the Belgian colonial government and sanctioned as a virtue by the powerful Catholic Church. The Belgians inherited the colonies of Rwanda and Burundi from Germany after the Versailles Treaty of 1918. They chose to rule through Tutsi kings and chiefs, showing scant regard for the rights of Hutus or of poor Tutsis. The fact that Tutsi chiefs served as a political and economic instrument for a harsh Belgian administration - to collect taxes, recruit labour, impose agricultural and health measures and inflict punishments - only fed Hutu resentment against Tutsi rule. The limited opportunities open to Africans in administration and education were reserved for the sons of Tutsi chiefs. Hutus, who constituted the majority, endured injustice and indignities, and remained politically powerless. In the 1950s, the Belgian government and the Catholic Church, worried about the inevitability of independence, suddenly switched their support to the Hutus, identified as the would-be victors in a democratic election.

Having promoted - and institutionalised - the prejudices, laws and practices that nurtured mutual suspicion between the Hutu and Tutsi, the administration and Catholic Church threw their formidable weight behind the determination of Hutu politicians to drive Tutsis out of power and positions of influence. By November 1959, parts of Rwanda had become a political tinder-box. Rumours about the murder of a prominent Hutu politician and subchief by Tutsi youths in Gitarama on 1 November were sufficient to trigger an explosion of violence. The initial targets were Tutsis in power, but within a short period, the entire Tutsi community was engulfed. Thousands of Tutsi huts were emptied and then burnt down. A United Nations team which investigated the violence in 1960 wrote: 'They burned and pillaged because they had been told to do so and because the operation did not seem to involve great risks, and enabled them to seize the loot in the victim's hut'.[1]

Retaliation by the King and his chiefs against Hutu leaders, several of whom were killed, reinforced the cycle of violence. The Belgian administration made no secret of its support for the Hutu cause, making little effort to contain the violence or protect the victims. Between November 1959 and January 1961, when the monarchy was abolished and most Tutsi chiefs dismissed, the scene was set for the culture of impunity which made the 1994 genocide possible.

This culture was first given legal content by a law passed on 20 May 1963. The law extended an unconditional amnesty 'for all the violations committed on the occasion of the Social Revolution during the period of 1 October 1959 to 1 July 1962 ... which, by their nature, the circumstances or the motives which inspired them, can be considered in the context of participation in the struggle of national liberation and thus suggest a political character even if they constitute violations of the common law'. The law went further; people 'who had, during this period, struggled against the liberation of the masses oppressed by the feudal-colonial domination' were excluded from the provisions of the amnesty. While the Hutus who benefited from the amnesty became members of parliament and mayors, a certain Tutsi chief, Mbanda, remained in prison until 1991.

---

1. UN Visiting Mission to Trust Territories in East Africa, 1960; Report on Ruanda-Urundi.

The reference to a 'national' struggle was a prophetic statement: Tutsis would be considered as outsiders in the newly-independent Rwanda. In 1994, thousands of Tutsis were drowned in the Nyabarongo river, or macheted and then thrown in. The killers renamed the river 'Ethiopian Airlines', saying these Tutsis were being repatriated to their mythical homeland, Ethiopia. The idea of Tutsis as 'foreigners' had been carefully nurtured for decades. Bélia Mukandekezi recalled the words that accompanied the violence of 1959: 'When Tutsis were being killed and their homes burnt, they were told that they were not Rwandese, that the Tutsis had governed a country which did not belong to them'.

With time, the ideology that underpinned the killings of 1959 and the early 1960s developed and intensified. History was falsified and the Tutsis demonised as a feudal minority to be written out of Rwanda's past and its future. The adjectives used to describe them - cunning, sly and deceitful - are reminiscent of the stereotypes attached to Jews before and during the Holocaust. In the minds of the largely uneducated Hutu population and the young, the idea took root that the Tutsis were 'snakes' who could be murdered without fear of reprisals. The history books taught in schools after 1959 were re-drafted; Tutsis were routinely described as 'invaders', refugees in their land of birth. Rwanda's educational system was largely in the hands of the Catholic Church giving such interpretations immense weight. In 1994, history repeated itself. A Catholic priest commented on the ease with which people turned on their neighbours. 'During the genocide, those who killed were convinced that they were killing an enemy, killing foreigners. They believed that they were acting in legitimate self-defence. The genocide flowed from that mindset'.

The events of 1959 also laid the foundations for the continuing story of Rwandese refugees; thousands of Tutsis left for Burundi, the Congo, Tanzania and Uganda. Others joined the exodus in the early 1960s, fleeing the cruelties of newly-appointed chiefs and subchiefs. But the nightmare was not over for those who remained. In 1960, Tutsis were expelled in massive numbers from the northwest region of Gisenyi and Ruhengeri, and forcibly resettled in the uninhabited southern region of Bugesera, a huge forest with swamps infested with mosquitoes and tsetse flies. The man behind the expulsions was Balthazar Bicamumpaka. In 1994, his son, Jérôme Bicamumpaka, served as foreign minister of the regime carrying out the genocide. He was not his father's son for nothing; he worked very hard to convince the world that the genocide was a non-event.

Since 1959, government officials who participated in pogroms against Tutsis knew that they would not only escape prosecution, but were likely to be promoted. Many of the people at the forefront of the incitement and killings in 1959 were Catholic teachers and catechists who were then promoted as chiefs and mayors. Killing Tutsis was not only just; it was a good career move for the ambitious politician and bureaucrat. The knowledge that 'success' in government depended on one's credentials in killing, dispossessing and marginalising Tutsis is, perhaps, the single most important belief that shaped the genocide of 1994.

One man who drew that lesson early on is Esdras Mpamo, a primary school teacher who became an auxiliary nurse in the 1950s. In 1960, the Belgians named him as a chief in Kibuye. He went on to become governor of Kibuye and then of Cyangugu, and always showed that he knew how to keep Tutsis in their place. The government of President Grégoire Kayibanda, Rwanda's first president, showed its gratitude by appointing him as an ambassador to Germany and to Uganda. After the minister of defence, Juvénal Habyarimana, seized power in a coup d'état in July 1973, he was appointed as mayor of his native Masango, represented Habyarimana's ruling party in Masango, and became a member of the party's central committee.

Despite his age, he remained mayor until 1994, becoming the doyen of mayors in the country. His long reign was marked by a policy of excluding and marginalising Tutsis, particularly from government employment and secondary education. His political star rose in 1990, in recognition of his contribution to the creation of the *interahamwe* militia. He devoted considerable energy - and the resources of the commune - to ensure that Masango's militia were well-trained, well-armed and motivated. Mpamo's devotion to his men became even more pronounced after his son, Georges Rutaganda, became the second vice-president of the *interahamwe* at a national level.

In 1994, Mpamo had a lot to teach his son about the mechanics of genocide. They became partners in crime and in a short space of time virtually annihilated Masango's Tutsi community. Godeleine Mukarugambwa, a teacher whose six children were thrown into the Nyabarongo river, recalled his exhortation: 'When you kill mice, you should not have pity on the pregnant ones'. Rutaganda is in the custody of the International Tribunal in Arusha; Mpamo remains a free man.

According to the architects of the genocide, the mass murder of Tutsis was necessary to safeguard the survival of Hutus. The Tutsis intended to wipe out the Hutus: it was, therefore, necessary for the Hutus to unite and strike first. The theme of genocide as a pre-emptive act of self-preservation dominated the airwaves in 1994. It had already been developed in newspapers sympathetic to Hutu extremism after Rwandese refugees based in Uganda formed the RPF and invaded Rwanda in October 1990. All Tutsis were an RPF fifth column who had to be neutralised in this preventive war. No distinction was drawn between RPF soldiers, the elderly or the very young; all were *Inyenzi*, or 'cockroaches'. All males, even babies, had to be slaughtered to prevent the emergence of future generations of RPF soldiers. Hutus were constantly reminded of their 'mistake' in 1959, when they let Tutsi boys go into exile. Those boys, they were told, included Fred Rwigema and Paul Kagame, the leaders of the RPF.

The description of Tutsis in Rwanda as 'accomplices' of Tutsis in exile is an argument that had enjoyed a long history in Rwanda. From the time Tutsi refugees launched their first attacks, in the early 1960s, reprisals against unarmed Tutsis living in Rwanda became the norm. They were killed, arrested or expelled from their jobs or area of residence. For politicians and bureaucrats, mobilising the Hutu population against the *Inyenzi* was a strategy for overcoming regional, political and party divisions among the Hutu. It was also a means for local leaders to build a following.

In December 1963, there were murderous assaults against Tutsi communities in many parts of the country. About 10,000 men, women and children are estimated to have been killed - hacked to death with machetes, spears and clubs by militia. Many of them were abducted as they left church after mass on Christmas Day. The killings were particularly pronounced in Gikongoro where the governor, André Nkeramugaba, publicly called for the extermination of Tutsis. The pretext was an attack launched by exiled Tutsis in Burundi on 21 December in the Bugesera region.

One of the most sought after priests in 1994 was Fr. Modeste Mungwarareba; he had escaped the killers in 1959, 1963 and in 1990. He outwitted them again, in April 1994. He hid for a month in the ceiling of Butare Cathedral, living on water and wafers before sneaking into a nearby convent. For him, there is no doubt that 'there is a link of cause and effect' between the massacres that have punctuated his life.

> In 1959, I was eight years old. I saw everything that happened. People were killed, houses were burnt, cows were slaughtered and there was looting. Then a whistle was blown. Everything stopped and we were told: reconcile.
> In 1963, I was twelve years old and a student at the Small Seminary. I was on holiday at home in Gikongoro when the massacres began. I ran to take refuge in the bush, but I was discovered. Beaten and left for dead, I was woken up in the afternoon by rain before being taken and saved by a Hutu neighbour called Berchmans, on Monday, 28 December. He used to tell me that I was in danger. But me, I could not believe that an adult could attack a child. I did not know that the adults had received the order to kill all male Tutsis. When I came back to school at the end of the holidays, I was even more scandalised to note that our teachers did not want us to talk about it. But one day, in a religious class, I decided to talk about it. Everyone listened to me, stupefied. But no one responded.
> When I went home during holidays, I was always astonished to see that the people who had killed, looted and burnt houses were not bothered. Rather, we were the ones who were afraid. They knew that we knew. They were only awaiting the occasion to make us disappear because we were their bad conscience.
> In the region of Gikongoro, the effectiveness of the 1994 genocide lies in the fact that those implicated in the genocide of 1963 had not been punished. Take a man like André Nkeramugaba. He was préfet [governor] and was the most virulent. But the population appreciated him to the point of electing him as a member of parliament. Others became mayors or local officials of the party.

On 1 October 1990, the RPF invaded northeastern Rwanda. On 4 October, the army staged a fake attack on Kigali and blamed it on the RPF. Between 8000-10,000 people, overwhelmingly Tutsi, were imprisoned as supporters of the RPF, particularly in Kigali. Many were tortured; all were detained for several months. Some died from the beatings, lack of medical care and food. As in 1994, educated male Tutsis - businessmen, priests, teachers and civil servants -

were the primary targets. The property of some of the detainees was confiscated; afterwards, those who were released were dismissed from government service and had their passports withdrawn. The arrests were accompanied by violent attacks in several communes, in particular in Kibilira, Gisenyi, instigated and encouraged by local government officials, leading to deaths, injuries and displacing many Tutsis from their homes. Again, local Hutus were incited to loot their homes and steal their livestock.

International criticism forced the government to give the impression of reining in officials who had 'gone too far'. A number of them were arrested in connection with the killings in Kibilira, but were soon released; some were given new posts in government. In the meantime, civilian officials and the military continued a steady campaign of violence and intimidation against Tutsis, culminating in a series of organised massacres in March 1992 in Bugesera. The killings in Bugesera showed the hallmarks of 1994 - the use of the newly-created militia, the *interahamwe*; reliance on Radio Rwanda to broadcast incitement and the distribution of incendiary tracts. The men at the forefront of the violence between 1990-1992 became leading génocidaires in 1994. They include Col. Tharcisse Renzaho, the governor of Kigali; Emmanuel Bagambiki, the governor of Greater Kigali and Jean-Baptiste Gatete, the mayor of Murambi.

One of the most effective strategies for creating the largest community of killers in 1994 was the appeal to people's greed. This intimate relationship between the material well-being of Hutus and the mass murder of Tutsis was, by 1994, a tried and tested strategy. In 1959-62, the message to Hutus was clear: not only did power now belong to the Hutus, but they could use this power to disinherit the Tutsis - of their land, their houses, their livestock and their possessions. Willy Ukwishaka was 26 in 1960 when his home was attacked in Nyamasheke, Cyangugu.

> Members of Parmehutu came during the day and took the belongings of Tutsis. During the night, they burnt their houses. My house was burnt to the ground and I took refuge in Zaire. The Belgian administrator did nothing to discourage these terrible acts.

In 1994, Rwandese officials followed suit. Every Hutu was encouraged to steal, loot and destroy the livestock, shops and houses of Tutsis with impunity; the only condition was to murder or burn the occupants and owners. Men, women and children stripped the dead and the dying of everything; most of the dead were naked by the time they were dumped in mass graves. The militia were rewarded with money, food and beer for their 'work'. The promise to inherit their land was, without doubt, the single most important incentive given to the peasantry for making Rwanda a Tutsi-free zone. Peasants had every reason to believe this pledge; since 1959 they had seen the powerful distribute the land vacated by Tutsis.

Antoine Ngiruwonsanga worries about the number of people who participated actively in the genocide who remain free men and women. 'The State must punish the killers to prove to us, the survivors, that there is no possibility of history repeating itself'. When Théoneste Karangwa was burnt to death, he left a three-year-old son, the age at which his father was murdered. Time will tell whether his son will in turn be murdered, or his death celebrated, by the descendants of Jean Nsengumuremyi, or whether the people Rwanda will finally confront the culture of impunity which haunts their lives and their country.

Testimony of a survivor of the genocide, Augustin Ndahimana Buranga

When the genocide began in April 1994, Augustin Ndahimana Buranga, 40, lived in Nyarutovu, sector Bisesero in the commune of Gishyita, Kibuye. He is currently working in a factory in Kigali.

I used to live just next to the road in Nyarutovu. A few days after the death of President Habyarimana, I saw militiamen, soldiers and policemen gathered together in Muhuhuli forest. They wanted to attack our region. I was frightened because I had seen that in the sector of Mubuga, they had already begun to kill the Tutsis and to burn their houses. I said to my wife, Berthilde Mukangango, and to my three daughters— Uwamahoro, 8, Uwera, 7 and Ingabire, a baby - that we had to quickly leave our

A genocide foretold

house and join the other Tutsis who had gathered on the hills of Bisesero.

We left all our valuable objects in the house; we thought that we would be returning to our things straightaway. As soon as we left our houses, the militiamen began to loot and destroy all the houses owned by the Tutsis in Bisesero. There were many of us on the hills; even so, the militiamen had no fear and they launched attacks on us every single day. We were also well-organised; we went to fetch stones, spears and swords so that we could defend ourselves. We put up a strong fight during the month of April. At the beginning of May, we managed to kill a lot of militiamen, soldiers and policemen.

We knew the militiamen who attacked us at the beginning. They used to be our neighbours. They would often call out our names during the attacks and tell us not to run so that they could kill us more easily. In the evenings, when they had gone, each Tutsi family would gather somewhere on the hill to decide how to look for food. My family and I preferred to meet in Kazirandimwe, where my wife came from. We would get together very early in the morning and would then go back to Muyira hill to be with the others.

On 13 May, I was in Kazirandimwe with my wife, children and mother, Adèle Nyiramahe. We had stayed there because the militiamen had not come for a few days. At about 9:00 a.m., I saw the Tutsis who were at the primary school of Gitwa in Bisesero running. I also heard gunfire. The militiamen had surrounded us and they were shouting a lot. They had arrived in a great number of cars. We trembled when we saw all this. I went behind my family and we ran together to Muyira. My wife could not run because she was pregnant and my children were small. Due to the bullets that were coming from all directions, we dispersed. As I was running, I fell in a ditch. Above me, there was a big rock; I stayed there, shaking with fear. I could hear people crying as they died.

In the evening, when the militiamen had gone, I left the ditch. I couldn't find the way because there were bodies everywhere. Thousands and thousands of people were killed that day.

I looked tirelessly for the bodies of my people. Very early on the morning of 14 May, I went with other survivors. We were rounding up the children who were crying next to the bodies of their mothers when we noticed that the militiamen were coming back. We left the children and ran. I hid in my father's banana plantation which was close to the road in Nyarutovu cellule. The militiamen continued to massacre all the Tutsis who had escaped the day before. In the evening they went home, either in cars or on foot, taking with them our cows.

As they were talking and discussing, they suddenly saw a large bush which was next to me. They searched the bush and found two Tutsis hiding there. They were seriously beaten and then they were forced to move the cows along with clubs. These Tutsis never came back.

Luckily, they did not see me. In the evening, I carried on looking for my children and wife. I wanted to bury them because the dogs and crows had already started devouring the corpses. I hid during the day and looked during the night. The fourth night I came across my daughter's dress. I began to look at the other bodies nearby. I saw a woman with no feet whose head had been torn away from her body. She was lying with her child who was also dead. I looked closely and I realised that it was my wife. The child still had its clothes on which I recognised. I immediately went to fetch my late wife's uncle so that he could help me with the burial. Together, we put a bit of earth on the bodies. We had no more energy left to dig a grave.

I was too weak to fight against the militiamen, so I went to hide in a bush in a place called Muyoboro. There was a large stone there that the militiamen used for sharpening their machetes. The businessman Obed Ruzindana told them that they would have to work night and day to be able to exterminate all the Tutsis before the French soldiers [of Operation Turqoise] arrived. He ordered them to burn all the bushes. As there were no more bushes to hide behind, I had to lie down and put bodies on top of me. When the militiamen attacked they did not touch the rotten bodies to find us. There was a terrible odour. It was impossible to breathe underneath the corpses. The insects which came to eat the bodies stung me. I stayed like this until the French soldiers arrived at the end of June 1994.

Moi's Achilles heel?

Kathurima M'Inoti and Lucy Hannan

President Moi is still hanging on to power. Can he be unseated by constitutional challenge alone?

On 31 May 1997, Nairobi hospitals were full of well-educated casualties - among them the entire law partnership of Kamau Kuria and Kiraitu. Gibson Kamau Kuria - constitutional lawyer, government critic and former detainee - walked out of casualty with a surgical neck collar. Kiraitu Murungi - forced into exile in 1991 and now a leading opposition member of parliament - was hospitalised with serious head injuries; and other high profile advocates, who regularly represent those falling foul of oppressive government laws, suffered the effects of a serious beating. A mugging? Sort of. They had all attended a public rally on constitutional reform in Uhuru Park, Nairobi. Ruthlessly crushed by government paramilitary forces and armed police, the rally was followed by rioting in the capital for three days. Unlikely as it may seem, Kenyan lawyers and lecturers have hit upon the Achilles heel of President Moi's power base in their esoteric calls for constitutional reform. Now the most effective rallying call for opposition groups since the turn of the decade, calls for constitutional reform are threatening President Moi's personal survival in a way that the introduction of multipartism never managed to.

That the political temperature is rising over the issue of constitutional reform seems to underline the desire to fight for change on the grounds of legitimacy and order - Kenya appears to prefer legal revolutions to popular ones. It is an approach which is eminently compatible with the interests of international donors. But how effective is it as a strategy for change? Kenyan lawyers have spearheaded calls for democratisation - whether as members of parliament, journalists, members of non-governmental and human rights organisations, or by using their legal practices to take controversial political cases to court. The 'legal guerrillas' of 1991 were roundly applauded by donors and international human rights organisations for their part in the push for multi-party democracy, which was led by a group known as the 'young turks'.

The problems of 1991

Change, however, turned out to be disastrously superficial in 1991. It took only an afternoon for President Moi and his KANU government to alter the constitution to allow for multipartism - and the opposition declared victory. But five years on Moi remains very much in power. After the concession of abandoning his one party state for multi-party democracy, he went on to make a remarkable recovery, won the 1992 elections, and now looks set to win again this year.

The secret of his success was very simple: Moi retained the tough colonial laws which were the foundation of his Kenyan African National Union's (KANU) one party state. Laws like the Public Order Act, the Chief's Authority Act, the sedition laws and powers of detention, were designed to instil political obedience, inhibit freedom of expression and assembly, and crush dissent. Using these constitutional gifts, he cleverly managed a technical commitment to multipartism while continuing to use sweeping presidential powers and a politically obedient administration to monopolise the political landscape. He never really had to abandon the *modus operandi* of the one party state, but could satisfy national and international pressure to hold 'democratic elections'. It hamstrung the opposition and kept 'multipartism' restricted to a vocal minority in parliament.

Opposition MPs found that under the current constitution they could not meet with their constituency without a licence, could not hold rallies, or demonstrate, and even, at times, were penalised and beaten for holding civic education seminars. Moi - like many 'big men' under threat - has recently conceded a little, and compromised a little, and successfully bought more time. Promises for the repeal or amendment of certain laws instantly divided the opposition - and yet again upped the chance of KANU winning in the forthcoming elections. Above all, there will be no over-night change in Kenya -

President Moi has remained resolutely the 'big man', over-shadowing vital institutions like the courts, the civil service, the police, the local administration and parliament. He has marched into the 1990s, a key survivor among the 'old guard' of African dictators. Opposition MPs discovered that though they had been elected to power in 1992, they didn't have any to enjoy. That's when they started to take constitutional reform seriously.

But having dropped the ball so early on, the opposition found it difficult to pick up again. Popular support fell off dramatically when personality politics, corruption and opportunism were seen to take over; the ability to pull crowds of hundreds of thousands in the heady days of 1991-2 have not been repeated. Political parties had evolved abruptly in 1991 - before 1990, it wasn't possible to point to any influential group that held a consistently different theory of government to KANU, and there was a jump to fill the gap. The 'new' political scene was dominated by the old, as former politicians like Jaramogi Oginga Odinga, Kenneth Matiba, Masinde Muliro and Martin Shikuku took charge of 'change'. As the bickering escalated and the real impotence of the opposition became apparent, there was a lot of talk of old wine in new bottles. The so-called 'young turks' quickly became allied with the old politicians, believing they could move into power on the coat-tails of an old vanguard. In the process they became assimilated and divided - and probably hastened the disillusionment of the general population with the very word 'change'.

So, despite the grand visions for a multi-party Kenya, little in fact changed for the average man and woman, other than the relaxation of some of KANU's more oppressive, invasive features. Citizens continued to be policed by hard-line and often brutal local officials loyal to President Moi, and intimidated by the security forces. Recorded incidents of human rights abuses towards ordinary people actually increased in the 1990s, and there were cases of torture and politically inspired detentions.

The 1997 generation

Today's drive for constitutional reform began in a small, urban arena. Its motor is a politically disenfranchised elite who are frustrated by the old political vanguard and by their own limited role. They have genuine fears about the future of the country. Lawyers and lecturers are again at the front of the march, but they know they need the ground-swell of popular opinion that characterised the beginning of the 1990s. Then, key opposition players operated under the forgivable illusion that they would be able to beat Moi with strong popular support, and convinced their supporters that a change of personnel at the top would be sufficient prescription for all ills. Now, they have the difficult job of packaging the message of reform so that it ignites real popular support. At the moment, the opposition is capable of causing disruption - as seen in the riots of July - but in the provinces, relatively few people are prepared to turn out for the sake of positive political expression. Closed shops and empty streets are an indication of fear. It's not that the issues don't have popular appeal, but there is a lot of work to be done to restore faith in the opposition. And, with general elections round the corner, it's rather late in the day.

On 19 June the legal revolution planned to march on parliament and disrupt the budget speech. Ambitiously, the National Convention for Constitutional Reform claimed 'over a million people' would converge on parliament. But on the morning of 19 June, the Convention was forced to back down in the face of a massive security presence. Paramilitary units equipped with tear gas, batons, shields and riot helmets sealed off Parliament Way, along with riot police on horseback. Members of the International Federation of the Red Cross and Red Crescent Societies toured the streets in anticipation of casualties. The streets around parliament were lined with volatile KANU supporters, notoriously hired by the government for such occasions and known by the opposition as 'private armies'. Over the last few years it has become a political fact of life that KANU supporters are able to turn out in force with mobile phones, knives and stones and hold a veritable KANU parade without so much of a mention of the word 'licence'. Moi - for the first time - only briefly stood up in the presidential car on the way to parliament and was unable to take time to do the traditional inspection of the Guard of Honour. As he disappeared into parliament to hear the reading of the budget, the city fell quiet. Businesses had closed down in anticipation of riots, and shop windows were shuttered-up with metal bars. Most people had chosen to stay at home to avoid violent scenes.

Ironically, it was the fact that so many people chose to stay at home and watch television instead of demonstrating in the streets that ultimately allowed the opposition to snatch victory from the jaws of defeat. For a full half hour - before the plug was pulled - the government-owned Kenya Broadcasting

Corporation showed live scenes of chaos in Parliament. As Finance Minister Musalia Mudavadi struggled to read the budget, opposition MPs thumped the benches, waved pro-reform banners, chanted anti-Moi slogans and refused to stand for president. When three opposition MPs tried to grab the Mace, the demonstration turned into a boxing match, with members from both sides of the house on the floor. Throughout the chaos, President Moi sat like Rodin's thinker, head on hand, in silence. It was a watershed for the government. For the first time during his nineteen year rule, anti-Moi slogans were shouted in the President's face - with much of the Kenyan population watching.

The big question now is what the opposition can do if President Moi continues to resist pressure to make far-reaching political reforms. At the moment the opposition has enjoyed a rare unity over calls for constitutional reform; but what is wanted is real change. In July, after riots had affected investment and tourism in the country, and civil disobedience became a reality, Moi made promises to reform - and it has thrown activists into a quandary. What now, to get him out? For as long as the president holds on to his considerable personal powers, the playing field for the forthcoming elections is anything but level - the opposition would once again be participating in an undemocratic election. Many opposition politicians still feel it is important to participate and use their elected positions to continue the push for reform. The legal activists have so far found themselves to be perfectly equipped for international membership of the 'new world order' - they have a natural constituency in international legal bodies and organisations and in the lawyer-dominated international human rights organisations - and it's not a position they will give up lightly. The question of strategic violence is an important watershed for the opposition. But a sizeable camp believe the only answer in the face of government intransigence and manipulation is to disrupt the election process. In order to do that, some opposition MPs are already publicly declaring that the opposition must be prepared to burn their election registration cards and use violence.

There is no reason to remain confident that the so-far peaceful methods of the 'legal guerrillas' will necessarily avoid organised violence. Non-confrontational methods, so anxiously promoted by donors through non-governmental organisations and 'civic education', get difficult after a certain point. The very laws that are opposed - like those which restrict political activity and meetings - have to be broken in order to campaign against them. The election parallel is not so far behind: undemocratic elections invite undemocratic resistance. When international representatives met recently with non-governmental organisations, some of the well educated activists lashed out at donors, saying they were trying to make them abide 'by apartheid laws'. There is a parting of ways on the horizon. Kenyan activists admit that they have in the past paid disproportionate attention to the wants and desires of their international constituency, instead of their national one - not just for funding, but also because there has been a strong legacy from previous decades in the belief that the international community represents a moral as well as strategic weight. Now, whatever divergent methods the opposition camps may support, there is uniformly far more reluctance in 1997 to see leadership in the donor community. Ironically, it cuts both ways. After riots in July 1997, President Moi dismissed pressure from 21 foreign missions based in Nairobi saying they had 'no moral authority' to criticise his government.

> 'Non-confrontational methods are anxiously promoted by donors through NGOs and "civic education"'

Because times are changing in Africa, Kenya is now surrounded by African leaders who are refusing to abide by the traditional relationship assumed by the international community. The so-called 'new thinkers' in neighbouring Uganda, Ethiopia, Eritrea and Rwanda have learnt they can say 'no' and still be feted by donors fumbling to find an appropriate role in the 1990s. For Africa, there is less and less reason to assume that the dictates and opinions of the major donors are 'right'. After all, these are the donors who supported hard-line one party states, followed by a widely voiced opinion by Western diplomats that Africa 'wasn't ready' for democracy in 1989, until the freezing of aid was suddenly used to insist on hasty multi-party elections. Armies of foreign election observers poured holy water on deeply flawed elections all over the continent. Africans are now living with the consequences. The inappropriate and confused principles applied by influential international bodies can be seen everywhere in the 1990s - recently there were demands made for hurried 'democratic elections' in post-genocide Rwanda, and in post-war Zaire. Following the so-called 'winds of change' after the collapse of communism in 1989, the African continent has gone through profound change; but there has been little sober effort on the part of external players to make important distinctions between war and violence, fugitives and refugees, old politics and new politics. Frantic external political predictions are frequently wrong, although donor governments, United Nations agencies, and non-governmental organisations continue to attach a habitual credibility to internationally generated analysis. The international 'old guard' are still trying to waltz while a whole new song is being initiated by African leaders.

Times are also changing for the 'old guard' of African leadership. Most have fallen, and fallen hard. The situation of former Zairean president Mobutu Sese Seko - one of Africa's 'biggest men', who ruled for 32 years with strong international support - hit home hard in Kenya. Kenyans have recently shifted from boasting about the country's stability, to making fearful predictions based on comparisons with Somalia, Rwanda and former Zaire. The parallels with Mobutu were not wasted on the frustrated Kenyan opposition, who boldly stated in parliament that Moi should see 'the writing on the wall'. Far from finding the similarities uncomfortable, Moi made his support for the old dictator so clear that he effectively knocked Kenya out of the regional negotiation game. Moi clearly sees his status as 'African elder statesman' being elevated as the rest of the old guard falls. Not unlike his friends, he has found a formula which has assisted his own personal survival, but has profoundly undermined the well-being of the nation - the emphasis on personal power has destroyed vital independent institutions like the courts, the police, the civil service, the health service, education and civic society.

After Kenya spiralled in July 1997 into one of its worse political crises since 1990 - with security forces brutally dispersing reform activists, and more than eleven deaths recorded country-wide - President Moi once again promised that the constitution would be reformed. He lined some of the party 'heavies' up - including Vice-President George Saitoti, and the greatly-feared minister in the office of the president, Nicholas Biwott - to announce that contentious laws would be repealed or amended by an act of parliament. He reiterated that the constitution - which grants him considerable powers - would be reviewed carefully and reformed after the election. The irony is that, far from being treated as a sacred document, the Constitution has been hurriedly changed some thirty times since independence, and turned into a tool for political survival. Even if it were changed in the coming months, the long-term damage has been done - Moi has cleverly used it to entrench KANU power sufficient to survive any 'democratic' election.

A repressive constitution

The most controversial components of the present constitution are the repressive colonial laws that independent governments adopted lock, stock and barrel for their own benefit. These laws contradict guarantees of rights and freedoms that the constitution otherwise contains. So, for example, although Section 80 of the constitution guarantees freedom of assembly, it enables the police to insist under the Public Order Act that a licence must be obtained from the administration in order to enjoy such a right. The government has used this to routinely prevent opposition politicians and ordinary people from holding meetings - which has had the additional effect of encouraging a brutal and corrupt administration. To get the right paperwork to celebrate a birthday means the chief must be bribed. Guarantees of freedom of expression are made a mockery of by using the law of sedition - which, for example, has empowered the police to dismantle and confiscate a printing press merely on suspicion that it was used to print something which may lead to political disaffection. It has intimidated the population, and has had the effect of making security forces and the local administration political agents rather than public servants.

Some of the most damaging changes to the constitution have been made regarding the independence of the Judiciary. Extensive changes meant that the appointment of the Chief Justice, judges and the Attorney General were vested in the president - as was the ability to appoint a tribunal to investigate the removal of the judges. Between 1964 and 1988 the government could get rid of disloyal judges without even having to go through the motions of appointing a tribunal. The main flaw in the system was the temptation of turning judicial appointments into presidential favours, and creating political loyalty in the courts. Behind the reassuring ritual of wigs and cloaks, the Kenyan justice machinery has been in crisis for decades. Political compliance of judges and magistrates in political cases is one problem; of equal concern should be the millions of ordinary Kenyan citizens who, in failing to get justice everyday from the formal machinery, turn to mob justice. Attempts to reform the courts will not be meaningful until the political environment changes.

The constitution that Kenya inherited at independence in 1962 has been described as a mongrel - it combines the trappings of the Westminster model with the American executive president. At independence executive powers were divided between a Governor General who was the Head of State and a prime minister who was the head of government. When Kenya became a Republic all those powers were merged and vested in the president - an arrangement which combines both the powers and functions of a monarch and those of a popularly elected prime minister. In terms of an evolving democracy, these presidential powers have proved lethal. Among other things, Moi has - as head of state and head of government - absolute control over parliament. Kiraitu Mirungi, lawyer and opposition MP, says that President Moi can summon, prorogue or dissolve parliament at will, leaving MPs depending on gossip and guesswork instead of a calendar. For all its noisy debate, Kenyan parliament essentially remains a rubber stamp.

The haste with which the constitution has been changed since independence is seen clearly by the frivolous tinkering with the emergency laws. Emergency powers, which were originally designed to be evoked in times of conflict, quickly became a permanent feature of Kenya's peacetime laws. While some other African countries have taken steps to declare repressive inherited laws unconstitutional (like Tanzania, Zambia and Zimbabwe), Kenya uses them. A state of emergency was imposed in the north-eastern province until 1991, and one was temporarily declared in parts of central province as recently as 1993. Emergency legislation was used this year (1997) in response to famine. Powers of detention without trial were used throughout the 1980s under Moi's one-party state, and were used again this year to keep opposition leaders under house arrest. The effect of these constitutional powers is that everyday law and order is governed by an emergency ethos, encouraging security forces to carry out arbitrary crackdowns throughout the country - or to feel licence to act with excessive brutality during demonstrations of civil disobedience. The behaviour of the local administration and government security forces in some parts of the country amounts to *de facto* military rule - especially in areas like the Elemi Triangle, originally 14,000 square kilometres of Sudanese land, forcibly annexed by Kenyan security forces in 1988. These marginalised and heavily policed areas of Kenya represent a side of Kenya not really seen or acknowledged by the international community.

Now, the demands by opposition MPs, lawyers, university students and political activists, that prohibitive presidential powers be replaced by an altogether more liberal and democratic constitution, seriously threatens Moi's ability to hold on to power so comprehensively. A wily political survivor, his opponents wonder what tricks he will pull out of his sleeve after promising to start the process of reform. As the stakes get higher, there are scenes of violence and disruption in Nairobi and political tension rises. Proponents of change feel less and less sure of the future. Diplomats may encourage the well educated activists to pursue change by avoiding confrontation, but there is little incentive left for proponents of change to comply with the shifty promises of a decaying regime. There are legal guerrillas who now, by different degrees, entertain the use of violence - the first step, according to Paul Muite, lawyer and opposition MP, will be to physically stop people going to the polls. Even the leaders who remain adamant that peaceful, electoral methods are the only way, know that the entrenched nature of the government makes violent scenes increasingly likely over the coming months. Coffee bar chat has started to turn to the subject of battle. Real battle. Here, the academic fear is the same as the popular one: is the scenario in Kenya one that avoids conflict, or invites it? What happens if polite requests for dialogue and reform continue to be rejected by a government who is staring electoral success in the face?

Is constitutional reform enough?

The lesson learnt from the early 1990s - when influential donors like the US played a crucial role in persuading reluctant sections of the opposition to participate in elections - is that flawed elections solve nothing. To pursue them under such circumstances is an anathema to their real function. Willy Mutunga, lawyer and leader of the National Convention for Constitutional Reform, believes the huge groundswell of popular anti-Moi opinion in 1991 was Kenya's popular revolution. If it had been allowed to run its course, he argues, genuine change would have come about - but it was hijacked by the needs of donors and aspiring politicians. By focusing so intently on changing Section 2a of the constitution to allow other political parties to stand for election, the greater picture of change was effectively sacrificed. Opposition MPs got their seats in parliament - the country got the prospect of another decade under President Moi. There is fear that the same mistake could be repeated with the recent focus on legal and constitutional reform. It may ultimately mean that a real popular movement - which despises the opposition as much as it despises Moi - is hovering on the wings of the stage.

So, as with many other African countries, the fever with which elections were introduced meant that Kenya never really had a chance to sail with the post-1989 Winds of Change. The election ritual was implemented long before the necessary political transformation had taken place.

Kenyans have suffered the fallout. While foreigners hopefully cling to the image of game parks and beaches on the Indian Ocean, the real Kenya is struggling. Over the past few years, thousands of people have been killed in Kenya over politically escalated land clashes. The demise of vital institutions like the justice system has accelerated incidents of mob retribution - so-called mob justice - to the extent that it has become a mundane, bloody feature of everyday life. Violent criminals, drug mafias and criminal gangs operate in the urban centres and the provinces, and the number of guns coming into the country continues to increase. Security forces, used as political agents, have become corrupt, ineffective, and brutal. Prisons are full to bursting, because of inefficiency and compromise in the judicial system. While a small, highly visible group do extremely well at the top of the pyramid, poverty has accelerated. According to World Bank figures, Kenya is second only to Brazil in the enormity of the gap between poor and rich. Abandoned by a government which now unashamedly operates on the basis of patronage and loyalty, many of the social institutions are shored up and financed through non-governmental organisations. There are valiant attempts to reform - sometimes initiated by the government, sometimes by its opponents. But it gets increasingly difficult to see reforms as significant as long as the political landscape remains the same. A powerful factor in Kenya's future will be the capability of the overburdened and fragile institutions to absorb the shock-waves when a political system dependent on personal power collapses.

For decades, Kenya has enjoyed the reputation of being an island of stability in a region racked by war and chaos. Now, Kenya is becoming an island of political turmoil in a region of change. It is surrounded by a new sort of African leadership where leaders like Yoweri Museveni of Uganda, Meles Zenawi of Ethiopia, Paul Kagame of Rwanda, and Isias Aferworki of Eritrea, have made a break with the past on the back of civil war, and are promoting new political groupings and leadership by armed proxy. While the results may not always be pleasant, the initiative probably holds far greater significance for the African continent than election fever ever did in the first half of the 1990s. Kenya moves into the spotlight. Can it make change politely?

African portraits

Photofeature by Jenny Matthews

Jenny Matthews' photographs of people from Rwanda, Eritrea, Ethiopia, Angola, Mozambique and Sudan portray a range of human life in Africa - young and old, at work, at play, studying, building, celebrating. These are images which go well beyond the stereotypes of victims, and show people who have survived immeasurable suffering and found the strength to embrace life. Heaps of skulls and the mutilated hands of the man and woman who lived through the Rwandan genocide of 1994 are living history (pp139-142). The little Sudanese boy reading on top of an anthill in Uganda (p133), and the father and child in the same refugee camp(p134), have an extraordinary serenity as they wait for their lot to change, but there is nothing of pathetic resignation about them. And the little Angolan girl, probably no more than 10 years old, looking after four smaller children(p135), already has the resilience seen in the faces of the Eritrean women returning home from refugee camps in Sudan to rebuild houses and to celebrate independence after a 30 year war(pp136 & 137). The Ethiopian men winnowing corn are a rare glimpse of men working in the fields rather than women(p138), but illustrate more importantly the widespread communal spirit in Africa and the unchanged agricultural techniques which the vast majority of the continent lives by.

VB, RO

Right: Uganda, Sudanese refugee school.

African portraits

Above: Uganda, Sudanese refugees, father and child
Right: Angola, near Lobito.

African portraits

Above: Eritrea 1993, celebrating independence.
Right: Eritrea, returnees from Sudan build homes

African portraits

Right: Rwanda, genocide survivor.
Below: Ethiopia, winnowing corn.

African portraits

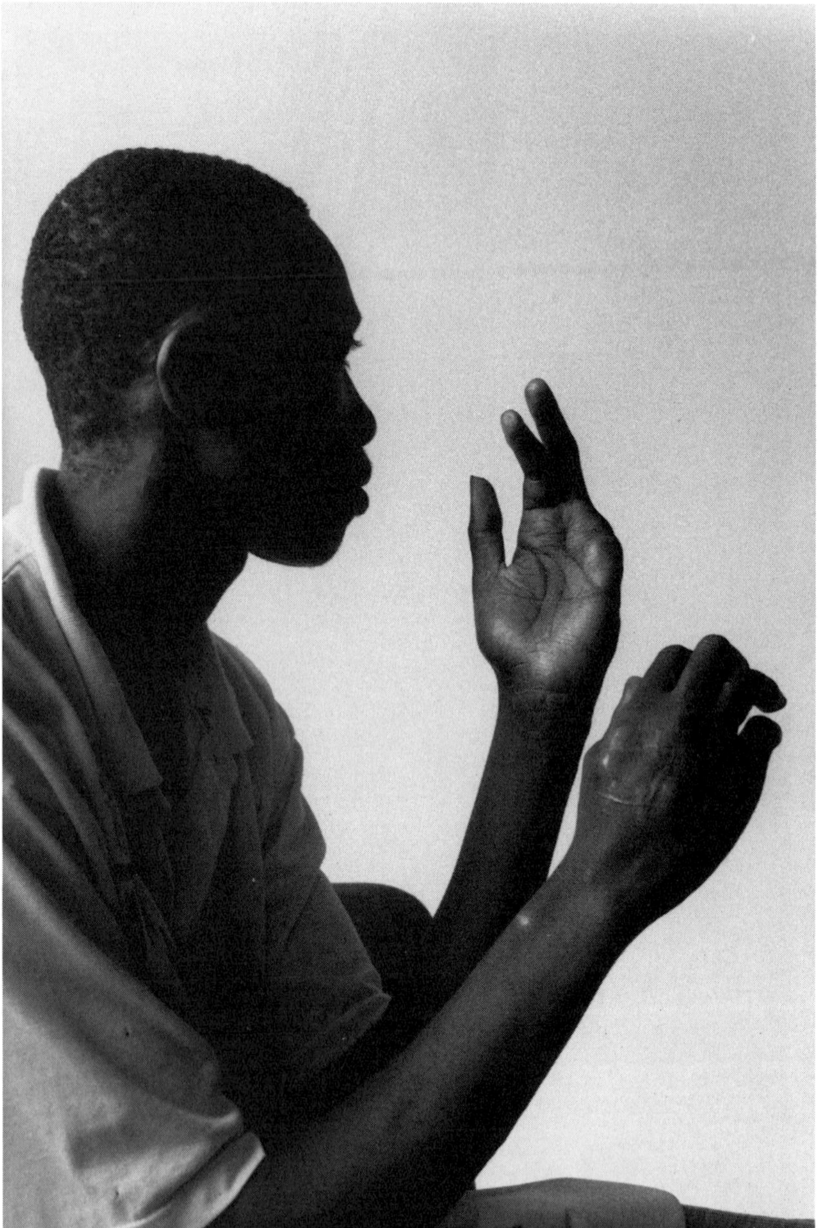

African portraits

Left: Rwanda, victim of genocide.
Below: Rwanda massacre site.
Overleaf: Rwanda, hands of genocide victim.

Soundings

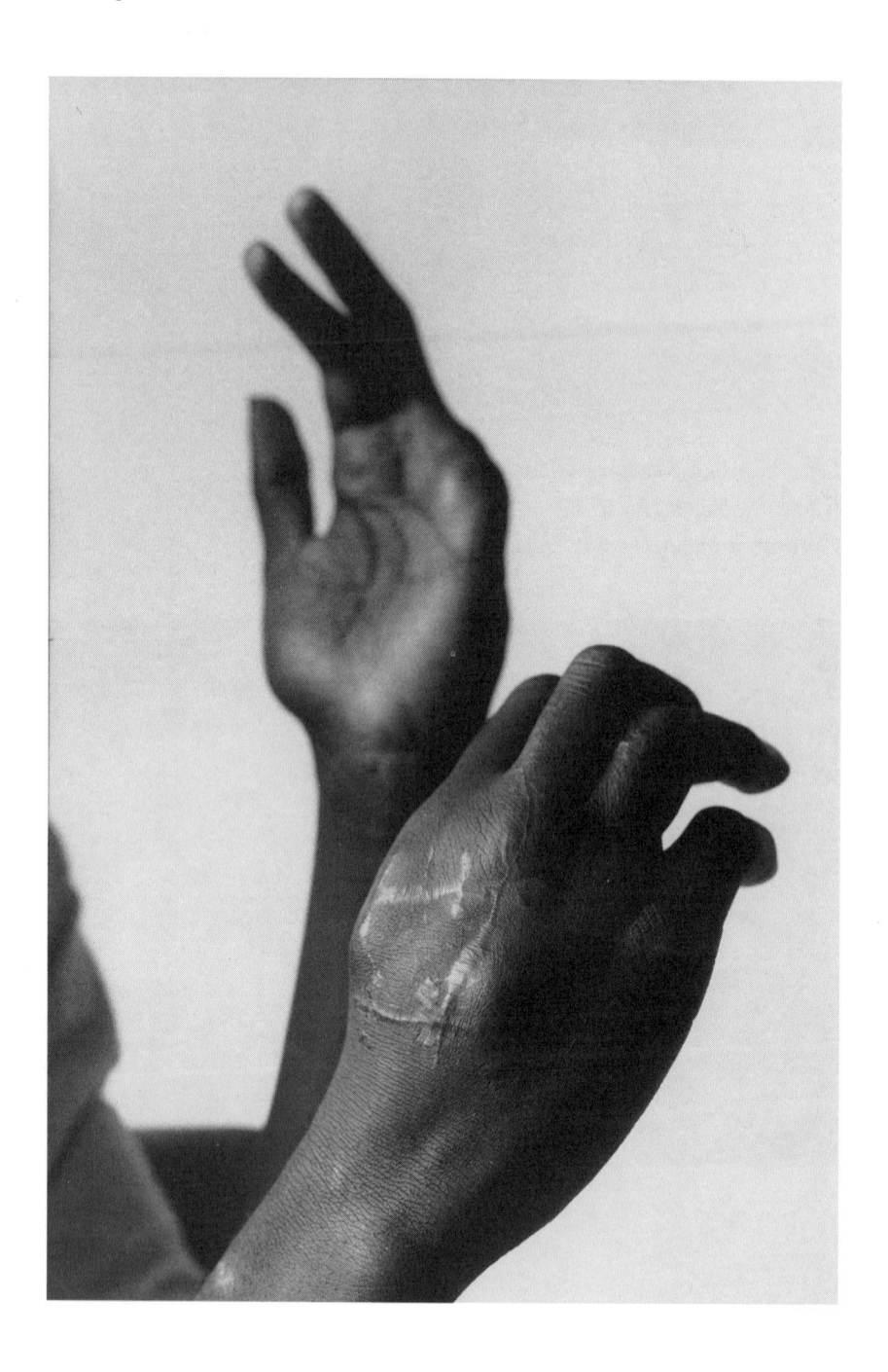

Angola under attack

Victoria Brittain

In an extract from her forthcoming book, Death of Dignity, *Victoria Brittain describes the assault on Angola in the 1980s.*

Arriving in Luanda from Europe in late 1984 for the first time, the airport was an instant warning that this was a world where people lived by other codes, far from my experience. It was stifling hot in the crowd pushing towards immigration, mosquitoes buzzed and bit, and it was completely dark at the entrance to the terminal, the only light far ahead behind the high screens of the immigration officials. I knew no one in Angola and spoke not a word of Portuguese. In the hour or so of squeezing towards the desk, falling progressively further and further to the back of the crowd, I had plenty of time to regret the curiosity which had driven me through the laborious process of getting a rare journalist's visa, and now appeared to promise two weeks completely out of my depth. My years of working in Uganda after Idi Amin, when the entire infrastructure had collapsed and journalists had to travel with their own food and petrol, or Sudan when it was overwhelmed with tens of thousands of Ugandan and Ethiopian refugees, Somalia during the war with Ethiopia, or the Sahel of the great drought which destroyed the centuries-old nomadic civilisation of a whole region of West Africa, suddenly seemed a poor preparation for the toughness of Angola. Waiting in the dark, the heat, and the crush, I went over the little I knew about Angola's war, and the stubborn determination to try to understand it which lay behind this visit.

Since independence from Portugal in 1975 South Africa had repeatedly invaded and occupied the southern provinces; a camp of Swapo refugees, including many children, had been massacred from South African helicopter gun ships at Kassinga; an ANC teacher at the University of Lubango, Jeanette Schoon, and her small daughter, had been assassinated by a South African letter bomb; tens of thousands of peasants had been killed, kidnapped, or driven from their villages by land mines - victims of Unita terror tactics. President Dos Santos had recently put the cost of destruction since independence at $10 billion. All this I knew only second-hand, from piecing together scraps of news out of one of the most closed countries in Africa. It added up to catastrophe, but it was a catastrophe out of sight, visited upon anonymous people whose pain never impinged on the rest of the world. Unlike Africa's better known disasters - famines, coups, border wars - which hit the headlines and the television screens for a week or a month, Angola's disaster had gone on for so many years that it was no longer news, triggered no outrage nor even much interest.

My visa had come with an invitation from the Angolan Women's Organisation (OMA). South Africa's ten year old undeclared war with Angola had the country on its knees, and the Angolan authorities were deeply sceptical about Western journalists, who mostly reported Angola out of Johannesburg, or through interviews with the fluent and media-friendly leader of Unita, Jonas Savimbi, at his headquarters in south east Angola, under the vigilant protection of the South African military; and none were allowed in except with a programme carefully controlled by the authorities. The relief at finally being met in the darkness outside the terminal by a woman from OMA was so extreme that neither her minimal English, nor the nastiness of my stuffy room on the tenth floor of a shabby hotel mattered that night.

But twenty four hours later I was in despair as I saw how little I was likely to find out or understand in this place which I lacked any key to. The hotel was state owned and mostly used then by foreigners from socialist countries here in Angola working as teachers, doctors, engineers or military advisers. The lady from OMA gave me vouchers which allowed me to eat in the down-at-heel restaurant on the 20th floor reached by one small lift which worked only intermittently. A slow procession up and down the narrow staircase went on for half an hour either side of the meal hours. The restaurant was filled with tables crowded with groups of chattering Cubans, East Europeans, Vietnamese,

Angola under attack

Chinese, and Angolans. I sat alone and no one spoke to me. Beyond the language barrier was the even bigger one that I, apparently alone in the hotel and probably in the whole country, was not part of the common fight by these tough people for the survival of Angola's independence. The meals were torture, not just because the food was hard to swallow, though it certainly was, but because I would stare at the faces and imagine the dramas of their experiences, their stories, their thoughts, and know I would never know them.

Once a day my minder from OMA took me out to a formal interview with a selected government official, or to an OMA project where the women of a poor barrio sang and danced for a visitor. It was a paradox that, although the single party, the Popular Movement for the Liberation of Angola (MPLA), or its offshoot OMA in my case, could organise entry into anything or a meeting with anybody, lack of imagination and flexibility meant they chose to organise my seeing things only at the superficial level of a prepared presentation. And I was too ignorant and too embarrassed by my ignorance to force a change in the agenda. The formality of these encounters as much as the language barrier meant the frustration of seeing these people living through the drama of war, upheaval, dispossession, bereavement and poverty, as though at the other side of a frosted glass pane. Because the realities were not articulated in any normally casual conversation I felt I was not grasping them, but merely becoming overwhelmed by a crushing sensation of the pain and injustice which underlay all these individual experiences.

There were flashes of something different. I had asked to see the Air Force Commander, Iko Carreira, a hero of the liberation war and a friend of one of my friends in Europe. There was no formality and no interpreters for the interview in his office in the Ministry of Defence. Sophisticated, amusing and extremely good looking, Iko was immediately friendly, and prepared to spend hours on the ABC of the current military situation, and to explain where Unita were pushing forward. Confident, optimistic, he went on to spell out their dependence on South Africa, and the illegal use of Namibia by the South African military, and to forecast that once Namibia was independent Unita would lose its lifeline and be easily defeated. He pointed to the maps on the wall and drew a line showing where the South African military were still occupying a stretch of the south of the country. Then, very casually, he gave me my first taste of how personally things get done in Angola: 'I'll get a plane to fly you down there before you leave and you can see for yourself they're still there, months after agreeing to leave'. No formal request would ever have produced such a gift of firsthand experience, but Iko did it and I did not see him again to thank him.

> 'On the streets people showed the strain of a society disrupted by war'

I used to stand on a chair to look out of my bedroom window in the hotel at a small slice of Luanda. Broken pavements, pot-holed roads, huge piles of rubbish, empty shop windows, crumbling apartment blocks, were a desolate background to the glimpse of the beautiful long curved bay which is the capital's focus. Palm trees against the blue water, and a fringe of sand on the far side of the bay, were like a hint of a normal West African coastal world. In contrast, on the streets downtown the people showed clearly the strain of a society disrupted by war. Country women in faded wraparound cloths, with babies tied on their backs, young people in the rather flash styles of downtown Lisbon, and ex-soldiers in tattered uniforms, usually on crutches, made their way wearily. Neither the sacked and looted towns of Uganda after Idi Amin in 1979, nor the dilapidated hotels and run-down streets of Accra when Flight Lieutenant Rawlings staged his second take-over in 1981, gave off the atmosphere of overwhelming melancholy of Luanda in the mid-1980s. Here the faces were set, hard to look at.

But one evening, picking my way with a torch between the garbage and the pot-holes among apartment blocks whose numbers were chalked at random, to find a friend of a friend said to live on the eighth floor, I began to find an exhilaration beyond the melancholy. Here were people whose matter-of-fact acceptance of an everyday life lived against the background of rare electricity, sporadic water supply, no telephone, no public transport, and all the shortages of a war economy, plus its sudden deaths, from the continuing invasions and sabotage by South Africa, had a resilience beyond my experience. My friend's friends were part of the mainly white and mestico intellectual circle of Luanda which had opposed Portuguese colonialism and supported the MPLA, often becoming ministers, ambassadors or other key officials in the early exciting years of independence, now vanished as the new war had gripped the country. The evening's conversation ranged from French movies to Algerian politics via American culture. Everyone there spoke French and some English - I was released from my prison of non-communication, though no one seemed to want

Angola under attack

to talk much about Angola.

Other evenings in Luanda in other flats of friends of friends, painstakingly found by tramping round with my torch ignoring the rats, brought me more of these cultivated engaging people, but still no real clues about Angola. I was beginning to learn that, as I had felt so overwhelmingly at the dark airport, this was not a society which worked by normal rules, nor which had much coherence. For one thing there seemed to be little overlap between the formality and rigidity of the MPLA, the party, the country's defence against the onslaught from South Africa, and these agreeable sophisticated people in the capital.

I had asked in my original formal visa application to go to Huambo, provincial capital of the Central Highlands, and now an island of government control surrounded by areas where Unita held sway. My minder from OMA got the tickets after several fruitless trips to Angolan Airlines, long waits in queues which never moved, and several cancellations of the departure date. The airport in Luanda was a different kind of shock this time. After a long wait for a much delayed flight there was a sudden rush as of a football crowd to the steps of the plane. The OMA lady proved to have sharp elbows and to be a determined fighter and pushed me through the crowd and onto the plane with extraordinary force. People stood aside politely for a foreigner. Several hundred weary-looking people, laden down with bags and children, were left behind on the tarmac, disconsolately heading back to the hard benches of the departure area to wait for another flight, another day.

If Luanda was melancholy, Huambo was desolate. The plane circled abruptly down to avoid Unita missiles, leaving stomachs behind with a lurch. The airport was a windy strip with dilapidated buildings and a tattered MPLA flag flying. The streets were even more broken down than those of the capital, shops closed, apartment blocks crumbling, offices empty. Tangled bushes of dusty bougainvillaea sprayed orange, purple and red flowers out across cracked pavements, the few vehicles on the roads seemed to be all military trucks. The sound of tapping crutches filled the silence, empty trouser legs flapped below the faces of soldiers so young-looking that the blankness of their eyes was impossible to meet without feeling you were intruding. Huambo was raw pain. It was the town which hooked me and ensured that Angola's tragedy would always be refracted to me at a special angle.

The town was under virtual siege by Unita and could be reached only by the irregular internal flight we had come on. The electricity and water supplies had been sabotaged, the railway from the coast was closed after repeated ambushes by Unita and stretches of the track being blown up. The Benguela railway was a key target for Unita and had suffered an estimated $60 million worth of damage from repeated sabotage. The town's factories stood empty. That night, in another hotel room just as dark and grim as that in Luanda, explosions and gunfire punctuated the darkness and made it impossible to sleep. In contrast with Luanda the highland air was cold, there was a bitter wind and it began to rain.

Miette Marcelino, head of OMA in Huambo, picked me up in her car the next morning and showed me around a day-care centre, the hospital, and, with an escort of two trucks of soldiers, one in front of the car and one behind, an orphanage a few miles outside the town. It was an empty shelter where the children were fed and sheltered, there was nothing beyond the barest necessities. On the way we passed a makeshift camp of thousands of displaced peasants on the edge of the town. We reached the hospital by mid-afternoon where a new crop of mine victims lay on iron bedsteads with no mattresses, faces stunned by shock and agony. Angolan, Cuban and Russian doctors passed in and out of the operating room where the amputations were being carried out, drawn with the exhaustion of working round the clock with minimal resources. Miette Marcelino leaned over the cot of a skeletal child with marasmus who an Angolan nurse told us had little chance of surviving, and touched his mother's hand with sympathy. It seemed as though all Huambo's pain was concentrated in that tiny shrivelled face of an innocent victim. (Ten years later visiting that hospital in a different era an Angolan doctor with a deeply lined gentle face came up and reminded me that he had taken us round that day. 'You were in an OMA delegation and you cried over one child who was dying ... all of us had long before given up crying'.)

Miette Marcelino, tall, slim, the mother of seven children, asked me to spend the evening with her family instead of going back to the terrible silence and cold of the hotel. It was a welcome escape from confronting my thoughts about what I had seen of shattered lives in that one day. Miette's husband, Fernando, was an agricultural scientist and head of the research station at Chianga just outside Huambo. Chianga was part of the university and a new generation of agricultural economists and botanists was trained here by his team to the highest of standards in the years after independence. The campus was set in a park of huge and ancient flowering trees, with laboratories, libraries of rare books, and a collection of soil samples in hundreds of glass jars which mapped the different fertility across Angola's contrasting land from northern forest to southern savannah. The night before I was to visit Chianga, Unita placed a mine on the approach road, blowing up the first car to arrive at the research station in the morning. That same night, on the other side of Huambo, they also blew up the International Red Cross office and the clinic at Bomba Alta which made artificial limbs for mine victims. The freshly blackened walls and charred remnants of artificial limbs, like the new gaping hole in the Chianga road, seemed suddenly to bring this war of random killing and destruction even closer than the tens of thousands of maimed and displaced peasants who so visibly peopled Huambo.

The Marcelinos, and their great friend Dr David Bernadino who I was to meet with them, were quite different from anyone I had met in Angola, either the formal Party contacts through OMA, or the cosmopolitan circle of my friend's friends. These people looked and behaved as though from another world - utterly dedicated to the ideals of the MPLA which they had carried since before independence, and so schooled in the acceptance of danger, hardship and sorrow that they were unmentioned. No civilians lived a life closer to the dangers and privations of the front line, but they had chosen that life in Huambo, in part in solidarity with the peasants who could not choose where they lived. Dr Bernadino was a socialist, a painter, a writer, a lover of music and ballet, as his small house in the centre of town immediately revealed when we went there that evening. On big panels on the wall he had painted Picasso-like dancing people with trumpets and horns against a background of blue lakes and black mountains; on another was a solitary, reflective zebra. His chosen work was in a small primary health care clinic which he had built on the edge of Huambo town, where the road disappears into high grass and a red earth track winds past mud and wattle huts, patches of maize, and the waving fronds of banana trees. Every day he was here, treating malaria, malnutrition, the diseases of the poor, and, under the wattle roof built to shade the adjoining courtyard, overseeing the huge pots of food for the dozens of skinny children who came in every day. But at the same time he was one of Huambo's links to the outside world where his specialised research on goitre was internationally known.

Ten years later, these three, whose fierce idealism had made them the soul of Huambo, were assassinated by Unita in two separate attacks. The killers got away with impunity. The quietly heroic lives of Dr Bernadino and the Marcelinos, and the manner of their deaths, symbolise the chance that Angola had and lost, to become a leader of a post-colonial Africa which put its millions of poor and deprived at the top of the continental agenda. That hope was brutally undermined in those years when South African-led destabilisation by Unita flourished and matured into a force which broke the state of Angola. These killings symbolised Unita's determination to have Angola on their own terms. Racism, culture, ideology all played a part in these assassinations. For David and the Marcelinos, their work, which gave their lives meaning, and their pleasures of classical music and movies like Babette's Feast, their libraries, their internationalism, their uncompromising honesty, gave them an unbreakable independence from any central power. The organisations they ran - Chianga, OMA, the clinic - were all ones which promised ordinary people, if not a taste of that independence, at least the chance of making choices and a better future for themselves. But the idea of choices and personal autonomy for Angola's peasants ran smack up against Unita's totalitarian concepts and practices - Huambo was marked for a disastrous clash. In 1984, though, no one seemed to foresee that the disaster could get worse. Everyone lived in the present, and it was made bearable by the thought that the war would be over just as soon as South Africa achieved majority rule.

The following week I flew north in a small plane, invited by the MPLA's Organising Secretary, Lucio Lara, who had had a letter introducing me from his old friend from the guerrilla struggle, the British historian Basil Davidson, and who was visiting peasant co-operatives organised by the Party. Lara, tall, spare, aesthetic, with a heavy Latin moustache, was the man who epitomised the heroic Angola which lived so long in the imagination of so many Africans across the continent. He was the leading ideologue in the MPLA from the years of the guerrilla struggle in the forests of Cabinda and the bush of Eastern Angola, and the man best known and trusted by the top Cuban leadership, many of whom were part of Angola's fight for independence from those days.

'L'Afrique profonde, that's what they always wanted Angola to be', he once said to me, much later, encapsulating decades of what he had fought against.

'L'Afrique profonde' sums up every stereotype of black Africa: Conrad's Heart of Darkness; Idi Amin's evil buffoonery; Bokassa and cannibalism; the savagery of Doe's beach executions and his own gruesome end captured on video - crude leadership of ignorant, child-like people. Savimbi was a similar figure: Unita's primitive fascism, in which all potential rivals to Jonas Savimbi were killed, and social control maintained by the terror of public burning of women as witches, and the kidnapping which wrested young men and girls out of family and community, created totally dependent people, devoid of free will, emotionally annihilated.

The town of Malange was holding the line against L'Afrique profonde in 1984. It was even colder than Huambo and lost in mist and rain. The pot-holed roads, broken buildings, and closed shops told the same story of a community under virtual siege. But the scent of despair was not there. This was a town fighting a war well understood as fired by imperialism. On the walls of the main street, huge painted murals of Angola's first President, Agostinho Neto, Fidel Castro, and Che Guevara, shouted defiance at the South Africans, Unita and their US backers. In the main square flame trees shaded a war memorial made entirely of old AK47 rifles and spent rounds, which commemorated the Cuban soldiers who had given their lives here. As in Huambo the defence of the town was assured by a Cuban garrison and there was also a clandestine camp of South African African National Congress guerrillas in the province.

> 'Unita's primitive fascism created totally dependent people, devoid of free will'

We stayed in the Governor's palace, a chateau crumbling from years with no maintenance, but with beautiful long rooms filled with old ornate Portuguese sofas, armchairs, and cloudy mirrors. Meals were at a long table filled with the Governor's staff and Party officials, and the talk, in several languages, was of the difficult, and deteriorating, economic and security situation in the province, and of the uneasy stand-off in the south of the country where, as Iko Carreira had explained, occupying South African forces had not begun to pull back over the border to Namibia as they had promised in negotiations earlier in the year.

Lucio Lara spent two days driving round co-operative farms with the province Governor and MPLA party officials, looking at water taps, tractors, ploughs and harrows, and listening to peasant leaders talk and talk of their

Soundings

difficulties. Shortages of fuel and spare parts for tractors, kerosene for lamps, soap, salt and other necessities meant that many of the co-operatives were doing poorly. The war was encroaching on their rich agricultural province, roads were no longer safe to travel, young men and boys had been kidnapped by Unita and never seen again, supplies of inputs needed for the farms, which should come from Luanda, were scarce. Through hours of sitting in farm courtyards Lara barely spoke, but listened as the complaints came thick and fast, with no fear of the man in authority. The peasants were angry and asking for more military action against Unita, against the South Africans, to safeguard their land and crops from further deterioration. Here was another vision of what the Party meant to people, quite different from the formality I had been shown before. Here the MPLA was the centre of people's lives, their security, their entry into a new world of organised farming, and the faith in the leadership was touching and unmistakable.

On the last day, as he went into the closing meeting with the Governor and Party, Lara sent me off to see one of Angola's wonders, the Calendula waterfall. We drove along a battered tarmac road past forests of huge flowering trees and fields of maize and coffee. When we got out of the car to walk down to Calendula for a moment, the realities behind the escort of two dozen soldiers, the strict orders not to step beyond the path because of the danger of mines, and to start back well before dark, were forgotten before the beauty of the huge, thundering falls, iridescent in the sun, and framed by giant ferns and flowering pink and white trees. It was a beauty that would be cut off from sight for years a few months later, as Unita moved deeper into the province cutting off Calendula and more roads and farming areas. Beautiful Calendula vanished into L'Afrique profonde.

They were better

Ngugi wa Mirii

Ngugi wa Mirii writes for audiences and performers in community theatre in both rural and urban areas, and his plays are performed in Zimbabwe in English or in Shona. His writing, like this new play, They Were Better, focuses on highly political issues, and aims to make them accessible to everyone, no matter how little education they may have had. This one is on a classic theme for him - the competitive relationships between foreign aid donors, the IMF and local elites, and the power relations between each of these and the ordinary people in whose name they claim to be working.

Fifteen years ago in Kenya, the Kamirithu theatre in Limuru was a byword in Africa for the plays written and directed by the novelist Ngugi wa Thiongo, and staged with local actors and much improvisation. Kamirithu was burned down by the Kenyan police, and Ngugi wa Thiongo was detained for the threat his ideas and their dissemination to peasants posed to the Moi dictatorship. He now lives and teaches in America. Ngugi wa Mirii co-wrote some of the Kamirithu plays, and he has recreated in Zimbabwe the spirit of the great days of Kenyan political theatre.

Soundings

Scene One

Rep   Ladies and gentlemen.
            I am pleased to be with you today.
            I think your leader has already briefed you on the purpose of my visit so without wasting my time ... I beg your pardon ... your time ...
            I would like to hear your development problems.

1st Peasant   We want boreholes
2nd Peasant   We want Clinics
3rd Peasant   We want schools
4th Peasant   We want pesticides
5th Peasant   We want land
All   We want food
All   We want roads
All   bridges
All   Medicine
All   jobs

Mai Fadzi   In addition to all the developmental needs of our people, we also demand that you and your government should stop arresting us for hunting antelopes for food and cutting trees for firewood. Is this not our country too?

Rep   These are indeed genuine problems ...
            I am very touched.
            I, being a messenger of my government, rest assured that your needs will reach the highest in this country.
            I promise you that we shall write these problems in the best English, Swedish, Danish, German, French, and in all other advanced languages of money, and take them to our donors who have promised to help.
            I am surprised to learn that you are gathered at this growth point without a single toilet.

They were better

> Wake-up men!
> You people must be extremely lazy.
> I won't promise that my government will build toilets for you, it's your duty to do so.
> Soon the trees will be scattered, you won't find a single place to hide your ... behinds while relieving yourselves ...

Mai Fadzi   And you call yourself a messenger, you want to tell us that you've never set yourself in an open space to pass stool?
(she demonstrates)
Yes, we know you have piped water in your house and a toilet inside there too.
You even don't use firewood anymore since your house is wired like a prison with electricity cables, but don't forget your roots.
You might be up there today and tomorrow ... who knows ... man made catastrophes might come your way too.
After all, we are not a party to determine where a growth point should be located!
Those who did should have planned on toilets too.

Rep   [The rep moves away from the people and beckons the community leader and inquires about the woman in a whisper]
Who is that woman?

Leader   Forget her Chief, she is just an old confused peasant ... who lost her two sons in the liberation war and a husband too during the drought and her last born daughter in the recent floods.

Rep/Afridel   I doubt that, that's the reason she talks like that, monitor her movements as from today and give me a feed back when you visit the city.
Tell your people to sing for me so that she shuts up now.

Soundings

[The leader starts a song as he rises to escort the rep. Meanwhile Mai Fadzi and a group of women are murmuring as they exit]

Second Scene

This scene opens with an American national anthem or 'God save the king'. It could also open with any other background song like 'Vachena' as the chairperson enters the centre stage dressed like a judge. As the music ends he/she calls the house to order.

Chairperson   Ladies and Gentlemen, welcome to the Paris Club.
The agenda of our caucus is to approve and adopt the new aid norms, rules and regulations to be imposed by the IMF and the World Bank, and all donor agencies and to the third world countries.
As you know, without these conditionalities, our economies would not survive.
Without wasting time may I call the IMF representative to present his/her case.
Later on we shall invite our counterparts from the third world to present their proposals for the perpetuation of their dependency.

Mr IMF   Time is money, money is time Madam chairperson, for this reason may I present the following methods and strategies for the second colonization of Africa.
One, the Central government must be responsible for the debts of all state enterprises regardless of the circumstances in which the debt was drawn and used.
Two, the Central government is responsible for the debts of private enterprises in its country.
This means even if it is Anglo-American, Lonhro, etc, the government must guarantee foreign currency for the repayment of loans.
Three, Madam Chairperson, the government must therefore

set aside, and/or provide, foreign currency with which private firms must pay their debts.

Four, when a country or its enterprises fail to honour their debts with interest on time, the lenders must harden the terms of the debt. Usually by imposing new service charges of about 2%.

Five, the trick, Madam chairperson, is that the crisis created by the hardened terms itself also becomes the pretext for raising all fees and charges for taking on risky clients.

Mr W Bank   Let us not go into details, the point is, third world countries should be encouraged to mortgage their lives to Europe and America through endless loans whereby they will never be able to set themselves free from payment of interest let alone the capital.

Ms EEC   You see ... we are very lucky ...
Africa is full of natural disasters. There is always a cycle of drought followed by floods, famine, diseases, etc.
We therefore are assured of permanent colonies.

Amedon   To make them more permanent our duty has been and still is to ferment regular civil wars, tribal clashes like those in Kenya and Angola today.

Chairperson   We set up the Paris Club in 1974 in order to coordinate our influence over the donor recipient countries' development policies while at the same time our countries continue benefiting by strengthening our sucking strings and straws of milk, blood, honey and minerals from the third world countries. As part of this coordination, our major sucking straws have been our industries and our development assistance to them.
But also of interest has been the World Bank economic development institute EDI which has assisted immensely in

creating economic robots among the third world civil servants.
They will soon be coming with their bowls for alms.

Germdon   I agree whole heartedly with Lord Amedon ...
We should ferment tribal, clan and religious wars in these countries.
We should accelerate border disputes and subsequent break out of wars among neighbouring countries
We should especially make blacks fight because these people are black in mind.
Such wars assist in keeping the countries disintegrated and thus assuring us of their economic vulnerability.

Donswe   We Swedish don't think these tribal wars are effective.
Look at what the USA did with Savimbi for almost two decades after the UN supervised elections, and yet the will of the people determined who was our best puppet in that country.
We wasted time and money in Angola, Mozambique, and I don't know for how long in South Africa!

Chairperson   As always, I think Sweden is making an important contribution.
Now with the collapse of communism, peace negotiations should be promoted.

Amedon   Point of information, Mr chairman, we didn't waste time or money. Our armament industries were boosted and depend on such lengthy and fruitless wars.
We must in fact be concentrating on brewing many similar destructive wars to sustain our economies and domination.

[*The third world reps enter the stage on their knees clapping in humility*]

They were better

Chairperson	As I told you earlier, the third world beggars have come ... Welcome. Welcome Ladies and Gentlemen from the third world countries, we have been waiting for you.
Afridel	On behalf of the third world people, I am thrilled to learn of your willingness to keep your development assistance flowing like blood in your veins to our naturally dehydrated countries. As you can see we are all gathered from Asia, Latin America and of course we from the dark continent. It's mainly us from South of Sahara who are hard hit by all forms of natural catastrophes. And you are gathered here in this club merely to think about aiding us ... This is very kind of you. May almighty bless you with more ... We are very kind.
Candon	I would like to first applaud my brothers from the US of America for toiling day and night through the CIA to destroy communism in the world. As for the natural beggars from the third world, they should learn to silence their disgruntled elements among themselves before spreading their bony arms for development assistance.
Amedon	And for food aid we want to build military bases for our marines in your countries.
Swedon	For Hospitals provision we get free testing ground on your people for our medicines.
Nethdon	For borehole drilling and windmills we shall invest in your countries while you protect our markets and interests.

159

Bridon	For scholarships we bring specialists and have hunting freedom in your game reserves. We will exchange experts/volunteers/expatriates.
Germdon	For the drought relief we get free land and minerals for our industries.
All	We demand free custom tariffs, free land acquisition and total unquestioning loyalty and commitment to us.
Del	We accept. We agree. Any time. Is your time. Your wishes. Are Our command.
Bridon	In that case, we will grant you a loan payable in 10 years at 10% interest which we shall re-negotiate from time to time.
Swedon	26 years at 6%.
Nethdon	28 years at 5%.
Germdon	Ours will be for 20 years at 8% interest.
Amedon	Only 25 years at 7% in exchange for dumping grounds.

[As the donors shout out their grants offers the third world reps are seen miming receiving the loans and signing agreements. They shake hands and leave the stage together with the donors singing a victorious song eg. 'For he's a jolly good fellow'

As the delegates exit and the song fades away]

IMF	Congratulations Mr Afridel that was a very good presentation of your proposals.
Afridel	[full of esteem] Thank you very much.
IMF	Anyway, for you to make your developmental programme a success, I suggest that you buy all the equipment and machinery you need from the USA. I have a list of the companies here with me. We can make arrangements for all the purchases.
Afridel	Noooooo! We have already identified indigenous companies which can do it for us. But thanks for your willingness to help.
IMF	(walking away from Afridel) Well, well, well ... If you don't consider buying from the USA, I am afraid we can make it a little difficult for you. I mean, it could become very difficult even for the approved loan to be deployed to you.
Afridel	(shocked, confused and in despair) But why? ... Why ...
IMF	If you want and if you are willing to cooperate, we can make things a little easier for you. Actually we can transfer 15% of the 1.5 billion loan to you. By the way, which bank do you bank with?
Afridel	Of course the national bank of my motherland.
IMF	[laughing] Motherland! Ah! you don't bank with Barclays International, Standard Bank or Lloyds Bank? Anyway, that is not a problem, we can open an account for you overseas with Lloyds Bank and deposit the 15% of the 1.5 billion dollars directly into your account.

Soundings

Afridel	[*amazed, excited and in disbelief*] 15% ... of 1.5 billion dollars ...
Voice	... and you call yourself a messenger!?
Afridel	[*possessed by the idea*] 15% ... of 1.5 billion dollars ...
Voice	... and you call yourself a messenger!?
Afridel	[*completely compromising*] 15% ... of 1.5 billion dollars
Voice	... and you call yourself a messenger!?
IMF	Is it okay with you?
Afridel	Fine, fine, fine, it's okay.
IMF	That's my boy ... thanks ... sign here

Scene Three

[*As the Rep enters, the workers freeze as he tries hard to revive them with presents and foreign donors but all in vain.*]

Rep   Forward with the workers!
Forward with the women!

I have brought you ... I have brought you ...
Sewing machines for women, ha ha ha ha ...

(silence) O.K, I have brought you a foreigner ...
I mean a donor!
I ... a Swedish ... Army ... American ... Fuck ... French white woman in a village ...
I mean ...

Your village.

Mai Fadzi   White for ... what for ... A sewing machine?
Is this what we requested?
This is blind fold! Just as you cheat us into payments of loans we know nothing about ...
What are we to give in return for their machines?
We have nothing left apart from the arid land.
They've taken all enterprises in this country, taken all the mines and our heritage. They've taken away our manhood ... everything!
Take away your simple machines, away with your handouts. Leave us our land, our sweat and wealth and we will never require anything from you except mutual understanding and friendship!

[*As she says this we see the rep beckoning his guard who in return manhandles Mai Fadzi out of stage. The workers then come back to life, they start singing songs and demanding the release of Mai Fadzi. In the process they chase the rep and his entourage out of stage.*]

The workers enter the stage singing songs, carrying posters and placards written: WE DEMAND 100 PAY RISE; WE WANT OUR JOBS BACK; DOWN WITH AID STRINGS SUCKING OUR BLOOD; DOWN WITH NEO-COLONIALISM; UP WITH PEOPLE'S POWER , ETC. *The workers are then addressed by the trade unionist.*]

TUREP   Fellow workers, we are here again to celebrate our day, 'Workers Day'! As we celebrate, we should not forget those of us who have been retrenched or retired in the name of our home grown World Bank ESAP.
The systematic devaluation of our currency which is affecting our living standards means a devaluation of our labour power and a reduction of the market value of the goods we produce.

Soundings

> We must stop producing cash crops at the expense of our food. It is meaningless to grow tobacco, coffee, tea, etc ,when we do not control the prices.
> It is also unrealistic to develop our country for foreigners instead of us and our people.
> The so called foreign investments are based on capitalistic interests over which we have little or no control at all.
> *[at this point the police come and arrest him/her]*
> Power to the people! A luta continua ... !

[The workers follow them off the stage singing. The students enter the stage demanding scholarships, re-introduction of bursaries, lecturers, and the removal of the detention without trial Act. Police with tear gas storm the stage and the students scatter shouting. The leader, though, is left struggling with the police and is seen being handcuffed and taken away.]

Scene Four

[The scene is at a prison cell where Mai Fadzi the peasant and the TUREP are looking miserable and bored. We see the student is then thrown in the same cell.]

Mai Fadzi   These people have been mentally enslaved. Why, my child, why have they brought you here?
I can understand my friend the trade unionist and
I know what I did, but a mere child ...

Stuleder   Mum ... I am not a child ... I'm no longer a future leader.
I have got eyes, ears and a mouth to shout for my rights too.
I am here for organising my fellow students against oppression in the campus and the country as a whole. I am here because I know our history ...

Turep   Don't we all?

Stuleder   I know and they know. Yet they acknowledge and sign contracts for our life and country. They've allowed foreigners to determine the quality of the air we breathe, the food we eat, the type of education we get, the drugs we take, and even, the other day, they gave us an ultimatum to abandon the planes they had sold us sometime back accusing them of being too noisy for their environment. Now they want to give us loans to buy other planes from them which have low controlled noise.

Turep   We are here for fighting against the unequal economic system in our country.
We are here in this prison for questioning the structural adjustment programme policies formulated and imposed on us by the IMF and World Bank.
These policies are designed to benefit a few while the majority remain poor.
The question is why? Why is the North so greedy? Why can't the North at least pay better prices for our raw materials: gold, diamond, nickel, cotton, tea, coffee and labour? Why can't they encourage and promote technological development in the 'third world'. The so-called market economies discourage consumption of indigenous products while at the same time benefiting the North.

Mai Fadzi   They think we are fools but we shall not be broken ...

The end

Cost-recovery, adjustment and equity in health

Some lessons from Zimbabwe

Kevin Watkins

Kevin Watkins looks at the problems caused by the imposition of inappropriate neo-liberal policies in Zimbabwe and other parts of Africa.

After independence, most governments in sub-Saharan Africa established equity as a fundamental principle of health policy. The World Health Organisation's 1978 Alma Ata declaration on Primary Health Care, with its commitment to achieving adequate health care for all by the year 2000, was embraced across the region (WHO 1995). Most governments continue to reflect the aspirations of the Alma Ata declaration in their national health policy plans. But as the year 2000 approaches, it is difficult not to be struck by the painful contrast between the ambition of the post-independence period and actual achievements. While health indicators have improved overall, they have done so more slowly than for any other region, and in many countries they are deteriorating. Poverty is the underlying cause of Africa's poor human welfare performance. Today, one in two Africans lives on or below the poverty line, resulting in high levels of vulnerability to illness and the highest burden of disease in the developing world.

At the same time, African states have been gripped by a deepening fiscal crisis, with governments unable to provide the basic services needed to address the causes and consequences of poor health. Nowhere is this more apparent than in the health sector. After almost two decades of declining *per capita* incomes, debt crisis, structural adjustment and reduced public finance for health, there is a deepening crisis in public health policy, with resources diminishing in the face of a resurgence of preventable diseases, the emergence of deadly new strains of viral infection and an HIV/AIDS pandemic.

Southern Africa is no exception to this broad picture. With the partial exception of Botswana, where diamond revenues have enabled the government to maintain growth and expand health care provision, the region faces a deepening crisis in public health policy. Governments and donors have embarked on major reforms in response to that crisis. Among the most important of these reforms has been cost-recovery, or charging for health services. Over thirty countries in Africa (and all countries in Southern Africa) have adopted user charges as a means of raising finance. Countries with a long tradition of attempting - admittedly often with limited success - to provide health services free of charge have introduced fees. Much of the intellectual support and financial impetus behind this policy shift originated in the World Bank and the wider donor community, where private finance solutions to public finance problems gained currency during the 1980s. Arguments advanced in favour of user-fees have placed great emphasis on potential efficiency and equity gains. More broadly, cost-recovery has been seen by many of its more enthusiastic advocates as the first step towards a health policy built on the foundations of neo-classical economic theory, with consumers exercising choice in the market place for health services. In this sense debates over cost-recovery are rooted in a broader approach to economic and social development - and they have implications which go beyond the health sector. Problems in health policy have been widely treated as an indication of the 'failure' of African states as agents for delivering services and achieving efficient outcomes in social and economic policy. An enhanced role for the market, and for private sector operators, has been the central policy prescription to emerge. The prescription has been enthusiastically swallowed by most governments in southern Africa, especially in the health sector. Cost-recovery has been introduced as one element in a broader strategy incorporating support for private insurance, decentralisation and community financing initiatives.

In practice, if not in neo-classical theory, the introduction of user-fees has often had a highly damaging impact on equity, with poor communities being excluded from basic services. Elaborate systems for exempting such communities from payments have foundered. Moreover, the evidence from many countries suggests that, despite their high social costs, cost-recovery schemes have failed to generate the resources needed to address the financing crisis facing public health systems. Given the importance of health care in defining opportunities for human development, and the symbiotic relationship between ill-health and poverty, these are serious public policy problems.

This article reviews the impact of cost-recovery in Zimbabwe. The case is an important one because of Zimbabwe's impressive post-independence track-record in improving human welfare. Health policies designed to promote equity and efficiency in access and service delivery were central to this achievement, with the principle of universal access to publicly financed basic provision a central feature. After 1990, the capacity of government to maintain health services was jeopardised by a chronic budget deficit, with stabilisation targets agreed under IMF-World Bank auspices leading to a sharp decline in social sector spending. Cost-recovery was actively encouraged by the World Bank as an alternative source of health financing. Introduced at a time when poverty and vulnerability levels were increasing as a consequence of drought, falling employment and declining real wages, the new policy had adverse implications for equity in health care, with poor communities excluded from basic services. An exemption system ostensibly designed to protect equity failed as a result of poor design and inadequate implementation. The Zimbabwean case raises serious questions about the uncritical adoption of national user-fee strategies. Greater caution and a commitment to monitoring the impact of policy changes on the poor is required. More broadly, the abandonment of equity goals and embrace of a market-based solution to health policy problems needs to be challenged, with governments seeking alternative financial solutions to maintain publicly-financed basic health provision.

The experience of Zimbabwe

Since independence Zimbabwe has achieved some of the most impressive human welfare advances in sub-Saharan Africa. Life expectancy has increased from 55 years to 64 years. Success in combating preventable disease has halved the infant mortality rate to 50 per 1000 live births (compared to 170 for sub-Saharan Africa as a whole). Parallel improvements have been achieved in maternal mortality rates.

These human welfare gains were the consequence of an explicit commitment on the part of the Zimbabwe government to pursue equity goals through increased public investment and improvements in allocative efficiency. During the 1980s, Zimbabwe pioneered primary health approaches which emphasised maternal and child health services, health education, nutrition, control of communicable diseases, water and sanitation provision, and family planning. Immunisation rates increased from 25 per cent to 80 per cent coverage of children. An extensive primary health structure was developed to meet local needs. In terms of health service delivery, one thousand rural health centres and fifty-eight rural hospitals provided the base of a pyramidical structure with six central hospitals at the top, and a range of government and missionary hospitals in between the two layers. Today, over 85 per cent of Zimbabweans live within 8km of a health centre, one of the most comprehensive levels of coverage in Africa. Political commitment to the creation of a health service accessible to all was reflected in a 1984 White Paper *Planning for equity in health*, and the *Health for all action plan*, which was produced three years later. It was also reflected in an increase in the proportion of GDP spent on health from 2 per cent to 3 per cent during the 1980s.

After independence, a directive on user-charges for health was promulgated but not implemented. However, during the second half of the 1980s, as public finances came under growing pressure in the face of slow growth and rising public debt, the failure to enforce cost-recovery came under criticism from the World Bank. One influential report recommended financial targets for user charges, with the objective of quadrupling, from 2 per cent to 8 per cent, the proportion of recurrent health expenditure derived from this source.[1] Recognising a potential threat to equity, the report advocated an exemption system, while placing the burden of proof on the patient, who would be required to produce evidence of low income in order to receive free treatment. In an almost surreal indication of the World Bank's distance from reality, it was

---

1. See World Bank, *Improving the implementation of cost-recovery for health*, Africa Technical Department, Washington 1992.

assumed that health facility clerks would provide the front-line service in differentiating between the poor and non-poor, using a variety of survey data on landholding size and type of dwelling to supplement wage data. To the extent that empirical evidence of ability to pay was gathered, it typically took the following form: 'There is strong anecdotal evidence (high out-of-pocket payments to private doctors, pharmacies and traditional practitioners) to suggest that many Zimbabweans would be willing to pay more for reasonable quality health care' (p5). The central conclusion to emerge from the World Bank's health policy evaluations was that fees were too low, collection efforts too lax, and evasion of fees widespread, with the result that significant financial resources were being lost.

There was little public discussion of the World Bank's health policy recommendations. But their importance became apparent in 1991, when Zimbabwe adopted a structural adjustment programme under IMF-World Bank auspices. At the core of this programme was the objective of reducing the national budget deficit from 10 per cent to 5 per cent of GDP within five years. In the health sector, cost-recovery was allocated a central role in containing public spending. Under the 1991-1995 framework for economic reform, the Government of Zimbabwe committed itself to quadrupling cost-recovery collections. Initially, action to this end focused on more rigorous enforcement and collection of existing fees. Then in 1994 a new fee structure was adopted. This raised the costs of registration at primary clinics from Z$1 to $Z6.50, introduced charges for ante-natal services which were previously free, and consolidated an escalating fee structure in which higher charges were applied for access to district level facilities.[2]

While retaining a commitment to equity in health policy, the health reforms adopted under the structural adjustment package constituted a radical departure from the consensus of the 1980s. In particular, the principle that universal health coverage should be achieved through services financed by general taxation was, for the first time, brought into question. This had implications which went beyond the health sector. During the 1980s, the human welfare achievements outlined above were achieved not as a consequence of increased per capita

---

2. M. Chisvo and L. Munro, *A Review of Social Dimensions of Adjustment in Zimbabwe, 1990-94*, UNICEF, Harare 1994.

income (which declined slightly) or the redistribution of assets, but through improved access to health and education financed through a broadly progressive tax system. Thus on both the income and expenditure side, budget spending incorporated important redistributive elements which the stabilisation plans adopted under structural adjustment appeared to threaten. By eroding the state's capacity to maintain a redistributive function, the stabilisation programme posed a direct threat to the human welfare gains achieved after independence.

The policy background

In Zimbabwe, cost-recovery was introduced in a context defined by four interlocking factors.

First, severe droughts in 1991/92 and 1994/95 depleted the assets of rural households. The 1991 drought left the vast majority of poor rural households with no marketable surplus and severely reduced assets. Livestock losses in excess of 50 per cent were reported in arid and semi-arid communal farm areas. When the 1994 drought arrived, households had correspondingly fewer assets and savings to cushion the effects, resulting in reduced consumption and an increase in off-farm labour.

The second factor, related to the impact of drought but exacerbated by structural adjustment, was a catastrophic decline in urban wages and employment. According to the IMF, real per capita incomes in the urban formal sector declined by 32 per cent between 1990 and 1993. Rural wages fell by 40 per cent over the same period, as drought undermined production on commercial farms. By the end of 1995, urban wages were still over 20 per cent below their 1990 level. This slump in wages did not protect employment levels, with over 120,000 jobs being lost during the first three years of the adjustment programme. Inevitably, in a country as urbanised as Zimbabwe, the collapse of formal sector employment and wages was transmitted to the communal farm areas in the form of reduced remittances. In 1991, remittances from urban family members accounted for around 20 per cent of total rural income, rising to over 30 per cent for the poorest households. As these remittances fell, it increased the vulnerability of the poor rural households to sudden shocks caused by losses of output or employment opportunities.

The third defining feature of the background to cost-recovery policies was a collapse in public spending. During periods of stress, poor households depend heavily upon access to public services to protect their welfare. In the case of Zimbabwe, structural adjustment was accompanied by a catastrophic decline in public spending and service provision - especially in the health sector. Between 1990/91 and 1995/96, health spending fell from 6.2 per cent to 4.2 per cent of total government spending. Measured in more relevant per capita terms, health spending reached a peak of Z$55 in 1991, more than any other country in Africa except South Africa, Botswana and Swaziland. By 1995, per capita spending had fallen to Z$32. Budgets for preventative health, the most cost-effective part of the system for protecting the poor, were cut by one quarter. Inevitably, the quantity and quality of health services provided declined, with drugs shortages becoming a recurrent problem.

The fourth factor conditioning the environment into which user-fees were introduced was HIV/AIDS. Zimbabwe has one of the world's highest rates of HIV/AIDS, which affects around 30 per cent of the sexually active population. AIDS is now the leading cause of death in Harare, and an estimated 7 per cent of children are born HIV-positive. Almost all will die before the age of five, most of them after protracted episodes of sickness. The AIDS epidemic has already led to a dramatic increase in cases of tuberculosis, which have risen by 350 per cent since 1990. Reports from City Health departments underline the extent of the public health crisis associated with HIV/AIDS. For instance, in Harare infant mortality rates have increased from 30/1000 to 52/1000, while perinatal mortality is increasing at the rate of 18 per cent a year. Nationally, HIV-related illnesses are now the second main cause of death and the single biggest killer in the 25-44 age range. The increasing demands imposed by HIV/AIDS on a health system undergoing deep budget cuts has created intolerable strains. Apart from tuberculosis, the epidemic is increasing the prevalence of respiratory infection, acute malnutrition and associated diseases, increasing the demand for health care at a time when provision is diminishing.

Each of the four factors mentioned above had the effect of reinforcing the pervasive poverty which characterises Zimbabwe. Around 17 per cent of rural children are malnourished, exposing children to risk from communicable, infectious and parasitic diseases. 'Poverty' afflictions such as acute respiratory infection and diarrhoea still account for half of all outpatient attendance at health facilities. Against this background, any loss of access to health services for poor people inevitably poses acute risks in terms of vulnerability to diseases.

Despite this neither the Government of Zimbabwe nor the World Bank appear to have considered the implications of cost-recovery. Instead, they assumed that an untested exemption system would protect the poorest and most vulnerable communities from the adverse effects of cost-recovery.

Adverse equity effects

The assumption was fatally flawed. Following the stricter enforcement of fee collections in 1991, it would appear that low-income groups were forced either to delay or reduce health care. One early study found that outpatient attendances dropped by 18 per cent by the end of 1991, while inpatient admissions went up by 12 per cent. One possible explanation is that patients started to seek health care only when it was absolutely necessary, thereby necessitating hospital care. Further evidence of the impact of cost-recovery in hospitals is revealed in the fact that average length of stay in government hospitals fell from nine days to seven days, and from four days to two days for maternity patients. Ante-natal clinic attendance also fell in 1991, whereas maternity admissions increased, along with a 10 increase in unbooked deliveries and babies born-before-arrival. Far from being a temporary adjustment to new market signals, it appears that the decline was part of a catastrophic long-term trend. Although ante-natal care registration started to recover slightly in 1992, by the end of the year attendance figures had still not reached their 1990 levels. The costs of non-registration are high, with unregistered mothers some four times more likely to die in childbirth.

Use of reproductive health services appear to have been particularly sensitive to the effects of cost-recovery. Admission statistics from Harare Central Hospital for 1991 to 1993 show an increase from 8.8 per cent to 13.6 per cent in the number of babies born to mothers who had not registered for ante-natal care. The associated human costs are not captured by cold statistics. They are reflected instead in the fact that the perinatal mortality rate for unregistered mothers (251 per 100,000 live births) is around five times higher than for those who had registered for ante-natal care. Reduced access to ante-natal care at the same hospital appears to have been behind a 21 per cent increase in the number of babies born-before-arrival (BBA), often because the mother was attempting to minimise the time and costs incurred in hospital treatment; or because of complications which had not been recorded because of non-registration for ante-natal care. In the six months after the introduction of user-fees, BBAs increased by 20 per cent. Mortality rates among these babies was considerably higher than the average. Evidence from other hospitals pointed to a similar picture of reduced health service use. At the St Paul's Mission Hospital, located in a poor communal farming area in Murehwa district, the number of BBAs increased by half over the six months following the adoption of the new policy.

By delaying or obstructing entry to the health system, cost-recovery imposed enormously high human costs on vulnerable people. Those costs are to be measured in terms of lost lives and the suffering associated with unnecessary sickness. The more immediate efficiency costs for the health system can be captured more simply in the additional costs of treating health problems which could have been resolved more cheaply earlier. Individual accounts of suffering and death are often dismissed by the World Bank and the Zimbabwe government, as 'anecdotal', or a consequence of specific problems in the health facility concerned. At one level, the observation is justified. There have been no large-scale controlled studies designed to isolate the impact of cost-recovery. An additional problem is that demand-diversion responses have not been examined, giving rise to the claim that reduced attendance at one health facility may have been complemented by increased attendance elsewhere. Viewed from a different perspective, the fact that such sweeping policy reforms were initiated by the Government and the World Bank without arrangements to monitor their effects through such studies suggests that some degree of self-criticism may be in order. But whatever the shortcomings of the research, the evidence of adverse social outcomes rests upon considerably more than anecdote.

Since March 1992, UNICEF and the Ministry of Public Service, Labour and Social Welfare have carried out five sentinel-site surveys under their Social Dimensions of Adjustment Programme. These surveys covered forty sites, interviewing 120-125 households in each site. They have produced the most comprehensive data on responses to cost-recovery. Among the most relevant findings, the following suggest particularly powerful causal links between cost-recovery and exclusion from vital services:

---

3. A. Renfrew, ESAP and Health, Silvera House, Social Series, No. 3, Harare 1992.

- The percentage of children whose diarrhoea was not treated at a clinic because treatment was regarded by parents as too expensive increased from 9 per cent of the total in 1993 to 22 per cent in 1994. This shift coincided with a 117 per cent increase in health fees at rural hospitals and health centres. In a sub-sample of 266 diarrhoeal cases treated at home, 58 per cent of families said they had not taken children to clinics because outside treatment was thought to be too expensive. One of the major reasons given by women for giving birth at home was that the cost of delivering at health services was too high.

- In January 1993, cost-recovery was introduced for condoms. In the same month, the number of condoms distrubuted by survey site health centres fell from an average of 53,033 in 1992 to 28,988 in 1993.

Before-and-after studies at specific health facilities reinforce the broader survey evidence. In January 1993, cost-recovery measures were withdrawn for six months in response to a series of epidemics. At one rural hospital, attendance at outpatient and ante-natal departments doubled in the six months after the withdrawal of user-fees. At the St Paul's Mission Hospital the cost of outpatient visit increased from Z$1.50 to Z$17 at the beginning of 1994. The cost of delivering a baby almost doubled to Z$120. By the end of February 1994, the number of inpatients and the number of deliveries had fallen by over 40 per cent each.

Failure of the exemption system

From the outset, the World Bank consistently stressed the importance of combining more rigorous enforcement of cost-recovery in Zimbabwe with the development of an exemption system to protect the poor. In practice, however, there was a considerable time-lag between the more rigorous enforcement of cost-recovery in 1991, and the emergence of a viable exemption system. This sequencing problem resulted in the partial or total exclusion of vulnerable communities from the health system at a time when poverty was becoming more intensive and health needs were growing.

The Government of Zimbabwe introduced the Social Development Fund (SDF) in 1991 with the support of the World Bank and other donors. There were two components in the scheme: and Employment Training Programme and a Social Welfare Component. The latter comprised food money, and assistance with school fees and health fees. Elaborate targeting mechanisms were established, imposing an intensive administrative burden on the Department of Social Welfare. Yet no new budget was agreed until 1992, and no extra staff were employed to implement the new system.

In 1993, an independent report into the operation of the Social Welfare Component of the SDF concluded that the food-money scheme was reaching only about 3 per cent of the target population and the school-fee scheme 20 per cent (Kaseke E and Ndaradzi M, 1993). The report concluded that eligible populations were being systematically excluded as a result of complex and cumbersome bureaucratic procedures devised without regard to the constraints facing poor communities. The following were among the most serious problems identified:

♦ *The high cost of applications compared to the benefits received.* Potential beneficiaries were required to go in person to DSW offices with extensive documentation to prove eligibility. In most cases, several trips were required to see an application through, resulting in high time and transport costs. Such costs are closely associated with the accessibility of welfare offices. In rural areas, it is not uncommon for the Social Welfare Office to be up to 100km away, rising to 200km in extreme cases. Poor people living in remote rural areas were unlikely to be able to afford bus fares to and from offices located more than 80km away. Even if they could, the cost of transport would outweigh the benefits.
♦ *Time lag in benefit payments.* Because approvals required authorisation from Harare, a gap of 6-8 months between applications and payments was normal.
♦ *Separate application procedures.* Instead of devising one standardised application for all three benefits, separate forms and procedures were required for each, adding to administrative demands and time/transport costs.
♦ *Lack of resource planning.* No attempt was made to link the size of the target population and level of benefits offered with the financial resources available, leading to shortfalls in funding.
♦ *Stigmatisation of applicants.* The report noted that many eligible parents were unwilling to apply because of the stigma associated with welfare benefits.

♦ *Local intermediary charges.* Confirmation of eligibility from headteachers and village elders was often provided only on payment of fees, further diminishing the potential benefits.

To these problems of administration and targeting can be added another: namely, an inability on the part of potentially eligible people to *obtain information*. At the end of 1993, only around one-half of the population had heard of the SDF (Government of Zimbabwe 1993). That number increased to around 75 per cent during 1995. However, of the respondents interviewed in UNICEF's sentinel-site survey at the end of 1995, only 21 per cent said they had applied for assistance, even though it was estimated that between 50-60 per cent were eligible. The main reason given for not applying was 'lack of knowledge' of how to apply.

Different procedures in different health facilities added to the general confusion. Some hospitals required letters of exemption from the DSW before waiving fees. Others applied more discretionary approaches. Some refused to waive fees even when presented with exemption letters, on the grounds that payments for treatment from the DSW would take up to eight months to materialise.

Health facilities were also forced to contend with the central paradox of introducing cost-recovery measures for communities characterised by high levels of poverty: namely, the law of diminishing returns. In some communal areas, in excess of 60 per cent of the population might have been exempt from user-fees on income grounds. But as one report noted for rural non-governmental hospitals: 'Exempting every patient would result in very little inflow of revenue given the fact that almost all patients fall below the Z$400 household income per month. Consequently, rural hospitals are encouraging patients to pay'.

The income criteria chosen for exemption was also problematic in at least two respects. First, any means-testing of household income is relevant only to the extent that it reflects the real availability of resources for family members, which is a function of the size and age distribution of families. A fixed income obviously translates into fewer per capita resources in a large family than in a small family. Yet the exemption system took no account of family size.

Second, the threshold levels chosen have not been accurate indicators of poverty. In 1991, when more rigorous enforcement was introduced, the exemption level was the same as it had been in 1981. World Bank estimates suggest that this was around 28 per cent below the rural poverty line and less than half the urban poverty line. In other words, the exemption level selected was weakly related to real needs. Moreover, the Z$150 exemption threshold was kept in place for operation purposes until the end of 1991, when it was raised to Z$400, where it remains today. The figure of Z$400 appears to have been picked almost at random. For instance, it is less than half of the income-tax exemption level, which might have provided an equally valid indicator of ability to pay. By 1994, the threshold level had fallen further below the real poverty line. Adjusted for inflation, the exemption level was around 20 per cent below the rural poverty line and 90 per cent below the urban. In the two years since 1994, inflation has averaged over 20 per cent, but the exemption line has not been adjusted upwards, further eroding the real value of the index.

The upshot is that many poor people have been excluded from claiming exemption because of the threshold criteria selected. Using the World Bank's poverty line data, around 25 per cent of the national population, rising to over 30 per cent of the rural population, do not have access to sufficient income to purchase an adequate consumption basket of food, shelter, education, health, and transport. If poverty is the determinant of ability to pay, this entire group would appear to merit exemption - an option which would impose an enormous administrative burden, while at the same time reducing revenues from cost-recovery. This is one of the central dilemmas facing any exemption system to compensate for the effects of cost-recovery in a situation of widespread poverty.

Alternatives to cost-recovery: the challenge

Considering the high social costs associated with user-fees, the benefits in terms of resource mobilisation in Zimbabwe have been derisory. Despite the introduction of more rigorous enforcement procedures, cost-recovery income has stagnated at less than 3 per cent of the recurrent health budget. Most district-level facilities were unable to raise more than 2 per cent of their budgets through this route. At the clinic level, UNICEF's sentinel-site survey found that fee collection had stagnated in real terms between 1991 and 1993. Taking into account the costs of collecting and accounting for fees collected, it is probable that cost-recovery resulted in a net loss of resources. This would imply that the quality and quantity of services provided deteriorated despite the additional burden being placed on households, calling into question one of the main benefits claimed for cost-recovery.

To its credit, the World Bank was relatively swift in acknowledging the problems associated with cost-recovery. In 1995, a Country Economic Memorandum conceded: 'There is evidence that the fee exemption system under which poor people are entitled to claim free treatment has not worked well, and that fees undermined access to health services for vulnerable sections of the population'.[4] The Memorandum went on to recommend the suspension of all fees for ante-natal, maternity and child health services, and free services for basic preventative care, immunisations - and treatment of infectious diseases. After initially rejecting this assessment, the Zimbabwean Ministry of Health conceded that cost-recovery had resulted in adverse outcomes, especially for the rural poor. It suspended cost-recovery for rural health clinics in 1995, except for a nominal registration fee.

Reflection on the Zimbabwean experience would also appear to have prompted a review in some parts of the World Bank. One recent research report on cost-recovery in Africa has recommended the withdrawal of user-fees on basic services, except as a last resort. However, more fundamentalist proponents of cost-recovery retain a powerful policy influence within the World Bank, especially in sub-Saharan Africa. Whatever the World Bank's current ambivalence, it might be argued that, in the absence of ideological blinkers, the outcome of cost-recovery in Zimbabwe would have been entirely predictable; and that more effective monitoring of impact and consideration of the evidence provided by UNICEF would have led to an earlier review of the policy advice which had been given. Such monitoring should form a fundamental part of any major change in health policy.

Future threats

Addressing the problems associated with cost-recovery, and developing alternatives, is a pressing social policy problem in Zimbabwe. The country is about to embark on the second phase of its adjustment programme with the

---

4. World Bank, *Achieving Shared Growth*, Country Economic Memorandum, Southern Africa Department, Washington 1994.

IMF and the World Bank, who stopped releasing funds in 1996 in response to government failure to meet targets for reduction of budget deficit. There is considerable pressure on government to resolve the budget-deficit problem. It remains to be seen whether or not it will be possible to meet the targets set within the time-frame allocated without inflicting irreparable damage on primary health care provision, education, and other priority social sectors, some of which are already on the verge of collapse.

The problem facing the government can be simply stated. In 1994/1995, the fiscal deficit amounted to just over 12 per cent of GDP. The aim of the new programme is to reduce it to 5 per cent by the end of the decade. This will require tight control over government expenditure. However, the room for manoeuvre is limited. Interest payments on public debt account for some 30 per cent of government expenditure - more than health and education combined. There is no discretion over these payments. Indeed, the rising cost of financing public debt has reduced the real value of the budgetary resources available for non-interest expenditures by over 40 per cent since 1990/91. Recurrent spending on wages and salaries accounts for another one-third of budget expenditures. When the value of the wages and salaries bill is taken into account, the real value of revenues left for capital spending has fallen by over 80 per cent. If amortisation payments are included, domestic debt servicing now accounts for 48 per cent of domestic revenue.

Between them, education and health account for slightly over one-quarter of total budget spending, making them obvious targets for reduced allocations. However, there is no scope for reducing public spending in priority social sectors without adverse effects for human development and long-term growth prospects. The real wages of health workers and teachers have been reduced by one-third over the past five years. Morale has collapsed in both sectors. During 1996, a major strike by health workers aimed at reversing the decline in salaries and halting the slide in service quality reflected a growing mood of desperation. Social-sector professionals are leaving the country in large numbers, with adverse implications for the quality of service provided. Cuts in the recurrent budget for the health sector have also contributed to chronic shortages of drugs and the virtual collapse of rural ambulance services, with vehicles left non-operational because of shortages of spare parts.

There is no question that the budget situation in Zimbabwe is unsustainable

- or that matters will get worse without action to reduce debt and contain future borrowing. Without moves towards a more sustainable budgetary position, it will not be possible to finance the delivery of social services, let alone to undertake the infrastructural investments upon which future growth depends. The question is, how can priority social services be protected during the budget stabilisation programme? The answer to this question is to be found in an three-pronged strategy aimed at *increasing revenues*, *reallocating resources* to achieve greater efficiency and equity in the social sector, and *changing the sectoral composition of budget spending*.

Increasing revenues Measures to increase government revenues are an immediate priority. Under the 1990-1995 adjustment programme, tax structures were reformed in a highly regressive direction, contributing to a decline in revenue collection. This has been reinforced by other measures introduced under structural adjustment which have brought windfall gains for some of the highest-income groups in the country, notably within the agricultural farm sector which is dominated by a small group of white farmers. Measured as a share of GDP, tax revenues have declined from 35 per cent in 1989 to 28 per cent in 1995, some five per cent *below* the target set under the adjustment programme. Comparing 1994/95 with 1989/90, income-tax revenues fell by Z$263m in constant 1990 prices. To put this figure in context, it was equivalent to around 20 per cent of the health budget. It was also many times in excess of the user-fees collected at rural health centres and district hospitals.

There is a strong case for the next phase of adjustment to include a strengthening of revenue administration and the introduction of progressive revenue-raising measures. Higher marginal tax-rates for high incomes are an obvious starting point, along with the withdrawal of generous tax concessions - such as those for company cars and housing loans - aimed at higher-income groups. The introduction of a graduated land-tax in the large-scale commercial farming sector would be justified on grounds of efficiency and equity. It would be justified on efficiency grounds because this sector currently uses land, the country's prime asset, highly inefficiently. In contrast to the densely populated communal farm areas, commercial farms currently cultivate only around half of the land they control. A graduated land-tax, allied to the charging of full costs for water and electricity, would encourage a more efficient allocation of resources.

Such a tax would also promote equity in revenue generation, since it would fall on high-income groups - a fact which helps to explain the reluctance of the government to consider a move in this direction.

Relocating social sector budgets Turning to reallocation within existing social-sector budgets, the challenge is to expand investment in primary level facilities where social and economic returns will be the highest. In the health sector, Zimbabwe performs better than most African countries in allocating resources to the primary level, but its $6 per capita spending is below the $9 minimum which the World Bank estimates is needed to publicly finance a minimum health care package - and the share is declining. Reversing this trend is vital if Zimbabwe is to achieve the goal of equity in health care, cost- recovery at the primary level is not an option consistent with this aim.

Where there is scope for increased cost-recovery is in the central teaching hospitals, and in charging private users, such as insurance companies, full costs for public services. Public spending allocations between the primary and the tertiary sector should also be reviewed.

Reprioritising budgets With regard to the third element of a budget stabilisation strategy, the inter-sectoral allocation of resources, there are tough political choices to be made. Subsidies to loss-making parastatal corporations constitute a major budgetary burden and these need to be reviewed and defence is another item of budget spending which is inflated in relation to need, in 1995/6 accounting for 9 per cent of budgetary expenditure.

Beyond Zimbabwe: issues for the region

Zimbabwe's experience is instructive for other countries in the region and elsewhere in Africa. Cost-recovery approaches to health financing are gaining ground in southern Africa, with the World Bank model of uniform national user-fee schemes remaining the dominant model. Chronic budget problems, the poor quality of state services and familiar arguments about the 'unaffordability' of publicly-financed basic health provision have all contributed to the political momentum behind cost-recovery. To the extent that broad lessons can be drawn from the Zimbabwean case for countries characterised by highly divergent levels of income, human welfare indicators and health problems, the most important would appear to be application of the precautionary principle. Cost-recovery has a poor record in achieving financial and efficiency objectives - and a disastrous record in excluding poor people from basic services. At the very least, governments in southern Africa might wish to review their collective experiences and reflect on alternative financing strategies and it is not only national governments which have a capacity to reduce the fiscal pressures driving increased recourse to cost-recovery. Both the World Bank and the IMF rightly stress the damage to social sector budgets caused by unproductive expenditures in areas such as armaments, loss-making parastatals and corruption. They have been less active in addressing the problems caused by unproductive expenditures made to themselves in the form of debt repayment. By the year 2000, slightly under half of Mozambique's budget expenditure will be directed to debt repayment, with the IMF the single largest recipient. At present, debt servicing absorbs more than twice the amount spent on health. This is in a country where one-in-five children die before the age of five, most of them as a result of infectious diseases which would be easily preventable were the resources available. In Zambia, for every $1 spent on health, another four are spent on debt servicing, with the IMF again the largest recipient. All of which points to a powerful case for providing early and deep debt relief, perhaps developing the Highly Indebted Poor Country initiative to reward governments willing to convert savings from debt into priority social investments.

Despite its well-rehearsed rhetorical flourishes on the importance of primary health and basic education, in practice the World Bank has failed to prioritise equity in social policy under its structural adjustment programmes. Like many of the governments it supports, the Bank - along with the wider donor community - continues to regard social policy as an appendage to market-oriented reforms. However, leaving things to the market is bad economics and bad for human development. Access to health provision is one of preconditions for establishing positive linkages between growth and social equity, creating the conditions in which the poor can realise their productive potential and take advantage of new opportunities. Conscious choices have to be made about how to establish these linkages. The evidence suggests that cost-recovery is the wrong choice.

Mozambique – under new management

Joseph Hanlon

How an African country came to be controlled by international businesses and aid agencies.

Mozambique has a striking similarity to the British high street. Diversity and local control have been replaced by international dominance, with direct ownership by outside interests, and with franchises. There is a facade of local control. Local people still work and shop there, but local managers must follow detailed directives from a head office.

In Mozambique, control of land and the economy is passing to international businesses, while control of government policy and services has been taken by a consortium of private companies, non-government organisations, foreign governments, and international agencies. Mozambicans are reduced to the role of hired managers who can be replaced at the whim of the foreign owner.

Of course there are exceptions. Just as a few local shops survive on the British high street, Mozambican local capital does retain a place in some economic sectors and some Mozambican officials and government ministers are able to maintain a degree of autonomy. But Mozambique is a particularly extreme example of a phenomenon variously described as privatisation, globalisation or recolonisation.

In this article, I will show how war and reconstruction have been used to break, fragment and dismantle the Mozambican state and hand control to a wide range of foreign interests. Through this discussion I will highlight the growth of a political or managerial or comprador class, which now plays a key role in the new Mozambique. I will also highlight two tools used by the industrialised countries - central planning and corruption - despite their rhetoric of opposition to both.

Initial state dominance

When Mozambique became independent in 1975 Frelimo inherited a bankrupt economy and major social problems. Portuguese settlers held all the key technical and managerial posts; even shopkeepers and taxi drivers were Portuguese. Most left at independence. Many Portuguese and other foreign owners simply abandoned businesses. Frelimo nationalised relatively little, but the state found itself running abandoned businesses, which accounted for the bulk of the economy. Meanwhile, the literacy rate was only 15 per cent and health and education were confined to urban areas. Frelimo's initial goals were to prevent economic collapse and to provide health and education to the bulk of the population, and by 1977 this had been accomplished. Frelimo declared itself a Marxist-Leninist party and Mozambique a one-party state; with eastern European and Cuban support, Frelimo moved for rapid modernisation.

State dominance of the economy was both ideological and a practical necessity. Because black Mozambicans had been banned from running businesses for much of the colonial era, there was only a tiny domestic capitalist group, so the state had no choice but to control the economy. By the late 1970s, however, the economy was growing again. Frelimo opted for a strategy of rapid economic growth based on big development projects and central planning. The peasants were largely ignored. But small businesses were handed back to the private sector, both because, in President Samora Machel's dismissive phrase, 'the state does not sell needles', and because there were now local entrepreneurs with the confidence (in themselves and in Frelimo) and experience to take over businesses which had been abandoned five years before.

It is important to put the late 1970s into context in several ways. Internationally, the concept of the developmental state was fashionable. And, after its defeat in Vietnam, and with Jimmy Carter in the White House, the United States was not aggressive and there seemed a genuine space for alternative socialist and social democratic development strategies, and even talk of a 'new international economic order'. Indeed, the late 1970s international thinking which lay behind the foundation of the South African Development Coordination Conference was to temper the Marxism of Mozambique and Angola with the Christian socialism of Tanzania and paternalism of Botswana, and provide a positive alternative to apartheid in South Africa.

Domestically, Frelimo seemed to be having initial success with its transformation of the Mozambican economy. (The degree and sustainability of that success is much debated, but it remains clear that, both to Frelimo and to the outside world, Mozambique in 1980 seemed a success story.) Most dramatic was the commitment and integrity of the new political class. Leaders genuinely believed that they were building a better country for their children, and that socialism would provide. Corruption was virtually non-existent, both because of social checks (it would be obvious if someone had unusual luxury goods, or sometimes even extra bottles of whiskey) and because there was a real belief that the state would provide for their old age and for their families so it was not necessary to be corrupt to build up a 'pension' and provide for the extended family.

In what follows, it is always important to remember how different the world was in 1980.

Reagan and destabilisation

The big change came with the election of Ronald Reagan as US president in November 1980. Whereas Carter had played down the cold war, put pressure on the apartheid regime in South Africa, and tried to bring Mozambique and Angola back into the western fold by positive means, Reagan immediately divided the world into the friends and enemies of the Soviet evil empire. Apartheid South Africa was anti-communist and so became the US ally in the region; Marxist Mozambique was declared the devil incarnate. Within days of Reagan's inauguration, and with full US approval, South Africa launched a war of destabilisation against Mozambique which was to cause one million deaths, five million refugees, and $20,000 million in damage.

South Africa targeted the state, both directly and indirectly. Frelimo's popularity rested more on social than economic gains, particularly the great expansion of health and education. So South Africa's proxy force, Renamo, gave priority to the destruction of the state health and education facilities, kidnapping teachers and pupils, carrying out massacres in hospitals, and burning schools and health posts. More than half the health and education network was systematically destroyed.

On the economic side, South Africa and Renamo targeted major economic installations, such as sugar mills and tea plantations, which were mainly state-owned. Travel was another target, with the destruction of bridges and roads, as well as attacks on both private and state-owned buses, trucks, and cars. Here, the state was probably not the main target, but rather the economy in general, and the country was crippled. By 1985, exports had fallen to one-quarter their 1980 level.

Using war to replace the government

The war continued for 11 years, until a peace accord in 1992. But during that period, the international community used the war to disempower the government and replace it with other, more malleable, agents.

The first action occurred in 1983 where there was a drought in southern Mozambique. South Africa targeted food relief and used the war to create famine. In January 1993 Mozambique appealed for food aid, but donors, led by the United States, actually reduced the level of food aid. Probably more than 100,000 Mozambicans died of starvation due to the donor strike. Mozambique had no choice, and it complied with a series of US demands in 1984: it signed a peace treaty with South Africa, it joined the World Bank and International Monetary Fund, and it allowed US and other foreign non-government organisations into the country for relief and development projects. The government was forced to cede to the US agency CARE a central role in the distribution of food aid - a particularly important concession because, for the first time, a foreign non-government agency was assuming governmental functions both of service delivery and of decision-making.

Aid increased and the war escalated. There was another drought and another donor strike in 1986, when donors withheld food aid; in October 1986 President Samora Machel was killed in a plane crash probably caused by South Africa, which also sharply increased its participation in the war. Again Mozambique knew that it had to make concessions. In January 1987 it announced its first structural adjustment programme, including major devaluations. Foreign NGOs and aid agencies were given much more freedom to do what they wanted in Mozambique.

My book *Mozambique: Who Calls the Shots?* (James Currey, 1991) details the subsequent struggle. But it basically had three strands:

◆ Non-government organisations and other aid agencies created parallel structures on the ground to undermine and bypass the state. Where once health workers, agricultural extension officers, and food relief distributors had been part of state systems, now they increasingly worked for independent agencies, usually NGOs, and sometimes even competed with state systems. The aid system insured that the foreigners had cars, computers, medicines, etc, which the state could no longer afford to buy. The state made valiant but decreasingly successful efforts to control and coordinate NGO actions.
◆ Bi-lateral and multi-lateral agencies began to force the state to modify its policies. Overtly political pressure was backed by the muscle of the donors; Mozambique had to agree structural adjustment when the donors went on strike and it looked like Mozambicans would starve. But demands were often quite detailed, involving health, education and agriculture policy.
◆ Government was decapacitated. Government workers were increasingly purchased and suborned by foreign agencies, either by simply paying them higher salaries to work for the new aid agencies, or by giving them bribes or perks such as foreign trips so that they would act in the interests of the agencies. Many of the most skilled and experienced Mozambicans began to work in much lower level jobs, even as secretaries, for the United Nations and for NGOs. This created a vicious cycle, decapaciting the government and backing the donors' arguments that they had to take over tasks the government could no longer do. To do these jobs, they often hired Mozambicans from the government - for five or ten times what the government paid them. In the most bizarre cases, the World Bank and IMF paid Mozambican technicians substantial salaries to return to their old desks as Bank consultants - doing the same jobs as before, but for a different paymaster. Smaller agencies and NGOs also suborned Mozambicans - either by simply giving them bribes, or by giving them 'top up money', trips abroad, or even just fancy radios - the quid pro quo was that they gave priority to projects of the NGO handing out the largesse. A particular trick was to

give well paid consultancies in which government staff did work for an NGO but on government time and using government resources. Donors often claim they are doing what they call 'capacity building', but Professor Reginald Green of the Institute of Development Studies accuses donors of consciously 'decapacitating' government - actively reducing its capacity by taking the best people out of government or making them ineffective or unable to work.

Central to this whole process were two linked factors - resources and demoralisation. In a rural district a foreign NGO was wealthy, with cars and other resources, while the local administration had nothing and became dependent on foreign agencies for favours if it was to carry out its work. Favours were available only to local government officials who were compliant. It became apparent, both to officials and to local people, who was in charge, which in turn made local officials demoralised and weak. Officials who could do nothing for their people began to worry more about themselves, accelerating the slide down the corruption spiral.

The same factors worked at provincial and national level. If national officials and even ministers did not do what donors demanded, they were simply bypassed. At national level the problem was compounded by demands from more than 200 donors, which ensured that ministers and officials spent most of the time responding to donors and had little time left to run their own ministries. Each visiting aid official demanded meetings with ministers and threatened to withhold aid if the same briefing was given by an underling. Each donor had different policies and different accounting rules. Mozambican ministers simply had no time for their own analysis and initiatives, so the donors took de facto power away from the state.

Stabilisation and peace

Pressure grew through the late 1980s, but initially Mozambicans held their own, setting economic policies which led to growth while keeping a key role for the state, and keeping some handle on social services. But two changes torpedoed any attempt at Mozambican leadership – the imposition of stabilisation by the International Monetary Fund in 1990, and the UN-led invasion in 1993 that followed the peace accord between Renamo and the government.

From 1984 until 1990, the World Bank had taken the lead, but the leadership passed to the IMF in 1990, and it imposed the first of its severely restrictive economic packages. I show in *Peace without profit: How the IMF blocks rebuilding in Mozambique* (James Currey, Oxford, 1996) that stabilisation had disastrous effects on the economy. But it also sharply undermined the state, in four ways:

◆ Policy changes included privatisation and deregulation, which effectively removed the state from the economy. Virtually all state companies were privatised, with the biggest going to Portuguese and South African companies. The banking system was also being privatised and by 1997 was largely in Portuguese hands. State services such as water and agricultural extension were being privatised; customs administration was taken over by two British firms. The state marketing board was virtually abolished. Deregulation meant that market forces rather than state policy determined all economic decisions.
◆ The World Bank took an increasingly detailed role in setting policy, particularly in transport, education and agriculture. The priority was put on export crop production rather than food.
◆ Sharp cuts in state expenditure reduced the ability of the state to provide social services.
◆ Sharp cuts in government wages pushed two-thirds of civil servants below the poverty line, forcing front line civil servants such as nurses and teachers to be corrupt in order to feed their families.

The end of the war in October 1992 brought a further onslaught on the state. The UN operation in Mozambique (ONUMOZ) was intended to oversee the peace accord, the integration of Renamo into civilian life, and the first multi-party elections. The peace accord explicitly recognised the legitimacy of the government, but ONUMOZ implicitly rejected it. UN Special Representative Aldo Ajello acted liked a colonial governor; the UN sent 8000 troops, vastly more than necessary, and enough civilian staff to fill an entire 8-storey hotel - the largest in Maputo. ONUMOZ cost $1 billion but Mozambique saw little of the money; UN staff and even UN Volunteers had resources undreamed of by Mozambican officials. In preparation for the 1994 election, I saw Mozambican election officials forced to beg lifts from UN Volunteers and foreign observers.

Barring government from rural areas

One consistent international goal has been to keep the state out of rural areas. During the war rural zones were made ungovernable and, if not controlled by Renamo, were turned into ungoverned or empty areas – one-third of the population was forced to flee to the towns or to neighbouring states.

The Mozambican government had attempted to coordinate emergency aid, but this was swept away under ONUMOZ, which took control of aid coordination. Huge amounts of money were given directly to NGOs, particularly by the European Commission, to work independently of government. Thus the international community and not the government was the dominant factor in the return of refugees to their homes.

A major effort was made to restore services in Renamo-controlled areas in ways that made clear that these were not government services; for example, government vaccination teams could only enter some Renamo areas when they wore NGO T-shirts and pretended to be NGO staff.

The IMF and World Bank are preventing post-war reconstruction in rural areas. World Bank money goes to upgrade main roads used to travel to neighbouring countries rather than to serve rural areas. IMF spending caps make it virtually impossible to rebuild the shops, schools, health posts and bridges destroyed during the war. Credit restrictions and the free market mean would-be rural traders cannot borrow the money to reopen rural shops. It means that in rural areas, peasants and especially returned refugees see only the aid agencies and not the state.

Another change is the role of big companies controlling land. Lonrho, which backed the government during the war (while also dealing with Renamo) was rewarded with huge plantations. James Blanchard III, a wealthy backer of Renamo's war, has been given a huge tourism concession in exchange for not backing Renamo in future. Private companies have colonial-style concessions giving them exclusive rights to buy peasant cotton.

Finally, Renamo and the international community have put heavy pressure on Frelimo to give greater power to 'traditional leaders' and chiefs as an alternative to central government at local level.

This is reinforced by the government's own weaknesses. It is proving impossible to decentralise as rapidly as the government wanted, which means that there will be local elected government only in towns and cities. Similarly, the new proposed land law will have formal land use titles only in areas near towns, while in more remote areas there will be a form of collective tenure which will, indeed, protect peasant use rights but which will also give power to traditional leaders instead of the state.

So a form of urban-rural duality is being developed, in which rural areas see less of a state presence and a more dominant role of big (often foreign) companies, aid agencies, and traditional leaders.

Central planning and corruption

It is important to note that the international community has taken control in Mozambique through two means it claims vociferously to oppose: central planning and corruption.

Central planners in Washington in the offices of the IMF and World Bank now have more detailed and more effective control over the Mozambican government and over the economy than Mozambican central planners ever had, and they continue to tighten that control. The international community has a rhetoric of democracy, but Mozambique's new multi-party parliament has no control over the state budget, the economy, agriculture policy, etc.

'Big projects' were dismissed as the foolishness of the socialist era, yet they are now being taken over by foreign capitalists. Lonrho, for example, is running a huge cotton project in the north in ways not dissimilar to that proposed by its original Romanian planners.

But it is corruption which has become the most important lever. When Mozambican officials were honest and acted in what they saw as the best interests of the people, outsiders had little power. Corruption has been essential to allow power to be shifted to outsiders, and it has been encouraged by impoverishing and disempowering Mozambican officials.

The new political class

I opened this article by comparing Mozambique to the British High Street. In both cases the transnational owners need local managers, and in Mozambique the new political class is taking on this role. Not yet fully formed, the new political class is a mix of the old Frelimo leadership and a newer, younger generation of technocrats with US or western European degrees.

At present the minimum wage is about £16 per month. Street pedlars and rural peasants are lucky to earn one-quarter of a minimum wage. By contrast, the new elite earns at least 50 times the minimum wage, and often much more - through consultancies, businesses, salaries as a member of parliament, or corruption. This is enough to live comfortably at a US or European standard, with a nice house, expensive four-wheel drive car, satellite TV dish, trips to South Africa, etc.

The new political class clearly benefits from IMF policies which have hugely widened income differentials. But little of its earnings come from the 'free market'. Maputo journalists talk of the 'goats' who eat whatever grass is available, but plant nothing; no privatisation occurs without at least one high level 'goat' being a partner. MPs award themselves high salaries. University staff and middle level officials earn more from consultancies than from their official salary.

It is a complex process by which the international community has forced Mozambicans to choose to do what the international community wants. It started with people saying, after the apothecary in Romeo and Juliet who reluctantly sells poison, 'My poverty, but not my will, consents'. From local officials up to ministers, Mozambicans agree to do what donors demand because, in the short term, people will be worse off if they don't - urgent food aid, improvements to a school, etc, will only happen if they maintain the good will of the donor. At local level, a blind eye to misconduct, accepting a violated policy, or wearing a donor T-shirt may seem a small price to pay for having a well dug for the local hospital or having transport to visit normally inaccessible areas. At national level, allowing donor officials to sit in what should be government-only meetings and accepting their suggestions of policy changes, buying from donor-favoured contractors, allowing the World Bank and IMF to put officials inside ministries, and even accepting national policy changes seem small prices to pay to prevent mass starvation.

And it makes life easier. Instead of fighting the donors to try to enforce government policy, it is easier to bend. Those who bend find they earn perks like more money, whiskey and video recorders, and even foreign travel. Soon officials feel less like Shakespeare's apothecary and more like Tom Lehrer's Old Dope Peddler - 'doing well by doing good'.

Those who don't bend can find themselves out of a job; at the very least, they don't earn the consultancies that are essential to survival. But those who adapt find themselves moving into the new bourgeoisie and having a much higher living standard, which must be maintained by consultancies or outright corruption. At one level, Maputo economists have become so accustomed to highly paid consultancies with the World Bank and donor agencies that the trade unions have trouble finding skilled economists willing to analyse alternatives to the standard neo-liberal policies – some cannot afford to take unpaid work, while others are afraid that if they write something that goes against the received wisdom of the donors, they will not get future contracts.

The result is a continuum of people. Some who could not stomach the compromises required went into private businesses or went to work for private companies or UN agencies, often abroad. Earning a PhD abroad is a good way to escape. Many try to do the best they can for Mozambique while accepting the lifestyle of the new class and the demands of the international community. Others have become genuine converts to neo-liberalism; they believe they deserve to be rich and that the unfettered free market and foreign dominance really are best for Mozambique. A final group has abandoned any concern for the Mozambican people and is only out for themselves and sees only opportunities for corruption and personal enrichment.

Corruption has become pervasive and corrosive in Mozambique – a far cry from the integrity of fifteen years ago. And it isn't only Mozambicans who are corrupt. Nor is it just small-time kickbacks and consultancies. Donors have been prepared to allow tens of thousands to starve to death in order to force policy changes; donors threatened to withhold millions of dollars in aid if favoured companies were not given land; one of the most important donors was prepared to ease up on pressure for hostile policy changes if the government signed an unfavourable contract with a particular company.

This is the new era of global free enterprise where everything has a price. It is an era in which the state has been reduced to implementing policies decided by central planners in Washington. And it is the era in which Mozambique's new political class feels it has no choice but to be reasonably well paid managers for foreign owners.

Corruption and the State

I Introduction

Laurence Cockcroft

The final flight from power of Mobutu was perhaps the most dramatic retribution yet wreaked on an African head of state for 'Grand Corruption'.[1] The analyses of his financial empire and businesses, which became public only as he fell, betray the extent of the connivance of the west in this most malfeasant of regimes. The fact that the Swiss banks, after thirty years of financial profit taking, were only prepared to freeze the assets of 'The Guide' as he fled Kinshasha is eloquent of this connivance.

However the fact that Mobutu was able to build up offshore assets of between $4 billion and $5 billion, accumulated at a rate of approximately $250m per year from the mid 1960s to the mid 1980s, is only an indicator of what can be achieved by a regime devoted to Grand Corruption. A level of extraction on a comparable scale has been achieved by several other regimes in Africa: in 1995 Dr Pius Okigbo, revered doyen of Nigerian economists, reported that in the previous three years approximately $12 bn had been syphoned off Nigeria's oil revenues, for which no account could be made. In Kenya from 1991-3 the current Vice President, who was then also Minister of Finance, George Saitoti, was closely involved in the 'Goldenberg' scandal by which $300m was syphoned from the public exchequer to provide an incentive premium for the export of

---

1. George Moody-Stuart, *Grand Corruption - How Business Bribes Damage Developing Countries*, World View Publishing, Oxford 1997.

gold and diamonds which, in fact, never existed. Yet, speaking to a public rally in Nairobi in 1995 President Moi could say: 'People say Saitoti has stolen, from whom has he stolen?'

Few countries have been immune to the actual or potential dangers of such deals, including those with a historic commitment to serving the common people. In 1994 and 1995 the Government of Tanzania was engaged in a serious negotiation with Siemens Plessey of the UK to purchase a complex radar system for military and civilian purposes at a cost of £100 m. In a deal put together by Bankers' Trust, the system was to be purchased by forward sales of gold over ten years at a fixed price and all of Tanzania's gold reserves were to be physically held in London by Bankers' Trust. Fortunately, the Governor of the Central Bank of Tanzania was able to fight the deal consistently over a period of a year, eventually aided by courageous domestic media coverage which was finally reflected in the international press. The government of President Mkapa has steadfastly refused to contemplate resuscitation of the deal. If implemented, however, it would have accounted for about 40 per cent of Tanzania's export earnings in any one year and is likely to have earned outgoing members of the previous government a huge commission.

Corrupt deals on this scale have a serious negative effect on the macro-economy of the country in question. Most of the income generated through deals of this kind finds its way into offshore financial havens in Europe and elsewhere. Where the scam is constructed around the purchase of equipment, especially in the military sector, deals will often be financed through export credits which have to be repaid over time, and accumulate as part of the country's external debt. The servicing of this debt, if it occurs, will constitute a direct burden on the foreign exchange earnings of the country. The majority of Nigeria's external debt is of this kind. The combination of capital flight, the erosion of government revenue, and a disastrous loss of export earnings are three of the key costs of Grand Corruption.

Yet these are frequently not the types of corruption which most concern the farmer in the 'shamba', or the market trader selling maize meal by the basket. Their concern, as recent polls have shown, is the extent to which bribes have become the key to accessing public services which were originally set up to be free at the point of delivery. The most exhaustive description of this process is contained in the report by Justice Joseph Warioba (a former prime minister) into the 'State of Corruption' in Tanzania in December 1996. A part of the English summary of this report is published below. It demonstrates in frightening detail how the worker and peasant in Tanzania - for whom a whole state system was constructed in the 1960s and 70s - is now victim to the need for financial survival of an ill-paid civil service.

The findings of the Warioba report were echoed in a survey recently carried out by the Zimbabwe chapter of Transparency International, in the form of a 'Vulnerability Assessment Survey', which explored the awareness of corruption in the public, private and NGO sectors. It found that: all of the people interviewed knew that corruption existed and 65 per cent admitted that they had been personally involved (either voluntarily or by force of circumstance); some saw corruption as purely functional as it enabled low paid functionaries to supplement their salaries; almost all saw corruption as adverse to development (only 6 per cent had the reverse view). It is evident that the issue of 'everyday corruption' is very alive in the public mind and that its dangers are recognised.

To recognise a danger, however, is not to diffuse it. As the Warioba commission suggests, and as observers of the Nigerian scene have recognised for some years, the extent of both everyday and grand corruption may now itself constitute the norm rather than represent some deviation from it. The implications of this for the web of loyalties to country and state which are an integral part of social construction, and deeply necessary in societies divided by tribe and clan, are gloomy. For example the courageous Kenyan NGO, Clarion, carried out a survey of 600 people in 1994 and asked the question : 'Who can be blamed most for corruption ?' Nearly 70 per cent of respondents considered government itself should receive the most blame.

There is no question that there are vital forces working within African society against corruption today. These include NGOs, politicians who have come to power in recent multi party elections, and, perhaps most powerfully, various denominations of the Church. The task adopted by these groups and individuals may be best described as turning the norm of corruption into the exception. Their progress will depend on reform-minded governments adopting the substance of their proposals, and on the extent to which politicians fighting for political power in elections see that the public will support those who are credible in their opposition to endemic corruption.

Corruption and the State

II The Warioba Report

Joseph Warioba

This is an edited part of the English language summary of the Warioba Report, published in Tanzania in 1996.

1   Our country has witnessed an alarming increase in corruption activities which are associated with public servants on the one hand and the citizens who are the consumers of public service on the other. Corruption has been accentuated by loopholes which are inherent in procedures, temptations, greed for power and profit, meagreness in incomes and erosion of ethical standards. Moreover, state organs which were expected to restrain this increase also have succumbed to this disease and therefore have left the people without an escape route.
2   The growth in corruption in the 1990s was accentuated by the close relationship between Government and Political leaders on the one hand and businessmen who engage in corruption on the other. This relationship was used to benefit the business interests of these businessmen and ultimately became a fertile ground for breeding corruption.
4   The Commission has found out that those who solicit and receive bribes are divided into two groups as follows:
(a) *The first group includes those who receive bribes as a result of their meagre*

incomes and low standard of living; and what they receive only helps make ends meet. This type of corruption is rampant in all sectors of the economy and social services as follows:

(i) *Education* : Corruption is demanded and given during the registration of children in schools; to enable pupils pass examinations; to enable students obtain placement in secondary schools and colleges; transfers and opportunity to repeat a class. Moreover, teachers give bribes in order to be promoted, to be transferred and to be given placements.

(ii) *Health:* Patients are forced to offer bribes at hospitals in order to: be treated, x-rayed, allocated a bed in the ward or operated upon.

(iii) *Home Affairs:* Policemen receive bribes to protect criminals; to arrest innocent people and take to court on framed charges as a way of soliciting bribes; and traffic policemen accept bribes from drivers who breach road regulations. Moreover, Immigration Officers accept bribes to issue: passports, visas and residence permits to undeserving foreigners. Prison Wardens solicit bribes in order to give favour to prisoners and remand prisoners.

(iv) *Finance*: Corruption is offered to employees of the Income Tax Department during tax assessment and tax exemptions. Executive Officers in the Ministry, Department and Parastatals demand bribes in order to authorise payment for goods and services supplied; and Auditors demand bribes in order to conceal deficiencies discovered during audit. On the side of Financial Institutions, clients are asked to offer bribes in order to be given or not to repay loans; or to be paid faked insurance claims. Retirees and retrenches are forced to offer bribes in order to be paid their benefits.

(v) *Judiciary:* Court Clerks demand bribes in order to open files or send them where they are required and to hide files of accused persons. Personal Secretaries and Typists accept bribes in order to produce copies of judgements for various crimes. Regarding Magistrates, corruption is offered in order to be given soft sentences, to reduce penalties, to withdraw charges, to give bail and order Court Injunctions.

(vi) *Office of the Attorney General:* State Attorneys accept bribes when attending to court cases; to authorise the signing of contracts which are against the national interest; and to give advice in favour of those giving the bribe. Moreover, independent Advocates give bribes to Magistrates and Judges so that they can give verdicts favouring their clients.

(vii) *Trade*: Trade Officers solicit and accept bribes from businessmen who trade without licences; and they demand bribes when issuing Trading Licences.

(viii) *Employment*: Personnel Officers receive bribes during recruitment of workers. Moreover, they demand bribes from junior officers so that they can promote them; to assign them responsibilities; to send them for training, seminars or duty trips.

(ix) *Lands*: Land Officers demand bribes during surveying and allocation of plots, valuation of crops and in issuing Certificates of Title. They also accept bribes and make multiple allocation of plots, to survey and allocate plots in areas reserved for community services. Moreover, bribes are offered in the allocation of Government houses to undeserving people.

(x) *Natural Resources and Tourism*: Forest Officers receive bribes to give permission for felling more trees than are allowed in the licences or to let free culprits who are caught with unauthorised forest products. Wildlife Officers also receive bribes to let poachers go scot free. On the fisheries side, fishermen caught using unauthorised fishing gear or explosives give bribes so that they can be let free.

(xi) *Energy and Minerals*: Employees of the state company TANESCO demand bribes in order to interconnect new applicants. Employees of the Water Department too receive bribes during water-rationing to favour certain areas or in order to connect clients to the main distribution pipes. Employees of the Mining Department demand bribes in order to issue mining or prospecting licences.

(xii) *Works and Communications*: Officers of the Ministry of Works receive bribes in order to give favour in awarding Tenders; to accept upward variation of contracts; to conceal the weaknesses of contractors; and in approving payments. Moreover, bribes are offered at road blocks in order to let the vehicles through; Telephone Operators and telecommunications technicians are bribed by unscrupulous businessmen so that they are allowed to make international calls using other clients' telephone numbers particularly those of Government offices and of Government servants and Parastatals. Moreover, Officers manning Weigh Bridges solicit and receive bribes in order to let through vehicles which are heavier than the carrying capacity of the road.

(xiii) *The Ministry of Labour*: Labour Officers demand and receive bribes from dismissed workers so that they can be reinstated and foreigners give them bribes so that they can be permitted to work in positions which could be performed by nationals.

(xiv) *Media Institutions*: Reporters accept bribes in order to publish or not to publish information which glorifies or destroys the reputation of certain persons or institutions.

(xv) *Local Governments*: Employees of Town and District Councils receive bribes during recruitment of staff, promotions, issuing of trading licences for unauthorised areas. Members of Ward Reconciliation Councils and Councillors receive bribes in order to give certain favours. Town and District Council leaders demand and receive bribes in order to approve and award tenders to private companies, to allocate plots and market stalls through favouritism.

(b) The second type of corruption involved high level leaders and public servants whose involvement in corruptive practices is a result of excessive greed for wealth accumulation and money. These are people whose earnings are adequate to meet their basic needs and they have enough property and money. This group uses various tactics to solicit and receive bribes:-

(i) Leaders who are supposed to take important national decisions are bribed by businessmen in order for them to take decisions which are in the interest of those businessmen; they offer Chairmanships and Directorships of Boards of Parastatals through favouritism and without taking into account professional knowledge, ability and national interest and they have interfered in executive decisions for such decisions like allocation of 'Hunting Blocks' or allocation of plots in areas not permitted by law.

(ii) Chief Executive Officers receive bribes in order to breach Tendering Rules and Regulations; to make various tax exemptions and to conclude construction contracts with private companies without due regard for the national interest. Chief Executives and Executive Officers have also been concealing sub-standard construction jobs and deficient equipment or services and have authorised payment so that one is paid commission; and the offering of scholarship for overseas studies through corruption.

(iii) Politicians offer bribes to Members of Executive Committees within Political Parties or to the people during elections so that they can vote for them or their candidates.

(iv) Members of Parliament have been offering bribes to voters so that they can elect them; lodging fake claims in their parliamentary activities; giving bribes to Reporters so that they can publish good stories about the MP's activities; and have demanded gifts from private and parastatal industries when they visit them. MPs who are members of various Parliamentary Committees demand from Chief Executive Officers of parastatals and Departments they deal with entertainment, money, and they are paid, as well as Board and Lodging.

Reasons for growth and expansion of corruption

4   The enormous economic difficulties that befell the nation in the early 1970s forced the Government to take political, legal and economic measures to deal with the situation. The measures were aimed at enabling a poor citizen to obtain scarce essential needs at fair prices. The scarcity of commodities resulted in inflationary pressures in the economy and the whole distribution system was disrupted by a few people who wanted to obtain extra benefits. Because public servants' activities were restricted by the Leadership Code, they started inventing ways of earning extra incomes to make ends meet; and in most cases the extra incomes were from illegal sources.

... ...

6   The liberalisation of internal trade policy was followed by changes in the political and social philosophy of our country. Businessmen began to draw near our leaders so that they could help them beat the legal system for private gain. By the beginning of the 90s, some of the top leaders had already been compromised and were engulfed by corruption.

People's view

7   Many people who gave their views to the Commission either in writing or by personal appearance said that corruption is rampant in the country for lack of a leadership committed to its eradication. Leaders appointed to help the President fight this scourge do not seem to realise the gravity of the problem in our social fabric. Whenever a citizen reports to leaders and senior officers incidents of corruption amongst the lower cadres under the said leaders, no action is taken against them due to either involvement of the leaders and senior officers themselves in the corruption ring or because they no longer care about the people's social problems and see the problem as something normal. Besides, the leaders divulge to the suspects the sources of the secret information reaching them. The people are thus worried that if they mention names of corrupt elements, they will become victims of persecution by State Organs in collaboration with the people they accuse or actually suffer bodily harm from the victims being accused of corruption.

Leadership and Ethics

14 It has become evident that the greatest source of corruption in the country is not the poor economy and low salaries; although these too have played some part. The greatest source is the laxity of leadership in overseeing the implementation of established norms. The absence of clear guidelines on accountability of leaders in their respective positions - be it in political leadership or senior administrative or management positions, is part of that weakness.

15 It is obvious that if we want to rid ourselves of corruption, we must begin by cleaning the top leadership ranks. We must remember that the most important job of leadership is 'to solve problems'. Therefore, a good leader is that one who puts in place elaborate systems of solving community problems - i.e. general problems of development; the economy; defence and security; etc. One important condition of good management systems is that they should be clear and should enable the leadership to take quick and just decisions. Moreover, good management systems of any institution - be it a public or private institution - which caters for the public, must be easy to understand and implement and, therefore, must not be a burden to the ordinary citizen - especially the underprivileged whose scope of knowledge and understanding is limited.

16 The biggest national task henceforth is to ensure that the country is led by people who believe in and respect ethical standards. The verdict on this principle is what the people are eagerly waiting for and that is what will also decide the fate of this country. It is a verdict which will aim at developing a 'National Culture' which shall enable the nation to clearly identify who between its many national leaders including those of Opposition Parties truly deserves to lead this Nation. We say including members of the opposition because all these leaders are standard bearers of our national trust. *If the leaders of the opposition parties will be people who give and receive bribes, they cannot criticise the Government and expect their voices to be respected.* It is not only the Government leaders who give and receive bribes, but this involves all the Tanzanian people as a whole.

... ...

19 There is no questioning the fact that the country's leadership is being accused of being involved in acts of corruption. There is an urgent need to take stern action to clean up the leadership ranks in order to restore respect and public confidence in the leadership. After the exercise of cleaning up the leadership, it is imperative to ensure that those who remain as well as the new leaders do not fall into the same trap. In fact, there is an urgent need to begin protecting the new leaders. Some of the bad habits include the practice of leaders and senior public servants, Government, Parastatals and Political Parties to make friends with rich businesssmen; the receipt of presents from such friends; the misuse of their positions by taking decisions which benefit them privately instead of caring for the national interest. Such habits inhibit the monitoring and control of the junior officers in their delivery of public services. It is thus recommended that the following steps be taken without delay:

(a) Leaders and employees of: Government; parastatals; political parties and civil organisations should be required to declare to authority the value of any present and ask the person concerned to pay for it; otherwise the present should be sold and the proceeds paid into the coffers of government or the relevant party or organisation.

(b) Leaders should be cautious in encouraging the habit of having private visits at their houses from businessmen and rich people who are not their blood relatives or friends of the leaders or servants concerned. On that basis, leaders and servants should take great care lest they lose their jobs because of receiving visitors at the home and presents sent to them personally or to their families. Indeed, they should strictly observe the rule that official business should be transacted in the office. It is up to the leaders and officers concerned to ensure that this is observed. They are the people who know the boundaries between relatives and friends and those who are after them because of their Government positions etc.

c) In order to ensure that everyone is held accountable for the responsibilities under him/her there is a need to define the boundaries or limits of responsibility between the Executive Officers of Ministries, Departments and Parastatals on the one hand, and Ministers or Members of Parastatal Boards of Directors on the other. The functions of the Minister and Members of Boards of Directors are to initiate or approve policies and to monitor the implementation of those policies. The responsibility for implementation lies with the Chief Executive Officers and the Heads of various Departments of Government and Parastatals.

(d) Leadership is a trust bestowed on an individual by the people. It is thus imperative that every leader should ensure that this trust is carefully guarded and is used in the interest of the people and the nation generally. For the respectability of any Nation depends on the respect that the people have for their leaders. Therefore, officers heading Departments; Ministries; or Parastatals, are expected to be accountable for any misdemeanour occuring in the institutions they lead or regarding their own conduct which bring shame to the Nation. It is therefore their duty to ensure that they establish Management Systems which will enable them to know what is happening in their respective domains and thus make sure that they make everyone accountable for one's misdeeds before such shame becomes their own responsibility. For example if people complain about corruption in a certain Department or Ministry or Parastatal, the Head of that Department or Parastatal should be accountable. This principle should apply equally to District and Regional Heads, i.e. District and Regional Commissioners as well as District Regional Heads of Department.

(e) In order to protect the President from appointing too many people, the procedures of using the Civil Service Commission; the Local Government Service Commission; the Police and Prison Services Commission; the Judicial Service Commission; the Teachers' Service Commission, etc.,should be strengthened so that the President is involved in the appointment of only a few top leaders or officers. Moreover, most of the appointments should be made after receiving recommendations from these Commissions through the Central Establishments Department which is versed in the principles. Jobs which require to be competed for by all government servants should be advertised and candidates processed through interviews conducted by the relevant Commission before recommendations are sent to the President for final appointment. In that way, Heads of Government Departments will be vetted before they are employed at levels where they will directly be responsible for advising Government. With regard to Parastatals, the President should be responsible only for the appointment of the Chairman of the Board. With the exception of Chief Executives of sensitive Parastatals like the Bank of Tanzania (BoT) and the National Bank of Commerce (NBC), all other Executives should be appointed by the respective Boards after they have been interviewed.

20 In the process of cleaning up the leadership ranks, it will be evident that there are some rich people who have been the source of corruption ... In order to ensure that the bad habits of these rich people too are stopped, it is recommended that the following steps be taken:-

(a) All those who are discovered to have been a source of injustice and breach of established rules and regulations should be severely punished by nationalisation and forfeiture of their property in accordance with the law. Live examples are erecting buildings in areas which were planned for public use, like Building of Shopping Centres, Dispensaries, Schools, Religious monuments, etc., or areas which were meant for public recreation. Obviously such decisions must have been made by breaching of regulations.

(b) The concerned rich people should also be required to account, in accordance with guidelines to be designed by Government, which of our leaders own shares in their companies and how they were acquired? If the shares were paid for by the Company, they should be acquired by Government. But if they were paid for by the leaders themselves, then they be allowed to retain them...

21 The people of Tanzania are very concerned by the growing corruption which is demanded by public servants in the lower ranks because of the difficult economic situation. The situation is so bad that the people have despaired and do not believe that they can receive any justice without giving bribes. For example, parents in the rural areas believe that they cannot register their children in schools without dipping into their pocket; that they cannot obtain justice in Government organs including the Courts without money for bribery, etc. The people have reached this misdirected conclusion because of two reasons. First, most people, particularly in the rural areas, do not know their constitutional rights. Corruption concerns the givers (the people who need services), and the receivers (public servants in Government and Parastatals). If the people generally know their rights properly and therefore refuse to buy those rights by giving bribes, corruption will die a natural death. The people need to be educated about their rights so that they can demand them wherever they think that they are being unreasonably denied or delayed. This is where the media assumes special responsibility to the people. The media is capable of educating the public about their rights in society. Indeed, because they are knowledgeable about the National Code of Ethics and possess the expertise and ability to do research, the media can help to expose all those who go against the national code of ethics by demanding bribes. If their information is accurate and true, it will be easy for the national leadership to call upon a leader to account for his/her actions.

22 The second problem, which is more serious, is that even if the people know their rights and therefore refuse to buy them by exposing the corrupt elements

instead, the public appear to have despaired because *the leaders in whom they had placed trust and who they expected to be their saviours, are themselves engulfed by corruption.* The Tanzania public has failed to expose those who solicit and receive bribes for lack of clean and responsible leadership in the Government Organs concerned like the Police, Judiciary, the Anti-Corruption Bureau and the Department of National Security. *Thus the greatest task before the Government itself, Parastatals and, indeed, the Political Parties is to clean up the leadership ranks currently in power. After that it will be necessary to take steps to develop a cadre of leadership which is genuinely committed to fighting the scourge of corruption at all levels by taking action against all who are exposed. By so doing, we shall have restored public confidence in the state apparatus and therefore encouraged the speed of eradicating corruption in the country.*

... ...

Immediate steps for implementation regarding leaders

29 Our country has been appointing Commissions to inquire into various problems. With the exception of a few Commissions - *viz.* the Nsekela and the Nyalali and the Mtei [and the Nyirabu] Commissions part of whose recommendations have been implemented - most of the Commissions' recommendations have ended gathering dust in the shelves of various offices.

30 There is a danger that this Commission too will end the same way; and especially when we recall that this is not the first Commission on Corruption. Besides, because corruption begins with the leaders themselves who are expected to oversee the implementation of this report, it becomes even more difficult. Therefore, any recommendation made concerning the implementation of this report must aim at overcoming past weaknesses.

31 ... Most of the leaders and functional officers with whom the Commission discussed do not appear to understand the seriousness of the problem and many of them believe that much of what is said about corruption is just hearsay aimed at tarnishing people's images. What is even more alarming is the fact that most of the functional leaders appear to believe that corruption is more widespread in the lower and middle grades of the public service. Their explanations of steps which have been taken in the past to combat corruption concern public servants in the lower and middle grades. For example, the Police Force has been taking steps against policemen connected with corruption and they submitted to the Commission a list of one hundred twenty three (123) policemen who had been

dismissed from the service because of corruption in the last six years (1991-1996). Of these, 120 are of the rank of Constable and only one was of the rank of Assistant Superintendent. Not a single Senior Officer was terminated from service because of corruption. But the opinions of many, including lower ranking policemen, say that the high ranking Police Officers are the greatest villains of corruption.

... ...

35 The greatest villains of corruption are not those who receive the minimum wage. They are people who are well paid ... For people like these, raising the salaries alone will not deter them from taking bribes. It will only help them raise the value of corruption!

36 On the side of top leaders, the situation is more pathetic. Every leader sees himself as being clean ... Government leaders blame the Judiciary and the Police as the corrupt ones. Judiciary blames the Government. Members of Parliament blame the Government and the Judiciary. Leaders of the Ruling Party blame the Government and its organs and leaders of Opposition Parties blame the Ruling Party, the Government and its Organs ... The utterances of leaders have become a strategy for power-mongering. Once these people are thrust into power, they change and assume a defensive stance. The Commission views this to be the most difficult problem of all in the struggle against corruption.

37 The Commission believes that in order to fight corruption, initial steps must concern leadership. When the President ascended to office, he declared his assets publicly; he refused to be hero-worshipped; he refused to have news about him to be in the front pages of newspapers; and he refused to have his portrait on the currency Notes. Except for the Vice-President, no other leaders have emulated his example. Instead, other leaders are behaving to the contrary. Members of Parliament are demanding protection; they want to be saluted; they demand so many other rights which to the ordinary citizen is just a dream - but they have not even declared their own assets.

... ...

38 The fight against corruption is everyone's responsibility and especially leaders. Every leader must be seen to be clean before the people; he should be seen to take stern measures against all corrupt elements in his area of leadership; and if he cannot do so, he should resign even if he himself is not accused of being corrupt. The struggle against corruption should not be left to the President alone.

The role of the NUM in South Africa

I Introduction

Vic Allen

The NUM, with 150,000 members, is the largest trade union in South Africa. It is also a disciplined, politically aware union that is capable of exerting significant pressure on the ANC government. It has a privileged access to the government in part because of its industrial power, and in part because of its role in the liberation struggle. The ANC has a strong sense of loyalty to those countries and organisations which assisted it in the fight against apartheid. The NUM is high on that list. It was formed in 1982 following a resolution by the Council of Unions of South Africa, a supporter of black consciousness, to organise black mineworkers. Many similar resolutions had been passed in earlier years but they had been unsuccessful.

The problems in the way of organising black mineworkers were multitudinous. The vast majority of them were in the gold, coal and diamond mines, which were largely owned by six mining conglomerates who, until 1982, were willing to use violence to prevent mineworkers from being organised. The mining houses which owned and controlled at least two thirds of the South African economy were represented by the Chamber of Mines. It represented an extreme case in the imbalance of class forces. On the other side of the class spectrum, the mineworkers presented acute difficulties for those who wanted to organise them. They were migrant workers from every country in southern Africa, who were employed on yearly contracts and compulsorily repatriated when their contracts expired. They spoke diverse languages. The vast majority were illiterate. Whilst in the mines they were incarcerated in mining compounds and housed in giant single-sex hostels which were policed by the mines and infiltrated with informers. More than 95 per cent of them were unskilled workers paid the same basic wage rate without any promotion. It was illegal until 1987 to allow any of them to perform a skilled task. In short, all the obstacles in the way of organising a union were encapsulated in the situation of the black mineworkers. In addition, to try to organise them, or to express a willingness to be organised were life-threatening until after 1982.

Cyril Ramaphosa, a legal assistant to CUSA, was given the job of carrying out its resolution. He obtained the help of about a dozen black personnel assistants who were working in various gold mines, and a financial grant from the Danish trade union movement. Within five months they had recruited 12,000 members, held an inaugural conference, and borrowed the name of the British NUM which Ramaphosa admired. In 1983 they obtained access agreements to allow union organisers into the compounds and recognition agreements to allow them to negotiate wage rates. The following year they held the first legal strike of black mineworkers in the history of mining, and engaged in a series of violent struggles against scabs and those reluctant to join the new union. Within five years the union had almost 300,000 members and was prepared to take the mine owners on. In August of 1987 the union called a national strike which lasted for three weeks until the mine owners, principally the Anglo American Corporation, threatened to dismiss every striker. Fifty thousand members of the union were dismissed and in many areas the union's structure was demolished. But the strike was not a failure, for the test had not been whether it would win but whether it could survive an attempt by the mine owners to destroy it. No other black South African union had survived that test. The NUM survived, rebuilt its organisation, recouped its lost members, and slowly grew again without making any concessions to the mine owners.

The NUM had not confined its activities to industrial matters, because it quickly recognised that without the destruction of apartheid none of its simple industrial aims were attainable. After two years Ramaphosa had rejected black consciousness. After three years he was actively campaigning for the ANC and the South African Communist Party, though it was illegal to do so. In 1985 the union resigned from CUSA and played a central role in organising COSATU as, in effect, the trade union wing of the liberation struggle. In 1986 the union elected Nelson Mandela as its Honorary Life President, though he was still in prison. The following year it adopted the Freedom Charter which was the ANC's policy declaration of 1955. Many of its officials and members engaged in the township struggles of the 1980s. Some were killed while many were arrested and imprisoned. So many of its officials joined the illegal ANC and communist organisations that when these organisations were unbanned black mineworkers formed their biggest industrial segments. Then when the first democratic election was held in 1994 the NUM was one of the few unions able to provide the ANC with finance and physical help. Its credentials in the struggle were impeccable.

Throughout these dramatic and traumatic changes the NUM never lost its political direction. It has maintained its class position and confronts both the mine owners and the government in its pursuit of its members' interests. But it is aware of the pitfalls in the way of achieving a democratic socialist South Africa, and has resolved to assist in avoiding them. It has a strictly socialist agenda and is already confronting the government over its acceptance of World Bank economic policies and its use of authoritarian measures to stifle political dissent. It is the only organisation in South Africa able to do this and survive.

The role of the NUM in South Africa II

James Motlasi

This is the presidential address by James Motlasi, President of the South African National Union of Mineworkers, at their ninth national congress.

When our last Congress met in March 1994 the country was preparing for the first democratic general election in the history of South Africa. We had struggled, fought and waited for 342 years for the principle that was embodied in that moment. It was a unique and historic achievement which we should always use as a measuring rod whenever we ask ourselves what is possible in the future.

The NUM played a key role in the struggle which led to the election and in the election campaign itself and we are proud of it. It had worked both through Cosatu and independently as a trade union standard bearer for the liberation struggle. In the midst of the township uprisings and the state of emergency in 1986 we defied the nationalist government by electing Nelson Mandela as our Honorary President and in the following year we went further by adopting the Freedom Charter and its Socialist aspirations. Our members were defiant and militant in the cause of freedom.

But we did more than put our collective power behind the struggle. Our union, along with other unions, was a training ground for leaders. During the apartheid years we were virtually the only legal bodies where young blacks could learn about administration and decision-making and at the same time practice leadership. After the unbannings, therefore, we were able to provide the movement with people to help take us through the transitional stage to a fully democratic society. Our union released a number of officials who did valuable work, but one of them, I think, deserves special mention at this point of time. There will be occasions when we will celebrate the others.

I am sure, Comrades, that you will agree with me that through our decision to release Cyril Ramaphosa we provided the ANC and the country with a person of unique qualities. Without Cyril's diplomatic and negotiating ability, in harness with the skills of Comrade Joe Slovo, it is unlikely that the transition to democracy would have been so smooth, painless, peaceful and speedy. Nor would we have had such an easy passage in getting one of the world's most progressive Constitutions adopted by the various political factions in this country. I think we would be failing as comrades if we did not pay special tribute to our former general secretary. Cyril Ramaphosa and the NUM have a special relationship. We grew up together; we matured together; we are like family. We cannot forget or ignore that fact. He is still one of us.

The achievements

The NUM has benefited already from the new democracy. Our right to act collectively and to strike is now enshrined in law. The new Labour Relations Act, though not perfect from our point of view, has removed racial discrimination from the field of industrial relations and provides us with the right to bargain again with our employers. The mine owners always treated bargaining rights as if they were their property to be handed to us as a gift provided we went on our knees and behaved ourselves. On numerous occasions mine managements have withdrawn bargaining facilities because we did not respond like puppets. But that is now history and we are going to make sure that it is never repeated.

Our greatest gain so far, however, has been the Mine Health and Safety Act. For the first time black mineworkers can participate on an equal basis with white miners in consultation with mine managers in the formulation and application of health and safety measures. Since 1982 we have been demanding the right to refuse to work in dangerous conditions. Now we have it. We also have the right to elect our own safety representatives. The Act by itself cannot prevent occupational diseases, accidents and disasters. But it provides us with a framework to make that possible.

There have been other changes. We no longer have to go on our knees to get access to government ministers. We just have to knock on doors and they open. They frequently come to us. This was illustrated clearly during the critical negotiations over the Labour Relations Act when the employers were pressing for the inclusion of a right to lockout. Our views prevailed for the first time. Nor are our feelings and sensitivities during and after tragedies ignored by the government as they were in the past. When the Vaal Reefs disaster occurred in May 1995, with the loss of 104 lives, the government declared it a national disaster and contributed R5 million to the Vaal Reefs disaster fund. This was important to us.

There is no comparison between this humane and civilised response to our grief and the callous treatment of black mineworkers after the Coalbrook disaster in 1960, when 437 were killed in a single roof fall and the government refused even to send condolences to the bereaved black families. Nor does it compare with our treatment after the Kinross disaster in 1986, when 177 were killed in a polyurethane fire. Then Gencor held its own Memorial Service in Afrikaans and the NUM called a national day of mourning in defiance of both the mine owners and the government.

It is not simply a matter of pride that these changes are important to us. They reflect a swing in power relations in our favour. It is a real gain that we have direct access to Ministers and even to the President. Big business still has too much power in relation to government but it no longer monopolises the arena of consultation with it. It is a great achievement that legislation which had always been used to suppress us is now rightly tilted in our favour.

These gains, however, have to be put into perspective. They are not gifts from the government. We have not been especially favoured. We have simply had our rights as citizens restored to us. Moreover, it would be wrong for the employers to think that they have been penalised. The balance has been tilted slightly from them towards us so that we are now in a better position to develop and protect the interests of our members on grounds of equality with them. But what we must always remember is that what we have achieved so far we have fought for and that if we are to improve our position we must continue fighting. There are no free lunches in our business. We have no guarantee that future governments will be as friendly towards us as this one. It is for this reason that we must give priority to building and strengthening our organisation so that it is a more effective fighting force. Our future lies in our own hands.

Understanding trade unionism

I cannot emphasis too much that we must view South African society not just in terms of the struggle between mineworkers and mine owners but in class terms with wide international implications. The oppression our workers suffer is common to varying extents throughout the capitalist world. It is, I must add, nothing to do with colour. White workers suffer along with black workers. This world-wide conflict, moreover, has been bitterly fought. Many thousands of workers have been killed in battles with employers, the police and the army. Most have occurred in the developed industrial nations but some of them have been in South Africa, as many of our members know.

I am talking about class conflict in this way so that you may understand the kind of opposition we face and why we need to be determined and vigilant. I have no intention of encouraging you, or anyone else, to go and fight at the barricades. I am not saying that you should go on strike on every possible occasion. There are different ways of waging the class struggle. It can be done through political action and industrial action. It can be done through negotiation and confrontation. It is my view that in the first instance we should always try and resolve our differences with employers and the government through negotiation and to use strikes only as a weapon of the last resort. But we should always keep our weapon bright, shiny and sharpened, ready to use at any minute.

We must always remember when we are negotiating with employers, managers and government ministers that we are not engaged in some kind of game. Nor are we there to serve our own ego or career ambitions. We are not on a gravy train or a stepping stone to political office. We are there solely to represent our members' interests. That must be our only purpose.

So whilst we may reach bargains with the employers we must never make private deals with them which sell-out the workers and undermine their solidarity. Those who do that are traitors to our cause and should be treated as such. All who work for the NUM should remember that it is bigger than any one of us. We are the cogs in a big machine. We are not the machine itself.

Some people understand all of this because of their own, personal struggles against poverty and exploitation. But most have to learn about it because employers and the state control the mass media and use it to convince workers that they should live in harmony with employers and not question the system which gives them the right to control their lives. We have to counter that type of propaganda. For this reason I want our union to launch an education campaign to bring a real understanding of the nature of capitalist society to our rank and file members, to our shop stewards and branch committees, to our full-time officials and to everyone who works for it so that the union will have a strong politically conscious foundation from which to serve its members.

The brain drain

We all know that many of the skills we require in our officials and staff come not just from formal learning but also from doing the job. Many aspects of what we do cannot be taught in a formal way. It follows that, provided we have adequate training, the more experience they have the more efficient they are likely to be. Here, however, we have a problem which is not of our making. We are suffering from a 'brain drain'.

I do not have to go into detail to explain what I mean by this term. You all know through your own experiences the kind of education we have had and how Bantu education has impaired our ability to do skilled and administrative work. You also know that as a result of the Bantu educational system, our country is desperately short of black people with skills in science, technology, organisation and administration. The problem the society is facing today is that the generation we are drawing on to administer the state, to run our public and para-statal services and to take over management positions in private industry, received Bantu education in the 1970s and 1980s.

In that period about 20 per cent of the black population had no education at all, 65 per cent were not literate in their own languages and as many as 90 per cent had not reached Standard Seven which meant they were not literate in English or Afrikaans. Only three per cent had reached Standard Ten while a tiny number, comprising 0.06 per cent of the black population, had university degrees, mostly in education and the social sciences. Hardly any blacks had degrees in science and engineering. When some years ago the union sent 19 mineworkers to Cuba to study mining engineering there were only two blacks in South Africa with mining engineering degrees and neither of them was a practising mining engineer.

We have had, therefore, a tiny pool of people from which to draw to help administer our country since the elections in April 1994. The result is that there are virtually boundless opportunities for young people with organisational and administrative experience to gain promotion, obtain high salaries and enjoy a standard of living which was unimaginable for them just a few years ago.

This is where trade unions, and the NUM in particular, enter the scene, for until 1994 we, along with the churches, were the only organisations which provided blacks with training and experience in administration and decision-making. Ours were the only organisations where blacks could handle budgets. Not surprisingly, we have lost and are still losing some of our most efficient staff - the heads of departments and skilled organisers - to work for government and para-statal bodies with conditions of work and salaries we can never hope to match. The result is that our union is suffering from a 'brain drain'. It is not, moreover, a one-off loss. We recruit new officials, train them, give them experience and then along come outside agencies with their tempting offers of employment and we have to start all over again.

I am not complaining about this process. In one sense I am proud that we are able to take part in it. The denial of education and training for blacks is one of the most destructive legacies of apartheid and unless we overcome it we shall not fulfil our election promises to the people. The NUM has a responsibility to help and wishes to do so.

But at the same time, I have to admit that this brain drain is holding the union back. We are not the worst affected union by any means but the problem, nonetheless, is serious, and we have to decide how long we can allow it to go on. At some point we have to ask where our priorities lie. Does it matter if our union acts as a training post for ambitious young people who want to rise in the ranks of management with the result that it staggers along inefficiently? Or do we want a strong, efficient and militant NUM which retains its skilled personnel because they are committed to what the union is doing?

My view on this is clear. I believe that a strong and militant NUM is vital for the democratic future of our society, for the transformation of the mining industry in the interest of mineworkers and for the economic future of the country as a whole. Let me take the question of democracy first.

Protecting Democracy

The most important test of democracy is the existence of the freedom of association leading to the formation of free trade unions and the right to strike. If trade unions lose those freedoms then no other freedom is safe. This has been the experience in every totalitarian country. It was the experience in Fascist Germany, Italy, Spain and Portugal where the first act of the dictators was to destroy trade union freedom by destroying trade unions. We have seen it happen in many Third World countries in recent years. It has happened in recent months in South Korea where the bitter battles between the trade unions and the government have been over the government's attempts to tame the unions. Politicians who want total power always start by destroying unions.

The trade union role in democracy is also important because unions are the voice of the dispossessed, the lowest paid and the most exploited sections of our society. The unions enable their views and resolutions to be heard alongside those of politicians and the business elite. Through the NUM, for instance, lowly-paid and poorly educated mineworkers sit opposite and argue with mine owners and government ministers. Their views are treated with respect.

Without the NUM the individual mineworkers count for nothing except as vote fodder. But within the NUM, they can move resolutions in their branches, their regional conferences and national congresses, which attack employers, governments and political parties without the risk of retribution because they have the collective support of their fellow mineworkers. If they tried to act in the same way as private citizens they could be disregarded and, perhaps, penalised.

We in South Africa are new to democracy and we may make mistakes along the way. We do not want those mistakes to lead to the loss of the freedoms we fought so long to obtain. We have not yet had time to build the infrastructures that would enable us to resist a return to authoritarian rule so we have got to have strong guards willing to fight any such tendencies. It is my belief that the NUM can and must be one of those guards.

Transforming the mining industry

It is true that mining has declined as an employer of labour in recent years, but it still employs about 500,000 people. It continues, however, to create great wealth, much of which goes to the government in the form of taxation. About half of our foreign exchange earnings come from the export of minerals. This will increase as we establish those industries which process the minerals and add value to them. The government has already taken steps to investigate the possibility of doing this in the case of diamonds. If, for instance, the global selling operations controlled by De Beers were transferred to South Africa it would add up to R19 billion to our foreign reserves. If we also processed the diamonds, the gold and the platinum we mine the benefits derived from mining would be enormous.

If this is the case why is it that black mineworkers are paid and treated like Third World peasants? Why are they amongst the lowest paid workers in South Africa and yet do the hardest and most dangerous work? It is interesting that when we complain to the mining houses about the poverty wages our members receive they always compare them with the wages received by mineworkers in Third World countries, because this enables them to announce that South African mineworkers are relatively highly paid.

They do not, however, compare their mining technology with Third World countries. They say that the South African mines compare with the best in the world. And when they boast about their Five Star safety ratings they are not comparing their safety standards with those of Columbia, Bolivia or Chile but with the advanced Western mining nations.

Moreover, in their campaigns to recruit whites from the developed countries to work in South African mines they do not offer Third World terms of employment but salaries and conditions which are better than they could get in their home countries. Well, I want the same standards to be applied to our members. I want black mineworkers here to have the pay, conditions and status equivalent to the best in the world. It must not be shameful to work in the mines but a source of pride. I realise that in order to achieve this we will have to change many aspects of mining. It is not necessary for me to say what needs to be done.

The Government's economic strategy

My final point concerns the context for the transformation for the mining industry. It is quite clear that we can only achieve our objectives within an expanding economy in which mining is profitable. We, therefore, have a direct interest in the government's Macro-Economic Strategy for Growth, Employment and Redistribution (GEAR) which has been presented as a blueprint for a prosperous South Africa.

Before the government formulated its policy document it invited proposals from the main interest parties. The South African Foundation submitted a memorandum called 'Growth for All'. This represented the views of big business in South Africa, for the SA Foundation is financed by 58 of the largest companies in the country, including Anglo American, De Beers, Anglovaal, Gencor, Gold Fields, Eskom, Iscor and Sasol. The document, therefore, is representative of the views of the mine owners and could easily have been written by the Chamber of Mines.

We submitted our own document called *Social Equity and Job Creation. The Key to a Stable Future*, which repudiated in detail all of the policies proposed by big business and suggested an alternative strategy to the government which put job creation, the redistribution of income and workers' rights as its central objectives.

Thus the government had before it two radically different sets of policies from which to choose. One from capital which represented the interests of no more than 5 per cent of the total population and one from labour which represented the rest. It set up a Technical Team to advise it comprising two representatives from the World Bank, five from the banking industry in Southern Africa, five from universities and two from government departments.

There was no one from the labour movement in the Team. Nor was there anyone in it to put a socialist perspective for the future of South Africa. The

Technical Team was dominated by monetarist economists and it is not surprising, therefore, that it produced a policy document which contains at least 95 per cent of the views of big business and 5 per cent of our views.

Let me make this clear, the GEAR document represents 95 per cent of the views of 5 per cent of the population and 5 per cent of the views of 95 per cent of the population. Something seems wrong here.

What is surprising is that the GEAR document has been enthusiastically endorsed by the government as its strategy for the future development of South Africa. When Trevor Manuel, the Minister of Finance, introduced it during the Finance Budget Vote on 14 June last year he said, 'The programme which we announce here today puts in place an integrated set of macroeconomic policies which will enable the government to deliver on the commitments we have made in the RDP.' He went on to say that: 'The package...is born of the need to enhance the quality of life of all South Africans...(and)...will unleash the potential for economic growth, job creation and redistribution that our economy possesses.' This is an ambitious claim.

He concluded by saying that the strategy is 'not up for negotiation at this stage', and appealed for close co-operation from the government's social partners. In saying this, he presented us with a serious challenge. We have to decide whether we can co-operate in the implementation of GEAR. It is vitally important then that we should be clear about what it entails.

What is in GEAR

GEAR is essentially a combination of World Bank policies which have already been applied in many countries in Africa and South America. We know their history and in every case they have been a disaster for the ordinary poor people. There are no exceptions. They have generated so much poverty and unrest that the main international voluntary aid agencies such as Oxfam, Save the Children Fund and War on Want have campaigned against them. No organisation anywhere which is concerned with aid, benefits, the fight against poverty and the rights of workers has anything beneficial to say about World Bank policies. The point is that these policies have a primary, hidden agenda to make the Third World countries dependent on the economies of the developed industrial nations. They have certainly not been designed to assist the ordinary people of the Third World. That much is crystal clear.

Why, with such a record of failure, should we even contemplate applying them here? I must say that the possibility of adding the South African working-class peasant farmers to the list of casualties more than worries me, it scares me, because there could be very serious politically destabilising consequences in five or ten years time that could be worse for the rural and township people than they experienced in the 1980s. For us to be asked to co-operate with big business, international finance and the government in implementing GEAR is like being asked to dig our own graves, jump in voluntarily and then wait to have the earth thrown in on top of us by the representatives of those interests. It would be mass suicide. The prospect is frightening. Let me explain why I think this way.

GEAR has been published so that each of you can read it and reach your own conclusions. The media has published various comments about it. Cosatu and the SACP have also published statements about it. I think that as President of a union that would be directly affected by the GEAR strategy I should explain to you what I think about it.

First, I have no problem with GEAR's 'long-run vision'. It wants and I want 'a fast growing economy which creates sufficient jobs for all work seekers'. I, too, want 'a redistribution of income and opportunities in favour of the poor', but I also want a much more equal distribution of the wealth which involves a substantial narrowing of the gap between the poorest and the richest. And I am also in favour of creating a society in which 'sound health, education and other services are available to all'.

My problem with GEAR's strategy begins with the statement that the growth of the economy and the achievement of its long run aims 'requires a transformation towards a competitive outward oriented economy'. In other words, it wants to create in South Africa a freely competitive economy where there are no impediments to the movement of capital or labour and no regulations to hamper production so that employers are free to exploit both in the interest of maximum profit-making. The role of the government in this setting is simply to provide the legal and fiscal framework to enable capitalism to work most effectively. It believes that a freely competitive market would allocate incomes and opportunities in a fair and equitable way.

Constructing this kind of free market mechanism requires a number of conditions and these are spelled out. It needs to keep inflation in check, have a positive balance of payments, reduce the budget deficit, increase the share of private capital in the economy, open up the economy to international competition, attract foreign capital and be given the co-operation of the trade union movement. It emphasises that all of these conditions have to be met otherwise the strategy will not work.

What is not in GEAR

What is not in the strategy is as important as what is in it. There is, for instance, no mention of the need to reduce the power of monopoly capital. Monopoly capital is a world-wide phenomenon but it is at its greatest in South Africa. If you look at the diagram of the financial interests of Anglo American on the inside cover of *Social Equity and Job Creation. The key to a stable future*, it is mind boggling. Virtually everything we do is controlled in some way, to some degree, by Anglo American. How can we talk of democracy when one unelected family controls so much of our lives?

When we examine the total monopoly scene we find we have a small elite of business executives deciding where we work, how we work, what we are paid for working, whether we work at all. If we are serious about making a reality of the rights enshrined in our constitution then we have to be equally serious about destroying the monopoly of private industry and creating a genuine democracy.

Next, there are no provisions in the strategy to ensure that income, property and wealth in general are transferred from the rich to the poor. It is sick and a travesty of justice to maintain the present gap between the rich and the poor. This transference, according to GEAR, will occur automatically as the economy grows. That, I must say with due respect, is a nonsense statement. It has never happened in the history of capitalism except where governments have intervened to make it happen.

Just look at the situation in the Western countries since 1979 where monetarist policies have been applied. The gap between the richest and poorest has widened, unemployment has increased, the number of homeless has grown and the percentage of the populations living in poverty has risen. As I speak, there are serious unemployment problems in France and Germany. If you judged monetarism by its record you would order its execution.

I must emphasise to you that there is no evidence anywhere that wealth can be redistributed through the free market system. It cannot. If you doubt me then let me make a further point. Capitalism with its market mechanism, which the government is so eager to perfect, is itself a monopoly. You can only belong to it if you have money. You have to pay for whatever you want and in order to pay you need money. People without money are excluded from joining. They cannot share any of the benefits that the market mechanism is alleged to provide. They have access to none of the goods and services that flow through it. In South Africa we have millions of people without jobs and, therefore, without money. Nothing is redistributed to them. Absolutely nothing.

Gear does not say so explicitly but it gives a clear impression that it wants weak, collaborative trade unions. It wants, it states, careful policy responses from us. In other words it wants us to do nothing to frighten off capital. It does not want us to rock the capitalist boat. If we follow that advice then we might as well pack our bags today and go home.

Delicious Organic Produce

FRESH FROM THE FARMS - DELIVERED DIRECT TO YOUR NEIGHBOURHOOD AT LOW PRICES BY ORGANIC ROUNDABOUT

Look after yourself and support the environment

Experience the fantastic tastes of this year's organic harvest. Choose from over 60 varieties of freshly cropped vegetables and fruit direct from the fields of UK organic growers and conveniently delivered to your neighbourhood. Available in LONDON, BRIGHTON and the MIDLANDS.

TRIAL BAG for £7.90 - A week's supply of produce (9-11lbs) for £7.90

DON'T MISS OUT - Become part of the UK's largest organic vegetable delivery service and join thousands of people who get organic produce direct from the farms. The scheme is run by Organic Roundabout, an ecologically committed co-operative. For details ring 0121 551 1679 or fax 0121 515 3524. For a trial bag of this week's best produce or for further information, please complete the form and send to: Organic Roundabout, PO Box 10014, London E8 3TY.

Name _____

Address _____

_____

Post code _____

Tel _____

Fax _____

Can you act as a pick up point for others YES/NO (please delete)

This is Issue 7 of Soundings
The Next Ten Years **was a special free supplement**

Soundings

Soundings is a journal of politics and culture. It is a forum for ideas which aims to explore the problems of the present and the possibilities for a future politics and society. Its intent is to encourage innovation and dialogue in progressive thought. Half of each issue is devoted to debating a particular theme: topics in the pipeline include: Active Welfare in Britain and The European Left.

Why not subscribe?
Make sure of your copy

Subscription rates, 1998 (3 issues)
INDIVIDUAL SUBSCRIPTIONS: UK - £35.00   *Rest of the World - £45.00*
INSTITUTIONAL SUBSCRIPTIONS UK - £70.00   *Rest of the World - £80.00*

Please send me one year's subscription starting with Issue Number _____

I enclose payment of £ _____

I wish to become a supporting subscriber and enclose a donation of £ _____

I enclose total payment of £ _____

Name _____

Address _____

_____

_____ Postcode _____

Please return this form with cheque or money order payable to Soundings and send to:

Soundings, c/o Lawrence & Wishart, 99A Wallis Road, London E9 5LN